THE LAST
AIRMEN

THE LAST AIRMEN

Exploring My Father's World

ROGER RAWLINGS

1817
HARPER & ROW, PUBLISHERS, New York
Cambridge, Grand Rapids, Philadelphia, St. Louis, San Francisco,
London, Singapore, Sydney, Tokyo

FIRST EDITION

Designer: Cassandra J. Pappas

Library of Congress Cataloging-in-Publication Data

Rawlings, Roger.
    The last airmen.

    1. Aeronautics—United States—History.   I. Title.
TL521.R28   1989   629.13′0973   88-45903
ISBN 0-06-016084-5

89 90 91 92 93 CC/HC 10 9 8 7 6 5 4 3 2 1

For my parents
and for Bobbie

Contents

NOTE

The identities of individuals mentioned in this book have been disguised except for historical personages (including pilots whose flights received extensive media attention) and members of the author's family.

THE LAST AIRMEN

Prologue:
An Airborne Boyhood

WHEN I WAS NINE, I SAW AN AIRPLANE CRASH. My mother was driving me home from school, and I was searching the sky through the car window, scanning for planes the way I often did. We lived near Mitchel Field, a small Air Force base tucked among the suburban tracts on central Long Island. Propeller-driven transport planes lumbered over our neighborhood several times each day, and sometimes I caught sight of bombers and fighters setting out on training missions. It was 1955.

I peered through the window and there, toylike in the distance, was a B-26 spiraling out of the sky. The wings of the twin-engine bomber paddled the air as the fuselage revolved, nose down. I remember the plane's descent as graceful, almost stately. No parachutes cluttered the scene; no sounds detracted from it. The plane simply came down out of the sky and vanished. It struck the ground a few miles away, too far off for us to hear the impact.

I suppose I knew as the plane descended that I was seeing men die. Inside the cockpit, the pilots struggled to arrest the plane's spin and pull the nose up. Or perhaps they struggled for a while, then tried to bail out. I imagined them yanking their seatbelts off, trying to move toward the hatches. But centrifugal force pinned them in their seats, holding them as the earth gyrated grotesquely outside their windshield and surged up toward them.

I knew, more or less, but it didn't register. My mother told me not to look at the plane. She pulled over to the curb and tried to divert my attention. But by the time she had parked, the plane had already come down.

No big deal; I wasn't upset. I'd seen lots of airplanes crash, after all. World War II documentaries were on TV constantly in the early 1950s: black-and-white footage of American victories in Europe and the Pacific. I watched all the shows—*The Big Picture, Victory at Sea*—but I liked the ones about the air war best. I saw our bombers pressing ahead to their targets, dodging black puffballs of flak and trading fire with enemy fighters. They fought their way through, then dumped long cascades of bombs while the music on the soundtrack swelled. Occasionally a bomber would be hit. Machine-gun rounds would pepper a wing, say, and the fuel tanks inside would detonate. Then the plane would wheel over and begin its balletic downward spiral. I'd seen it lots of times.

And I'd heard about it. My father had been in a crash—or a crash landing, anyway. It was my favorite bedtime story. Evening after evening, I asked my father to tell me the story again, and sometimes he would: He'd tell how his B-17 had been shot down in 1944. He had been in the Eighth Air Force, flying strategic bombing raids from an English airfield. One day while he and his crew were headed toward a target in Germany, enemy fighters attacked them, wounding several of the crew members and damaging the plane's controls. They tried to fly back to England, my father said. Dropping to low altitude, they turned toward the west and picked a route across the unfamiliar landscape. They made it as far as central Belgium, but then a second group of fighters pounced. My father said that was the end. The B-17 was crippled now—almost unflyable. He eased it down on its belly in a wheat field.

The fuselage and one of the wings were on fire when the plane skidded to a stop. My father lowered himself out the window beside his seat and went forward to the nose compartment. He helped the bombardier get out, then he went back in and brought out the navigator. Both men had been hurt. The bombardier had a large wound in one leg. The navigator had lost an eye.

Other members of the crew emerged from hatches and windows near the rear of the plane. Some of them, too, were wounded. Farmers who had been working nearby converged on the crash scene and led the injured crewmen away, supporting those who could walk, carrying those who couldn't. Then a half-track filled with German soldiers drove into the field. My father and the other uninjured crewmen scattered. Some of them ran into the adjacent fields. Some ran toward the town, where Belgian families sheltered them. My father ran to a small woods where he could conceal himself among the trees.

The next morning he began walking southwest. He planned to cross into France and then make his way to neutral Spain. He hiked for weeks, eluding German patrols as he went. He traveled during daylight hours, then knocked on the doors of isolated farmhouses in the evenings, asking for something to eat and a place to sleep. It sounded like great fun to me. He disguised himself in peasant clothes, foraged in orchards, and taught himself French. Eventually he made contact with resistance fighters in France, who helped him to reach the Pyrenees. He entered Spain, proceeded to Gibraltar, and got passage back to England where the Army Eighth Air Force gave him a medal and sent him on a tour of air bases to lecture on escape and evasion techniques.

My father became an airline pilot after the war. I remember a striking figure, tall, in a dark-blue uniform with gold stripes on the sleeves.

When he left for his trips, he carried a suitcase in one hand and, in the other, his flight bag, the leather case that held his flight manuals and air charts.

Naturally, I wanted to be just like him when I grew up. I reserved one of the bookshelves in my bedroom for plastic models of the airliners he flew: the Martin 4-0-4; the Douglas DC-3; the Lockheed 749 Constellation. The "Connie" was my favorite plane—a graceful flying machine with an arched fuselage that seemed to strain upwards, as if impatient to climb into the sky. She was a beauty.

My father flew for TWA. On the bulletin board next to my bookcase I kept a large TWA route map on which I could trace his trips. They were long trips, generally; he was often gone for fourteen days or more, traveling to Europe and the Near East. He would fly to London—a day-long flight—and rest up there. Then on to Rome, or Paris, or Athens. And then perhaps to Cairo or all the way to Bombay. He would lay over for one or two nights at most of these stops. Then, having reached the farthest point of his journey, he would turn his plane around and head back home.

I took his absences in stride, for the most part. It seemed natural to me that he should be gone at Christmastime or on my birthday. If I thought at all about the difference between my situation and the family lives of my friends—kids who had conventional workaday dads—I figured the balance lay entirely in my favor. None of *them* had a bona fide aviation hero for a father. None of *them* had a father with gold filigree on his cap brim and gold-plated wings over his breast pocket. (I never bothered to find out what most of my friends' fathers did for a living. Boring stuff in offices, I assumed. But movies like *The High and the Mighty* didn't get made about accountants, I knew that much.)

My father's uniforms symbolized all the advantages I thought I had. I took parts of the uniforms from his closet whenever I could and wore them around the house or, better, outdoors where my friends could see me. My father didn't like me fooling with his current uniform, but

I could play with his old Air Force gear or his worn-out airline suits as much as I liked. I remember raiding his closet on several Halloween nights. While my friends gathered outside wearing stupid store-bought costumes—pirates or ghosts—I transformed myself into an authentic aviator. I thrust my feet into a pair of my father's huge black-leather boots, put one of his caps on my head, and draped one of his old flight jackets over my shoulders. I was scarcely able to move in this outfit— the jacket sleeves reached well past my knees—but staggering out the front door, I felt terrific.

For day-to-day purposes, I made do with a substitute outfit. I had a large collection of tin pilot's wings, the kind airlines gave away to children. I would stick a pair on my shirt almost every day, and often I would pin a bath towel to my shoulders. My favorite game was to act out Superman adventures: Holding my arms out horizontally ahead of me, I would fly down the block at sidewalk altitude. I couldn't have said for certain whether I was the Man of Steel or my father, but that didn't matter. I was an airborne crusader, ridding the world of injustice. Sometimes I actually did become airborne, at least momentarily. I liked to climb onto the roof of our garage and, with the towel flapping loosely behind me, jump off.

I also took other, more orthodox flights. All the members of my family did. My mother, sisters, and I could travel free anywhere on TWA's routes, so we flew a lot. We took annual vacations by air and we flew to Kansas City frequently to visit our relatives there. My father came with us on some of these trips—like the other pilots, he could "deadhead" on any flight that had a spare seat. But his schedule didn't often jibe with ours. Sometimes he had to take out a flight a few days before one of our trips began. Sometimes he was "on reserve"— he had to stay home near the telephone, ready to accept a last-minute flight assignment. (The phone would ring, my father would talk to someone in the crew scheduling office, and shortly afterward he would head for the airport. I pretended it was like Air Force pilots rushing out of their ready room when word of war came.) So, more often than not, we traveled without him.

The kids in the neighborhood made a satisfying fuss over my free flights. "Get out of here! For free? You mean, no money?" I told them sure. "We go all over the place," I said, "and we get all kinds of free food and everything. We just drive down to the airport and sign up for any flight we want."

It was almost true. We would sign up, but only for standby seating. After checking in at the ticket counter, we would walk to the gate. Then, as the passengers filed out the door and climbed the stairs to the plane, we would wait for the boarding agent to call our names. Frequently he didn't. The door closed, the stairs were pulled away, and we watched the flight depart. Then we had to return to the ticket counter and submit our names for the next flight.

Even when we did get aboard, we stayed edgy. Few flights went long distances without at least a few intermediate stops, and for us each stop represented a threat. Whenever the plane touched down, there was a chance that we would be bumped off to make room for paying passengers. That meant we would have to sit around for hours in some out-of-the way airport—Lancaster or Dayton or Terre Haute—waiting for another flight. Sometimes the wait extended through the night. Trying to sleep on a hard couch in a fluorescent-lit terminal was no fun.

But I played down these frustrations when talking to my friends. Between innings in our stickball games, I strutted and waved my arms. "See that sports car?" I asked. "The planes go ten times faster than that. A *hundred* times faster."

I stressed speed until I was about twelve. Then, having grown old enough to notice stewardesses, I started stressing them. "You should see them," I said to my friends. "They're knockouts! Listen, if you see one coming down the aisle, you sit with your arm like this, sort of sticking out in the aisle. Then, when she tries to get past you . . . ."

I was lying, of course. The women *were* knockouts, but they were also far beyond my pubescent designs. So I kept my eyes down and my elbows in. Still, when I stood telling lies on the street corner, my friends' eyes would expand, and that was a victory.

Strangely, I never thought to tell my friends about the things that actually made flying enjoyable for me. The drama of takeoff, for instance. I loved sitting in a plane that was poised for takeoff at the foot of a runway. The pilots revved the engines and the cabin filled with the sound, and as the walls and floor shook I could see the passengers around me getting nervous. I would look left and right along my row, smiling at the fear on people's faces. Then the pilots would ease the throttles back and release the brakes, the sound would rise again and the plane would begin rolling, and I would lean forward to stare out the window. Airport scenery slid across the plexiglass: hangars and fuel trucks and parked planes, rushing backward past us, faster each moment. Trying to take it all in, I ran newsreel commentaries in my head. *The brakes are off. The plane is charging forward.* I tried to feel the plane growing buoyant as the wings gained lift; tried to anticipate the moment when the wheels would leave the runway; the exact moment when the ground would drop away. *Sixty miles an hour,* I estimated silently, *seventy* . . . . The plane rotated, nose gear rising first, then the main gear, and we welled upward. *The plane is climbing fast. Now we can hear the landing gear coming up.* Everything shrank and spread out. The towns surrounding the airport slipped into view as we climbed, and all the objects in them—houses, cars, trees— progressively diminished. I liked to pretend that it wasn't real scenery at all but train-table stuff, marvelous H.O.-gauge miniatures, as if I weren't rising above Long Island but above a superb diorama at some ultimate world's fair.

The view got still better when the plane reached cruising altitude. The horizon seemed to dip down—the sky became immense and the earth itself expanded. I could see hundreds of miles at a glance: geometric patchworks of green-and-brown fields and subtly textured townsites. There were strange distortions; nothing looked like itself. Hills flattened out; bodies of water—lakes, rivers—became strips of gleaming metal; cities became jumbles of reflections set off against dull gray backgrounds. I liked coasting, detached, above such dissociated forms. And I liked playing games with the clouds. Sometimes a deck of clouds would form below us, cutting us off from the planet. I pretended we were a million miles high; I pretended there was no solid surface anywhere below. At other times the clouds converged on us—a gray film would suddenly wash across the windows, darkening the cabin. *The sun has gone out. The universe is dark.* Then we would burst into the sunlight again and the clouds would rearrange themselves as a floating landscape of bulbous hills and steep, indistinct canyons. Pressing my forehead against the plane's window, I imagined stepping out onto that landscape, marching off to explore its hidden places.

Occasionally I was treated to a special view of the earth and sky and clouds. We often flew with pilots who knew my father, and from time to time one of them would invite me up into the cockpit. That was the jackpot. I would stand just inside the cockpit door and gape. I loved the visual complexity of the control panels: the myriad dials and switches covering the walls and ceiling. The crew would chat with me, explaining various instruments and their functions—the artificial horizon, the vertical speed indicator, the turn-and-bank indicator. I would nod and, to be polite, ask a few questions. But mainly I wanted to look out the windshield, to get a pilot's-eye view of things. Beyond the nose of the plane, I could see the horizon ahead of us: a distant pale-blue rim with the deeper blue of the sky arching above it and the mottled earth unrolling beneath. I would stare at that indistinct junction of sky and earth until my time was up and I had to return to the cabin.

I'm not sure when I gave up the intention of becoming a pilot. My interest in flying remained strong throughout most of my childhood.

Strong enough to annoy my friends. No matter how exciting one of our games might be—bottom of the ninth, tie score—if a plane flew overhead, my attention would shift upward and I would follow the plane with my eyes until it faded in the distance. But even at such moments, I did not visualize myself as the pilot of the plane. My concept of pilots was too exalted for that. At some unconscious level, I had already decided I couldn't measure up to that concept, so I treated piloting as a fantasy only. I daydreamed about it and played at it, but I refused to think of it as a goal that I might pursue in my real, waking life.

I remember standing aloof from the "my-old-man-can-lick-your-old-man" arguments that my friends got into sometimes. I was so sure of my father's superiority, I saw no reason to debate the point. But his superiority and his occupation were interlocked: I was awed by my father, and I felt nearly the same awe for all other pilots. I don't think an accountant's son is likely to feel anything comparable about accountants. He might admire his father and want to grow up like him, but would he harbor a profound admiration for every one of his father's colleagues? That's what I did with pilots. My father was the best pilot, of course, but I assumed that all other pilots came pretty close to his level. I thought of them as Gregory Peck in *Twelve O'Clock High,* James Stewart in *The Spirit of St. Louis.*

I remember the first time I flew in a plane piloted by my father. He had been a copilot for nine years after joining TWA, but then he switched from overseas flights to domestic U.S. routes and he was promoted to captain. Whenever my mother planned a family trip after that, she tried to arrange for us to go at least part of the way on one of my father's flights.

She arranged it during the summer of 1956, when we were headed for Kansas City. I remember we took off from LaGuardia Airport on the north shore of Long Island, then banked and climbed to the west. And as we passed above the Bronx, my father's voice came over the P.A. system, giving the estimated arrival time for our first stop en route. Hearing my father make this announcement threw me. I had heard pilots make hundreds of in-flight announcements before, but somehow I couldn't quite believe that the man sitting in this plane's cockpit, speaking these words and commanding this flight, was my father.

It was a small thing, it passed quickly. My father made additional announcements as the flight continued and I grew more accustomed to each one. In a way, though, this was worse. Previously, I'd compartmentalized my father: There was Dad, the guy I knew at home, and there was The Pilot, an archetypal figure in my imagination. But now, listening to my father perform as a pilot, these two conceptions merged. I felt I was overhearing my father in his true life, and the distance between that life and my own seemed immeasurable.

I had opportunities to change my mind and prepare myself to become a pilot, but I didn't take them. My father and I spent a certain amount of time together when I was a teenager. He owned a sailboat, a large sloop in which we cruised the bays along the south shore of the Island. We swapped turns at the helm. Typically, one of us would man the tiller and sheets, sailing the boat, while the other descended into the cabin or stretched out on the foredeck to enjoy the sun and wind. Then after a while we would exchange places.

We were quiet much of the time. I had picked up my father's habit of reticence, speaking only when it seemed essential. On the boat, it rarely was. We spent many afternoons sailing long distances in almost complete silence.

But when we did talk, our subject was often the sky. Like any sailors, we continually studied the sky, trying to decide what the weather held in store for us. My father used his flying experience to draw conclusions from the shape and color of the clouds and the direction of the wind. I remember afternoons when he said the weather looked quiet below but challenging aloft: Our cruise would be smooth—too smooth, maybe; we might be becalmed—but any planes passing through those clouds we could see on the horizon would probably get bounced around pretty hard.

Occasionally he told me about weather conditions he'd observed as a pilot. Rainbows were circular when seen from the air, he said; and if you looked closely, you might see several concentric rainbows, a dwindling series of them, one within the next. He said the winds inside thunder clouds, updrafts and downdrafts, were astonishingly strong: Your plane would be hoisted toward the roof of the storm one moment, then thrust back down the next. Lightning rarely looked like jagged bolts when seen from the air: Usually all you saw were harmless blossoms of light, violet or white, inside the clouds. He said that sometimes on a night flight, in humid air, static electricity would pile up around a plane's nose: A glowing red column of charged particles would extend forward into the darkness while colorful wreaths of St. Elmo's fire glistened on the windshields and propellers. If you were flying between two layers of clouds at sunset, sometimes the sun would throw the shadows of the lower clouds onto the upper clouds: The shadows looked like huge blue-purple stalactites. If you were flying high above a cloud deck, you could look down and spot the shadow of your plane, and it would be surrounded by an iridescent pattern of light called a glory.

I stared into the sky while my father spoke, trying to visualize the things he described. I wanted to see such things in reality. But if my father's comments contained an implicit invitation, I ignored it. I didn't ask many questions or own up to the strength of my interest. When my father finished speaking, I let our customary silence return.

Toward the end of 1985, I read a newspaper article that said the airlines were scrambling to hire new pilots. Jobs were opening up both because airline deregulation had created a huge increase in air travel and because large numbers of senior pilots—men around my father's age—were retiring. "Pilot Shortage Hits Airlines," the headline said.

I was amazed at the ache I felt. It was more than twenty years since my father and I had last sailed together—twenty years since I had last toyed with the notion of becoming a pilot. I'd gone on to college and then graduate school, then landed a good job, then a better job. I had a comfortable life now—I was, as far as I knew, satisfied. But reading the news article unhinged me. I wanted one of those piloting jobs. I wanted to march into an airline personnel office, slap down my résumé, and lay claim to my place in a cockpit. I couldn't, of course. I had no qualifications; I'd never even taken a flying lesson. But with an intensity that startled me, I wished the facts were otherwise.

I had a melancholy evening of bourbon-fueled introspection. Then I tried to put my regrets away. I told myself I'd been hit by an ordinary attack of midlife remorse: A boyhood dream had surfaced momentarily to taunt me before receding again. I wasn't going to fulfill that dream any more than I would fulfill the others that I'd once nurtured—fantasies of skippering an America's Cup defender or of soaring to rock-and-roll stardom. But they were childish dreams, anyway; I told myself they were best forgotten.

The next morning I drove to work the same way I did every weekday. I carried on with my life. The effects produced by the article lingered, though. I couldn't suppress my regrets completely, and eventually they led me to ask myself some questions that I hadn't confronted before. I wondered what my life would have been like if I'd been less intimidated by pilots when I was a boy. I wondered how I would have made out if I'd asked my father for flying lessons and then pursued a flying career. I wondered, also, about the men I'd looked up to when I was a boy. What were they actually like, as individuals, behind the image that my fantasies had projected onto them?

I began mulling over these questions, and gradually I came to feel a sense of urgency about seeking some answers. The senior pilots were retiring. If I wanted to learn about them and about the lives they'd led, I'd better do it soon, before the past was beyond recall. Still more urgently, I realized that I needed to deal with some of the unfinished business in my own life. I realized that I was wrong to put piloting in the same category as my other boyhood dreams. Clearly, for me, this dream was special, and I needed to understand why it had returned with such strength so long after I thought I'd dismissed it. I needed to come to terms with it—which meant, I knew, that I needed to come to terms with my father and, if possible, with myself. I was nearly forty years old; it seemed to be about time.

So, I've tried. Early in 1986, I began meeting with active as well as retired airline pilots, including some who began flying years before my father, men who set the pattern for his profession. I traveled around the country attending air shows, and loitering at airports, and visiting pilots in their homes. And, far more than I'd done in years—more, really, than I'd ever done—I had long conversations with my father. The following chapters are my report on these meetings.

Contact

CLARENCE MULHOLLAND IS A CERTIFIED OLD-TIMER. He showed me the certificate: his first piloting license, signed by Orville Wright. I met Clarence at an air show near his home in Michigan. We sat on canvas chairs at the edge of the airfield and watched acrobatic biplanes spin and loop above us. And in the intervals of relative silence between the planes' stunts, we talked about his first airline job, piloting Ford trimotors across the Midwest in the late 1920s.

"When I started out," he said, "we thought we were doing pretty well if we managed to get to our destination at all. I don't mean on time. I don't mean close to on time. I mean *at all.*

"It wasn't a matter of just flying from here to there. The weather held us up a lot more than today, so we might never take off in the first place. Or once we got going, we might have to make an emergency landing in a farm field or some such place. That was pretty common. The airlines went around making contracts with farmers so they wouldn't sue us if we came down on their property.

"I had to land that way, one time. How it happened was, it was winter and I was in Chicago getting ready to take out a flight west. But a teletype message came into the office saying 'Take Mulholland off the westbound flight and put him on the eastbound flight instead. He'll get it through.' See, they were having snowstorms in the East and the company wanted somebody foolhardy enough to fly into that mess.

"Now, I was just a young pilot, a very young pilot, and you've got to understand that when your boss sends a message like that, well, it's liable to hit you in the ego a little bit. I mean, I was bound and determined to get that plane through.

"Anyway, we took off, headed toward Ohio, but we never got very far because after a little we ran into a snowstorm. And it was quite a storm, I will say that. I mean, I hadn't really thought about what kind of weather I was going to run into, I was just pleased that the company wanted me for the job.

"But I started to feel less pleased when we got into that snow. The clouds came down lower and lower, and the snow blew so hard I couldn't see three feet ahead of me, I don't believe. So I kept dropping the plane down lower and lower, trying to keep under the clouds. I was looking as hard as I could for the train track that I knew was down under us somewhere. I could see straight down pretty well by sticking my head out the window, even if I couldn't see ahead much.

"Luckily there was a train on the track, so I picked up its lights. So then I let down farther and started following that train. In those days there was really only one rule: You weren't supposed to fly lower than three hundred feet with passengers on board. Sometimes we had to bend the rule a little, though, because the only kind of flying we knew was contact flying, meaning we had to keep our landmarks in sight. Or, like in this case, I had to be able to see that train."

Contact flying. Clarence interrupted himself to define the term. During the 1920s, airmen picked their way across country by staying in visual contact with the ground (while trying to avoid a more conclusive form of contact). Like Mark Twain committing each twist and bend of the Mississippi River to heart, they memorized the terrain they flew over each day: towns, fields, roads, lakes. These were the pragmatic points of their compass.

"Do you know what I'm talking about?" Clarence asked. "You kept your eyes peeled and you stayed below the clouds where you could see the ground.

"Scattered clouds weren't a problem. You could fly above them as long as there were gaps you could look through. But if the clouds built up so that there weren't any gaps, you'd better duck below them. Otherwise the winds could blow you off course and you'd have no way of knowing it. You might end up three miles north of the airport you were shooting for or twenty miles south of it. If you couldn't see the ground, you wouldn't know, and that meant that when you started your descent later on, you wouldn't know what the hell was under you. You might come down through the clouds and smack into a hill that you never knew was down there.

"No, you kept the ground in sight. You knew the landmarks, so you could hold yourself on course. Or if you did get a little lost in spite of everything, you were low enough to look around for a sign on some-body's roof. That was about the only kind of navigational aid there was in the beginning. The Guggenheims [the Daniel Guggenheim Fund for the Promotion of Aeronautics] paid towns to paint them. They had the name of the town and small arrows that pointed north and bigger arrows that pointed toward landing fields.

"*Some* routes had beacons that you could follow if you were flying after dark. But you weren't always on a route that had them—and even if you were, fog or something might block them out. But they were godsends when you could see them."

The beacons, which were operated by the Bureau of Lighthouses, blinked one-letter Morse-code signals. The first beacon on each air route blinked the letter W, the next one blinked U, and so forth. Each set of ten beacons coruscated with the letters W U V H R K D B G M, and each succeeding set of ten repeated the same sequence. Airmen kept the gibberish straight by repeating the mnemonic *When Under-taking Very Hard Routes, Keep Direction By Good Methods.*

Unfortunately, no rooftop signs or airway beacons were within eyeshot while Clarence followed the train through the snowstorm.

He resumed his story. "The snow was getting worse and I kept dropping lower as the visibility fell off. Well, pretty soon the copilot started getting kind of disturbed, for which you can't blame him. He held himself in about as long as he could, I guess, but finally he bellowed out 'Get us down out of this damned mess or you're going to kill the whole lot of us.'

"I said, 'Well okay, but where in the hell am I going to put you?'

"So he said, 'If we are where I think we are, there's a farm field back there behind us a mile.'

" 'All right, then,' I said, and I whirled the damned plane around and headed back where the copilot said this field was. And before long, sure enough, I saw it. Or I saw a fence, you know, and a white space beyond it that looked to be empty and fairly level. So I banked over toward it and got lined up to land.

"I came down over the fence and was getting ready to set the wheels down when all at once the copilot bellowed again. He said, 'There's a haystack right in front of us!'

"It was snowing so damned hard, I couldn't see the damned haystack. I don't know how he did. But I gunned the engines a little bit to get up past the stack, and then I kicked us into a sideslip, and I pulled off the power, and I fishtailed the plane a couple of times to kill the speed, and then we set down into the field.

"Now, what I didn't know was that beneath this smooth-looking snow the ground had been plowed up into some pretty sizable furrows. As soon as the wheels bit through the snow, it felt like we were rolling over a scrub board. We jangled enough to loosen our teeth, just about—it was a real buggy ride.

"The copilot and I both grabbed the brake and we groundlooped the airplane [i.e., spun it around in a tight circle]. That slowed us down and kept us in the field. But what also happened was that the plowed ground piled up in front of the wheels and tipped us over. When we got ourselves stopped, the plane was tilted forward onto its nose at about a forty-five-degree angle.

"I told the copilot, 'You go back there and keep every one of those passengers sitting in their seats. Because if they get up and go to the rear, this plane is going to flop down and that will bend the fuselage.'

"Then while he took care of the passengers I slipped out over the side and went up to the farmhouse that I could see over in the next field. The snow wasn't too deep; I could walk it all right. So then I banged on the door and got the farmer. He looked surprised to see me, but he went with me down to his barn where we hitched up his wagon. Then we rode back out to the plane.

"The passengers were still in their seats, not looking exactly happy. We let them out, though, one at a time, and told them to climb into that wagon. Then we took them up to the house and I called for some cars to come out for them. When the cars came, they got in without any complaint and that was the last I saw of them.

"So then we just had the question of how to get the plane back out of the field. But I had an idea how to do it. When the snow let up enough, we took some poles out of the barn and set them under the plane to prop it up. Then we put a rope around the tail wheel and hauled on it while we let the poles down real gently. That way we could lower the plane off its nose without bending it.

"Next we dragged the plane backwards to the corner of the field where there was this old tree that had been sawed off. We took the rope that was tied to the tail wheel and wrapped it good and secure around that tree. Then I started up the engines and I really gave them the gas. The plane tried to get rolling but the rope held it so that we sat there straining against the rope, which made our tail come up. Now, I had told the farmer to get an axe and to stand beside the tail. So when he saw the tail was up and the engines were really pulling, he chopped that rope and we were off.

"It was the roughest takeoff you ever saw. We bounced across the field so hard, it felt like our heads would jump off our necks. But we got the speed we needed before too long, because of getting our tail up like that. So that's how we got out of there."

The airline Clarence flew for went bankrupt after a few turbulent months. Its service wasn't worse than other airlines'; merely typical. Many airlines opened for business in the '20s, and many failed. Among the short-lived concerns were companies like Boeing Air Transport (BAT), Southwest Air Fast Express (SAFE), and Ford Air Transport Service (FATS). Of the bunch, Transcontinental Air Transport (TAT) intrigues me most. Formed in 1928, it was a joint venture of a group of airline promoters and a pair of railroads, the Pennsylvania and the Sante Fe. The plan was that TAT would offer coast-to-coast passenger service using a combination of trains and planes. At night, passengers would stay safely on the ground, riding in railroad sleeper cars. Then, after sunrise, they would transfer to Ford trimotors, the preeminent airliners of the period. Two nights of railing and two days of flying would (if all went well) get the passengers from one seacoast to the other.

TAT excited widespread public attention, at least initially. The idea that ordinary citizens could sign up for long-distance trips through the air seemed fantastic. Aviation in the 1920s was the province of daredevils: barnstormers, air racers, polar explorers. For every aerial success recounted in the newspapers (Lindbergh's flight to Paris; Byrd's flight over the North Pole), several failures were reported (the ditching of the first plane to attempt a flight from California to Hawaii; the wreck of the Navy dirigible *Shenandoah;* the many crack-ups at air meets). So the public was intrigued—and, I imagine, more than a trifle skeptical—when TAT began advertising its services.

"People thought fliers were kind of nuts," Clarence Mulholland said to me. "I guess they were right, in a way. There was a kind of circus atmosphere to it sometimes. But it wasn't only the 'dangers' that got people interested. A lot of people had faith in aviation. It was the coming thing. You could see it when TAT got started. People really made a fuss, even though another company [Universal Air Corps, a predecessor of American Airlines] had already tried carrying passengers across the country. But people still got worked up when TAT started because they thought something important was going on."

TAT's inaugural flights—one westbound, one eastbound—became sizable news events. The departures were carried live on radio, much as space launches would be carried on TV in later decades. Large crowds gathered at the TAT terminals, and celebrities of various stripes—politicians, movie stars, famous aviators—participated in elaborate bon voyage ceremonies. The hoopla began at Penn Station in New York City, where the first small batch of passengers were scheduled to depart on the evening of July 7. They would ride a night train to Columbus, Ohio, then begin their first day of trimotored flight. The world's foremost female aviator, Amelia Earhart, was present at Penn Station—she cracked a bottle of Prohibition grape juice over the nose of a trimotor that had been towed over from Newark Airport for the ceremony. Then Dorothy Stone, a Broadway star, performed similar honors, christening the train that would make the Columbus run. Finally, at 6:05 p.m., an electric gong sounded, a band rendered "California, Here I Come," and the train—"The Airway Limited"—pulled out.

The gong sounded in response to a cross-continent telegraph signal sent from the office of the governor of California. Charles Lindbergh, the Lone Eagle himself, sat at the governor's desk and pressed the telegraph key. Lindbergh had played a central role in the development of TAT. He had spent months conducting survey flights to map out TAT's routes, and he'd drawn up the technical specifications for much of the equipment that the company needed to buy or develop before beginning commercial operations. So he was chosen to send the transcontinental signal. And on the following day, a few hours after the passengers from New York arrived in Columbus to board their plane, he entered the cockpit of a trimotor parked at the Los Angeles airport to begin TAT's first eastbound flight. A crowd of nearly fifty thousand watched Lindbergh take off and turn toward Kingman, Arizona.

Lindbergh's participation contributed greatly to the interest the public showed in TAT. The Airway Limited left Penn Station just two years after Lindbergh soloed the Atlantic, an event that made him far and away the most idolized American of the century.

The standard explanation for Lindbergh's immense popularity is that he was a loner who prevailed against the odds. Before taking off for Paris, he had been ridiculed as the "Flying Fool"—people thought he was nuts for pitting himself against better-financed rivals in the race to fly the ocean nonstop. But when he unexpectedly succeeded, the ridicule switched to celebration. Europeans took him to represent an infusion of hope and energy from the New World. Americans decided that he represented the best that they saw within themselves, or the best that they hoped they saw. They made him the latest edition of the archetypal American hero. Modest yet self-reliant, he was the can-do little guy who shows up the big dudes.

The standard explanation is true enough, I guess. But there was also something else behind the adulation Lindbergh inspired. Most adults alive in the 1920s had been born before the first powered flights were made. For them, the idea that man could travel through the sky still seemed (to use a cliché of the period) miraculous. They still felt some of the wonder and excitement they had felt when aviation had its beginnings. The original reports of the Wright brothers' flights in 1903 had been assumed to be hoaxes. People couldn't bring themselves to believe that a man-carrying machine had actually risen into the sky. Later, when the Wrights and their rival Glenn Curtis made public demonstrations of their aircraft, large crowds gathered to watch in amazement, and reporters filed breathless accounts. When Curtis managed a successful flight from Albany to New York City in 1910, the *New York Times* devoted six pages to his accomplishment.

All the pioneering flights had seemed miraculous, and romantics thought they discerned a great promise in them. Man had acquired wings: For the first time, he could act out the ancient desire for transcendence, rising from this grubby sphere to enter a realm that seemed clearer, finer. An avenue into the heavens had been opened, the romantics said. An author writing in 1910 gave the following report of the emotions Chicagoans felt when for the first time they saw an airplane flying above their city: "Not a man but felt that this was the beginning of such a mighty era that no tongue could tell its import, and those who gazed felt awestruck, as though they had torn aside the veil of the future and looked into the very Holy of Holies."

Such words seem almost unbearably corny now. Even at the time they were written, they must have rung false. Perhaps technological progress could contribute to mankind's betterment, if not spiritual then at least material. But aviation technology was almost laughably crude at first—it's hard to see how anyone detected any sort of promise in it, much less intimations of heaven. The pioneering airmen flew only tentatively, hurling themselves boldly from the ground but then quickly fluttering down again. When the Wrights delivered the first military airplane to the U.S. Army, they could coax it no higher than one hundred forty feet into the sky. They flew low, slow, and wobbly. Similarly, Curtis was forced to land twice on his famous trip from Albany to New York; his "flying" machine didn't fly so much as skitter across the state. And then there was the sobering example of the first-ever transcontinental flight, a sixty-nine-stop journey from New York City to Pasadena, undertaken in 1911. Sitting at the controls of a flimsy aircraft built by the Wright brothers, Calbraith Rodgers had needed eighty-four days to complete the trip. He crashed so often en route that, when he finally reached California, every part of his plane had been replaced except the rudder and one wing strut. Rodgers himself was almost as battered as the plane: At various stages of his journey he suffered burns, cuts, broken legs, fractured ribs, and a concussion.

Aviation was absurd. Not only was it unlikely to usher in a mighty new era, it was unlikely to convey you from one town to the next without breaking your neck for you en route. But slowly during the 1920s the absurdity lessened, somewhat. Plane designs improved, somewhat. Flights became higher, faster, longer. Each year brought new endurance and speed records, all of them given banner coverage by the press: relatively sober magazines as well as the most intemperate tabloids. The July 1924 issue of *The National Geographic Magazine* was devoted entirely to aviation. One article recounted the first nonstop flight across America, accomplished by two Army pilots. Another article was titled "Man's Amazing Progress in Conquering the Air." The theme: Aviation was coming into its own; aircraft were being put to practical purposes ranging from carrying the mail to aiding map makers and archaeologists through aerial surveying.

The culmination of air progress seemed to come when Lindbergh conquered the Atlantic, linking by air the greatest city in America with the most magnificent city in Europe. His flight was considered one of those epochal events that will surely change the course of history. It was thought to be a heroic enactment of human aspiration, an achievement that, by advancing civilization, would improve humanity's sorry lot.

"It makes me sad to think back to it," Tom Clifton said to me. Tom is several years younger than Clarence Mulholland. I met him in Illinois where he now lives after retiring from a long airline career. A short, fair-skinned man, Tom seemed charged with scarcely contained energy. His eyes moved continuously left and right while he spoke, touching on an object—a plant stand on one side of my chair, a floor lamp on the other—and then darting restlessly away again.

"We thought Lindbergh had changed the world," he said. "Aviation had been progressing and progressing, and it was big news, *big*. But it was still shaky. But then, *wham*, here was this amazing thing. One guy got in a plane by himself and went over the North Atlantic, all the damned way to Paris. Christ.

"If you took all the astronauts and rolled them together, that's sort of how people felt about Lindbergh. The only thing anybody could talk about after his flight was flying. It was an overreaction, but everybody was excited. It was like, if you could get your hands on an airplane, you could go anywhere or do anything you wanted.

"We were fooling ourselves. The future looked pretty rosy. Everybody was going to start flying everywhere, there was going to be all this business for the airlines." Tom waved his hand, a gesture I couldn't interpret—it seemed dismissive, but I thought it also could have been a salute.

"That's what led me into flying," he continued, "because of Lindbergh. I wanted to be like him, you could say. And I'm not sorry about it. I enjoyed flying, I always did. But we got ahead of ourselves with all our optimism about how big flying was going to be.

"You're too young to remember how there was so much talk about 'the freedom of the air' and 'airmindedness.' Everybody was supposed to be 'airminded.' There was this optimism like I never saw again. I think people get excited about something like flying, something they like to dream about, and then it dies down, and then they get excited about it all over again later on. I've seen that over and over. But the high point was right after Lindbergh.

"Did you know that before he died, he turned against flying, and technology, the whole bit? He thought progress was going to improve things for everybody, but then he got disillusioned. Myself, I didn't know what he meant for a long time, but then later on I did. Everything got built up so high, there had to be a letdown.

"I remember people coming down to the airports to look at the planes. It was a big deal. Families would come out on the weekends and make an afternoon of it. We thought aviation was going to come along like gangbusters. But people were too scared to actually buy tickets. Most flights went out half-empty. People liked to *think* about flying, but not many were ready to try it.

"I suppose they were smart. Now, today, flying is all right for the passenger, but back then was a different story. It was pretty much by-guess and by-golly, most of the time."

Many airliners of the 1920s and '30s were built of wood and canvas (the absurdity of early aviation had lessened only somewhat). They were appallingly fragile. Their wings sometimes "shingled" in flight—layers of plywood suddenly peeled off and blew away. Some of the planes were also susceptible to a still worse condition: They developed dry rot inside their wings. One of the most publicized crashes of the period occurred when a wooden airliner carrying Knute Rockne among its passengers lost a wing over Kansas. The plane flipped over and pinwheeled to the ground, killing everyone aboard. Investigation revealed that the wing had been weakened by rot.

Largely because of that crash, the airlines rushed to convert to sturdier, all-metal aircraft. The Ford trimotor was the most famous of these new machines. Built of corrugated sheet metal, with a stubby fuselage and thick, high-mounted wings, the trimotor established a reputation for rugged indestructibility. "It looked tough," Clarence Mulholland said to me, "and it was. You got the idea that if one of those ships ran head-on into a mountain, the mountain would come off second best. The trimotor was that strong-built.

"Besides," Clarence continued, "it was one of the most stable airplanes I ever saw. It would bounce you around, I don't mean it wouldn't. But it had good flying qualities. A trimotor would recover itself from bad attitudes instead of tumbling down like some planes would. If you took your hands off the wheel, it wouldn't go over on its side or something like that. Instead, it would seesaw up and down a little until it found a stable flying attitude, and then it would just fly straight on ahead. It was worlds better than anything else flying at the time."

Henry Ford, the car king, decided to build the trimotor early in the 1920s. He figured air travel was set to become a profitable business, and he wanted to be in on it. So he had his engineers create a simple, sturdy airliner that might become the Tin Lizzy of the sky.

The scheme fizzled. The trimotor (nicknamed the Tin Goose) sold well—it *was* better than other airliners of the period. But that's not saying much. Few people who flew in a trimotor once volunteered for a second go. The plane dragged itself lethargically through the air—it was scarcely faster than most intercity passenger trains. Equally vexing, the plane had a range of only a few hundred miles—for long trips, it had to land every couple of hours to refuel. Worst of all, the trimotor subjected its passengers to a continuous onslaught of physical abuse. The engines (one in the nose, the others hanging beneath the wings) made a stupefying racket. Exhaust fumes from the nose engine blew through the cabin, choking everyone inside. Because the plane had no heating system, passengers had to huddle under heavy blankets during winter flights, while on summer flights they had to open the windows in hope of a cooling breeze. And in any season, the plane buffeted sickeningly—all trimotor flights were conducted at low altitudes, where swirling winds produced constant dips and heaves. (Technically, the trimotor was able to climb several thousand feet above sea level, but this capability was rarely exploited. The cabin was unpressurized, so passengers tended to pass out from lack of oxygen if a flight climbed into the thin upper air. In any case, pilots wanted to stay low where they could see where they were going.)

The rigors of trimotor flight were epitomized by the three items each passenger was handed when boarding: a stick of chewing gum, a wad of cotton, and a large paper cup. You were supposed to start chewing the gum the moment the plane's wheels left the ground and to keep at it until they touched down again. The idea was that vigorous jaw movements would make your ears pop, releasing the air pressure that otherwise would built up inside your skull as the plane changed altitude.

The cotton wad was provided because the cabin walls lacked sound-proofing. You were supposed to jam half the wad into each ear to help block out the uproar of the engines. (The din inside the cabin was so overpowering that the only reliable way for passengers to communicate with each other—even if they declined to plug their ears—was by passing notes.)

The paper cup was for airsickness. Everyone got a cup, and almost everyone needed one. Some flights were such gut-wrenchers that the cabins had to be sluiced out afterward with hoses.

"It's a shame," Clarence said. "The public was ready for air transport, I believe. But what with contact flying and the uncomfortable planes, *we* weren't ready for *them.*"

In 1963, a *New York Times* reporter went along on a commemorative trimotor flight tracing the old TAT routes. He got off at one of the first stops and refused to reboard. He said he couldn't take any more.

TAT lasted only a year and a half. The company had dubbed itself "The Lindbergh Line," trusting that its association with the hero of the age would help drum up business. But neither the slogan nor a series of fare cuts did much good. A modest rush for tickets after the inaugural flights soon tailed off, and thereafter the company lost money steadily. The owners held out as long as they could, but in October of 1930—with the nation's economy sliding into depression—they conceded defeat by merging TAT with a competitor, Western Air Express. The new, financially stronger air carrier that resulted was named Transcontinental & Western Air, TWA. This is the outfit that, a decade later, my father went to work for.

I remember an afternoon in the 1960s when my father told me about his first job with TWA. We were sailing together south of Long Island, and intermittently aircraft headed for Kennedy Airport passed low over us. They were large, howling jetliners—707s and DC-8s—sleek machines that cast sweptback, racing shadows on the surface of the water. After one especially low flyby, my father commented how different these jets were from the plodding, piston-powered aircraft he had seen flying above Kansas City when he was a boy. Those had been trimotors, and DC-2s, and every so often a plane that had appeared colossal to him, a glistening new DC-3.

Almost all of them had been TWA planes, he said. The airline had established its headquarters in Kansas City—as many as a dozen TWA flights a day rose out of KC's Municipal Airport, just a few miles from the house his parents rented. Walking along the streets in the neighborhood, he would hear the drone of engines and spot the planes' silhouettes through the branches of the trees.

He said the planes fascinated him. He dreamed of flying in them. From time to time he would play hooky from school, hop a trolley car, and ride down to the airport to watch the planes come and go. He would study the baggage handlers loading cargo, and watch the passengers as they climbed the short boarding stairs. Then smoke would belch from the engines of one of the planes, and ground personnel would pull the chocks from its wheels, and it would taxi away from the terminal. A great show.

My father wanted to become a pilot, but he didn't see how he could. Flying lessons were too expensive—there was no way he could scratch up the money for more than an occasional joyride. Still, his fascination with planes grew and he decided he wanted to hang out around them, so when he got old enough he took a job as a clerk in TWA's hangar. It was dull work for the most part—fetching things for the airline's mechanics, keeping track of spare parts. But he got to walk right up under the planes instead of peering at them from outside the airport fence. And he could overhear the pilots talking with each other as they prepared for their flights. And sometimes he actually got to climb aboard the planes.

Mainly, he entered the planes during lunch breaks, when no one was around to tell him not to. He would climb into the cockpit of a DC-2 parked inside the hangar and lower himself into the captain's seat. Then, eating his sandwich, he would imagine how it would feel to shove the throttles forward and take the plane out.

He said he was careful not to actually touch any of the controls; he knew he'd be fired on the spot if he broke anything. So he would reach toward various switches, study their positions and functions, but hold his hand a tantalizing half-inch short.

He told me he scared himself one time, though. One afternoon while sitting in a cockpit, he thought he felt the plane suddenly drop toward the hangar floor. He was looking out the windshield, he said, and suddenly, distinctly, he saw the plane's nose swing downward.

Panic. He thought he had made the landing gear collapse somehow. He was in *major* trouble. He braced himself, expecting the plane's belly to smack down hard on the concrete. He shut his eyes and gripped the edges of the seat. But nothing happened. No shriek of aluminum buckling. No clamor of propellers splintering. Nothing. So after a moment, he reopened his eyes and peered through the windshield again. And as his heartbeat subsided, he realized that he had been victimized by an optical illusion. The plane hadn't moved downward. Somebody had opened the hangar door, sliding it up on its metal tracks.

My father said he ate his lunch somewhere else for the next several days.

Generally, the pilots I contacted during the last three years received me warmly. I would arrive at their homes with references: I would mention other pilots whom I'd already met, and allude to my father, and speak of my own interest in aviation. And generally they welcomed me in. But despite the best intentions all around, our conversations frequently stalled. Few of the pilots were like Clarence Mulholland, natural talkers who delighted in recounting their adventures. Most were just the opposite, quiet men who seemed uneasy at the prospect of conversation. A pilot would lead me into his living room, motion me to a chair and supply me with a mug of coffee or beer, and then he would sit staring at me, waiting for me to ask my questions. So I would ask, and he—looking away, or toward the ceiling, or into the distance beyond me—would answer. But often the answer was clipped, almost elliptical. The pilot wasn't trying to hold out on me. He wanted to help me; that was why he was giving me his time. But when it came down to it, he didn't find talking easy. Chitchat wasn't his style.

The best approach, I soon learned, was to talk to each pilot only about the airline he flew for. Rarely would a pilot know—or care— much about any line except his own. But if we confined ourselves to the history of that one line, his interest would sometimes ignite and the words might start coming. I went to the library and boned up on airline histories, then tried to put the histories to use when I visited pilots. TWA pilots would sometimes light up if I mentioned Lindbergh or TAT. Eastern Airlines pilots sometimes reacted the same way if I brought up Eddie Rickenbacker, the World War I fighter ace who became Eastern's president. Pan Am pilots sometimes turned on if I referred to the *China Clipper* and its captain, Eddie Musick. But if I mentioned TWA when meeting an Eastern pilot, or United Airlines when meeting someone who flew for USAir, the response was usually a blank look of boredom. Boredom or scorn.

They were proud men, almost without exception. I was never tempted to mistake a pilot's reserve for diffidence. Almost every pilot I met made it plain that he thought his particular airline was just about the finest corps of airmen ever assembled. And I got the distinct impression that, although he wouldn't say so, he thought that he personally was about as talented as any pilot the world had yet seen. Few of the men bragged. Few made explicit claims of excellence for themselves. But the way they held themselves—erect, with a characteristic air of self-confidence—and the way they tended to bite off their words, and, above all, the claims they made for their airlines (they wouldn't brag on their own behalf, but they would do so on behalf of their lines) conveyed their pride unmistakably.

I don't mean to generalize unfairly. There were certainly strong similarities among most of the pilots I met, but that's not to say the pilots were indistinguishable from one another. There was considerable diversity. Some of the men were tall, some short; some slim, some heavyset; some were voluble, some would scarcely communicate beyond nodding or shaking their heads. There were differences, too, in the degree of self-esteem the pilots exhibited. I got the impression that, as a rule, retired pilots took more pride in their careers and in their airlines (sometimes far more pride) than pilots who were still flying. And retirees from some of the larger lines seemed, as a rule, prouder than those from the smaller lines.

One group of pilots seemed to feel an especially sharp pride: men who had flown for Pan Am. It's hard to remember now, when Pan Am is rocking on the brink of bankruptcy, but there was a time when it was incontestably the most important airline in the world. While other lines were struggling to establish short overland air routes using small two- and three-engine planes, Pan Am pioneered a vast network of ocean-spanning routes using a fleet of magnificent four-engine flying boats. For many years throughout much of the world, Pan Am *was* air travel.

The career of Pan Am's most famous pilot, Ed Musick, typified the company's predominance. In the mid-1930s, Musick assumed a stature rivaled by very few pilots before or since. When his picture appeared on the cover of *Time* in December 1935, the caption read "To him, Lindbergh's dream is old stuff."

Musick began flying as a teenager, in a plane he built himself. He fashioned the plane's wings from bedsheets stapled to wooden slats; for landing gear, he used the wheels from his bicycle. When he'd finished work on the plane, he carted it to the infield of a deserted race track near his home. He spun the propeller to start the engine, then jumped into the cockpit. The plane charged across the grass, bounced once or twice, and came apart in a flurry of tangled cloth and splintered wood.

His later flights were generally more successful but no less daring.

He became a barnstormer (billed as "Daredevil Eddie Musick"), performing eye-popping aerobatic maneuvers over fairgrounds in the Midwest. Then, moving to Florida, he took a piloting job with Aeromarine, an embryonic airline that offered seaplane service in the Caribbean. When Aeromarine folded, he kept body and soul together by flying bootlegged rum from the West Indies to Florida.

He loved adventure, but there was also another side to his character. He prided himself on control. It was said that he could hold a plane exactly on its compass heading, at exactly the speed and altitude he wanted, no matter how violent the weather got. He could meet any test of airmanship, other pilots said, and he could do it with easy nonchalance, mastering himself as thoroughly as he mastered the machines he flew. He was the consummate airman.

Impressed by his flying skills, Pan Am hired him as a seaplane captain and then tapped him to conduct long-range survey flights. He became the airline's chief test pilot, working out the procedures needed to fly overseas routes safely. There was plenty to work out. Contact flying remained the norm for overland flights but it was useless on oceanic routes, so Musick and his crews used various alternative techniques to find their way. Primarily, they relied on dead reckoning, carefully following precomputed compass headings. To doublecheck their progress, they took sightings of the sun or stars with a specially designed octant, and they tossed "drift bombs"— cannisters full of dye—out the window so that they could estimate the direction and speed of the wind by observing the movement of the dye stains on the water. Later, they augmented these techniques with the first radio direction-finding equipment, picking up radio signals broadcast from shore and then calculating their position by triangulation.

Musick also tested the planes Pan Am intended to use for overseas travel. They were flying boats, built by companies such as Sikorsky and Martin to specifications drawn up by Pan Am's engineering department. The airline wanted flying boats rather than conventional airplanes for several reasons. Many of Pan Am's proposed routes would terminate in regions where no airports existed. It would be cheaper to build planes that could land in bays or lagoons than to construct airports in distant parts of the world. Moreover, flying boats offered a promise of increased safety. If the engines of an ordinary plane failed somewhere out over the ocean, anyone aboard would be a goner. But a flying boat could put down on the waves and, with luck, remain afloat until a rescue party arrived.

Musick demonstrated himself to be unflappable, admirably methodical, and brave. The sole complaint against him was that he was awfully close-mouthed, even by the standards of a terse profession. On April 16, 1935, he conducted the first test flight across the Pacific, from San Francisco to Hawaii. Before takeoff, he agreed to radio periodic reports of his progress. He fulfilled the agreement, after a fashion. He made the reports, but they were cryptically brief. "Sunset," one of them went, "6:39." Period. End of report. No information about the plane's condition, no specifics about longitude and latitude. The Pan Am officials clustered around radio receivers must have gritted their teeth. But I suppose they consoled themselves with the thought that if Musick was calmly noting the moment of sunset, he must still be alive—his plane must still be out there, somewhere, droning along through the Pacific sky.

Pan Am's brass forgave Musick his idiosyncracies. The man might be difficult, but he sure could fly. He pulled off the test flight to Hawaii successfully, and he completed several subsequent tests in the same triumphant (albeit tight-lipped) manner. Then, on November 19, 1935, he piloted Pan Am's first operational transpacific flight, a trip from San Francisco to the Philippines via Hawaii, Midway, Wake, and Guam. The plane he used was the *China Clipper*, a ninety-foot-long flying boat that—because of this flight—would become the most famous aircraft since the *Spirit of St. Louis*. (When Warner Brothers made a movie about the aerial conquest of the Pacific, they named it *China Clipper*. Humphrey Bogart played the character based on Ed Musick.)

Fireworks cracked and a hundred thousand spectators cheered as Musick guided the *Clipper* through its takeoff run in San Francisco Harbor. More than a dozen escort planes swirled overhead (they would turn back after accompanying the *Clipper* along the first few miles of its flight). Fireboats sent streams of salt water skyward, and oceanliners sounded a salute with their horns. The departure was covered by nine radio networks from North and South America, Europe, and Asia. It had been preceded by the reading of telegraphed messages from the governor of Hawaii and the president of the Philippines. The postmaster general of the United States had been on hand to read a message from President Roosevelt.

Two years after piloting the *Clipper* across the Pacific, Musick was dead. He was killed while conducting another test flight, this time surveying a route to New Zealand. His plane developed mechanical problems following a takeoff from Pago Pago, so he shut down his number four engine and turned back. Then he began dumping fuel to reduce the plane's weight before landing.

Normally, dumping excess fuel would have been prudent. But in the type of plane Musick was flying that day—a Sikorsky flying boat—it was potentially calamitous. Technicians had known for some time that the Sikorskys had a design flaw that allowed fuel vapors to gather inside the wings when the dump valves—located on the undersides of the wings—were opened. The risk was judged to be acceptable, however, and Musick was not informed about the problem.

Musick opened the valves and fuel began flowing in thin streams from the wings. Then, as the plane approached Pago Pago, he lowered his wing flaps. The technicians had misjudged the risk. Fuel vapors inside the wings ignited when a spark leaped from the electric motor that operated the flaps. The plane exploded and fell into the sea.

Air Sense

I'VE VISITED MY FATHER SEVERAL TIMES NOW TO TALK WITH HIM ABOUT HIS CAREER AS A PILOT. We were both uncomfortable during the first few of these visits. We weren't accustomed to sitting together in a room, talking; we weren't sure how to do it. So, instead, we got out. We drove to Kennedy Airport to walk through the TWA facilities there, or we drove out to some of the small airports on eastern Long Island, fields used mainly by private pilots. And as we drove, I would ask my father questions, and he would reminisce.

He said he held his job as a hangar clerk until shortly after the attack on Pearl Harbor, when he enlisted in the Army. He took and passed the tests to become an air cadet, then was shipped to Texas where the Army gave him the flight training he couldn't have afforded on his own. He said he hoped he would be selected to fly fighter planes, but he was assigned to heavy bombers instead. So he wound up in Europe, in a B-17 squadron. After the war, he returned to Kansas City, where he applied for a new job with TWA, as a copilot this time rather than a clerk.

Conditions on the airlines were markedly different after the war, he said. Trimotors landing in farm fields, seaplanes exploding over Pago Pago—it wasn't that way anymore. The daredevil days were pretty well over. "The airlines had much better equipment by the time I got started," he said. "The war probably compressed twenty years of aeronautical progress into just four or five years. Everything was accelerated because of the pressure to keep ahead of the Germans and Japanese. So when the war ended, airline work was a different deal. The planes were better, the navigation gear and the radios were better—everything had improved.

"Flying was settling down. It was still challenging and interesting. But a certain amount of the adventure had gone out of it."

I asked if he hadn't found this disappointing. I'd always assumed one of the main reasons guys became pilots was in order to seek adventure. Wasn't that what he wanted? To whip a plane around the sky, to charge off into the wild blue?

"Not really," he said. "Or if I did, I got enough excitement in the war to last me.

"I think I hit the airlines at just about the right time, actually. The '40s and '50s were great years for pilots. Earlier, the planes were so primitive, flying could be pretty miserable. And today it's gone to the other extreme. Everything is so automated, it's almost boring. But there was that period in there when the planes were great to fly, and you actually *flew* them, you didn't just sit and watch some computers flying them. It wasn't rip-roaring excitement, but that wasn't what I was looking for. It was good, solid flying."

His answer sounded familiar. Other pilots of his generation had said much the same to me. The new conditions on the airlines had suited them fine. They felt no desire to perform wild-assed aerobatics or to punch their way through snowstorms or to pioneer routes to places like Pago Pago. They claimed they liked nothing better than to conduct routine, wholly unremarkable flights: depart on time, reach each checkpoint along the route on time, get to the destination on time. They were proud that they had never damaged an airplane, never hurt a passenger. They said they flew cautiously—they wanted to give their passengers a comfortable ride and then turn in for a peaceful night's rest.

Some of the men had gotten angry at me for questioning them on the point. When I used words like "daring" and "adventure," they frowned and set me straight. Airline pilots have no daredevil impulses, they informed me. They are meticulous, buttoned-down aviators. They are professionals.

I believed them, for the most part. I thought I believed my father. But I caught a gleam in some of the men's eyes; and I heard some stories . . . . As a matter of fact, the stories I heard from pilots nearly always belied the image that the pilots seemed to want to project. The pilots made themselves out to be staid, conservative, serious. But when they got to talking, they usually told comic stories about pilots who were anything but. There was often a note of censure in their voices when they told these stories. There was also a note of something else, though.

My father told me a few such stories as we drove Long Island's highways. "I knew one captain in the 1950s," he said, "who used to descend to just five hundred feet above the ocean on his way to Europe. He flew the plane about as close to the water as he could. He would only do it at night, so his passengers never knew the difference.

"Maybe there was some justification for what he did. The air is warmer down there, anyway—less chance of picking up ice. But it was obvious that, no matter what his other reasons were, mostly he was sneaking down low like that for the sheer hell of it."

My father and I both laughed. "Of course, it wasn't really funny," my father said. "He was dangerous.

"But other guys cut loose sometimes, too, although usually in smaller ways. One time when I was a copilot, the captain I was flying with suddenly started whipping the [steering] wheel left and right and shoving the yoke [the hinged column attached to the wheel] in and out. I couldn't figure out what he was doing—the air was calm and there wasn't anything wrong with the plane. But of course as a young copilot, I knew better than to question this authority, this *god,* who was sitting there beside me. So I just watched him.

"He kept it up for a while, working the controls like he was fighting to save the plane. Then he started to ease up, and after a little he was flying quietly again. He didn't say anything for a minute, he just flew along. Then he turned to me and winked. 'Rough air,' he said."

I heard many similar stories from other pilots. In fact, I was treated to some particularly colorful stories over and over: stories that, I gathered, had passed into flying legend. For example, several men told me the story of Harold Gilman and the bridge in Kansas City.

Gilman had a reputation as a throttle-bending, natural stick-and-rudder man. He was said to fly his plane full-out, throttles all the way forward—balls to the wall. "He was hell on the equipment," one of his former colleagues told me. "I mean, you wouldn't want to be the mechanic who had to overhaul the engines that Gilman had ridden hard for a few hours. But then, guys always said he could get an airplane to do things very few other pilots could."

Like all legends, the story of Gilman's flight under the bridge is hard to pin down. I heard so many versions, some of them distorted by such obvious exaggerations, that I grew less sure of the facts each time I heard the story repeated. Maybe no one recalls anymore what really happened; the myth may have wholly overwhelmed the facts. So I won't swear that the following version is true. Let's just call it the version that emerges after the most conspicuous embellishments have been stripped away.

Sometime during the 1950s, Gilman was taking off from Kansas City in a Lockheed Constellation when one of the plane's engines quit. This was not a big problem. You don't *want* to lose an engine on takeoff, but the condition isn't necessarily critical in a four-engine plane like a Connie. Gilman told his flight engineer (the crewman responsible for maintaining the plane's engines and other systems) to feather the defective engine—lock the propeller and adjust the pitch of its blades so that they paralleled the airstream. The engineer complied and Gilman pushed on, steering the Connie out over the dike that protects KC Municipal Airport from the waters of the Missouri River.

Then, just as the landing gear came up, a second engine quit. Now this *was* trouble. Fully loaded Connies weren't supposed to be able to climb with half their engines out. And this Connie had no airspeed to speak of; it was hanging onto the lowest stratum of the sky by its fingernails, just a hundred feet or so above the river.

Worse yet, the second engine refused to feather. Instead, its propeller started spinning at the wrong pitch and speed, creating drag that was sure to force the plane to stall. So Gilman was going to crash. Only he didn't. Somehow, pressing his remaining engines to and beyond their limits, he kept the Connie going. He banked her around and, dumping fuel, lined her up with a runway. He edged her over the dike, lowered her landing gear, and brought her in. *The Connie sagged toward the concrete—and then the wheels were down—and she had landed.*

It was a miracle of airmanship. Gilman deserved a commendation; he deserved a parade down Main Street and a blowout at a local bar. So, naturally, what he got instead was a suspension and an interminable round of hearings. Nitpickers from the Civil Aeronautics Administration pointed out a few discrepancies in Gilman's performance. It seems that he forgot to close the dump valves before landing, for one thing: Gas was still flowing from the wings when the plane set down. He forgot to get clearance to land, for another: He didn't radio the control tower on his way back to the airport. He just turned his plane around and landed her, trusting that any other planes on the runway would clear out of his way.

And then there's the question of the bridge. A long, lovely, low-slung bridge that spans the river between the airport and downtown KC. On his way back to the field, Gilman evidently slipped the plane under this inviting structure. Maybe he had no choice. Maybe he was so low, and the plane was so unmaneuverable, that he could do nothing but plow under the bridge before beating his precarious retreat to the airport. *The bridge was right in front of him—it loomed in his path—there was no alternative.* But the investigators doubted it. They figured they knew Gilman too well. They figured that like any born-and-bred cowboy pilot, Gilman had always wanted to fly an airliner under a bridge.

The plane was staggering through the air. Gilman was lower over the river than he'd ever been, and as he roared at the engineer to cut the horseshit and feather the goddamned engine, the bridge loomed up ahead. In a flash of purest inspiration, he realized that this was his chance. He bled off a little more altitude and, maybe waggling his wings ever so slightly, eased under her. Just to keep the day interesting. And then he came around and landed, pretty as you please.

The investigators were apoplectic. It was the most harebrained, death-defying, hellfire magnificent piece of flying any of them had ever heard of. No, delete magnificent. They were determined to condemn such mad-macho shenanigans. What was he trying to do, kill everybody on board? Nobody could survive such antics. But Gilman had them there. He told them he couldn't rightly recall whether he'd gone under the bridge or not. But as to surviving, "Well," he said, "I'm here, aren't I?"

Occasionally when I visited a pilot, he would introduce me to some of his friends—other pilots whom he'd invited to sit in on our conversation. These were always interesting sessions. As the outsider, I was usually the focus of attention at first. But I tried to back away from that position—I thought I'd learn more if the pilots forgot about me and talked to each other as they would when there were no nonpilots present.

A few times, it almost happened. The pilots never lost track of me altogether, but on a couple of evenings in a couple of living rooms, I heard groups of pilots do a bit of "hangar flying," swapping tales and rumors about their colleagues. One pilot would tell of a particularly admirable, or preposterous, or damnable piece of flying he'd heard about somewhere, and then the other pilots would pitch in with their own favorite tales, and before long my presence faded.

What intrigued me most about hangar flying was the tone of voice the pilots adopted when they told each other stories. It was the same tone I'd heard my father use recently. There was a strong trace of condemnation in it: One of the pilots would tell about a wacko aerial hotdog—a pilot who buzzed his friends' homes or who liked to fly at the edge of stall speed in order to make his flights "more interesting"—and all the other men in the room would shake their heads and pass judgment. "He must have been nuts," they said. "Only a jackass would fly like that." But then they would all compete to top that story with one that was still wilder. And often, as with the retelling of Gilman's exploit, admiration would become evident in their voices. "Mind you, I wouldn't want to do it myself. Under a bridge? Christ. He must have been one crackerjack pilot, though, to get that plane back to the airfield."

The amount of admiration the men expressed seemed to be proportional to the age of the story. Stories that were decades old were received with good spirits and laughter, while stories about the present tended to elicit frowns. This puzzled me for a bit, until I recognized that there was an unspoken statute of limitations in force. The passage of time had removed the sting from questionable flying performances that occurred long ago, whereas present-day screw-ups retained their power to embarrass. The pilots wouldn't countenance mistakes by guys who were still out on the line. They clearly felt that such episodes threw their profession into disrepute, and they wanted no part of that. Time hadn't softened the offense yet. But the old pranks were different.

Only one form of flying seemed immune from even the faintest hint of criticism. This was the airmail piloting of the 1920s and '30s. The pilots I encountered seemed fascinated by it. They told about lone airmen who had gone aloft in single-engine planes, in all weather conditions, carrying small consignments of airmail. They told how the mail pilots frequently crashed or got lost. They told how sometimes, if an engine quit or a plane caught fire, a mail pilot would bail out, leaving the mail bags behind to burn when his plane plummeted to earth. They enumerated the mail pilots' misadventures, and they laughed over them, but they were never critical. Instead, they seemed envious.

The men I heard telling these stories were too young to have any direct knowledge of airmail flying. So they weren't being nostalgic, precisely—they had never sat at the controls of a mail plane, never faced the challenges the mail pilots had faced. For them, the '20s and '30s were a period of fables, not memories. But they obviously loved the fables. Maybe they wouldn't have wanted to fly like the mail pilots—in tiny planes with scant instrumentation and faithless engines—but they certainly enjoyed imagining it, and I thought I knew why. A little daredevilry wasn't a sin on a mail flight. Just the opposite: It was a positive requirement.

I tried to find oldsters who could give me firsthand accounts of the airmail days. For a while, my luck ran against me. One man I contacted said yes, he had flown the mail; but no, he wouldn't talk to me. Another former mail pilot agreed to meet me, but when we sat down together his memory proved so sketchy that I didn't learn much.

Eventually, though, my luck changed. I met Timothy Smithfield one morning in 1986 when I was a visitor at a reunion of retired airline pilots. He spoke up during some impromptu hangar flying that developed in the hotel lobby—a bald, bearded man who repeatedly trumped the other pilots, telling stories that went farther back than anyone else's. When the group dispersed for lunch, I introduced myself to him and asked if we could talk privately. He said he supposed that would be all right. We walked to a restaurant down the street from the hotel, and, after we'd been seated, I asked him to repeat some of the stories he'd told at the hotel, especially the ones about airmail flights.

"Back in the '30s," he said, "there weren't many passengers willing to ride in airplanes. But the Post Office paid pretty well for us to carry the mail, so that's how the airlines made their money. We wouldn't have kept bread on the table without it.

"Some airlines didn't even fool with passengers, they flew the mail and nothing else. That was the whole reason they went into business. Others started out that way but then switched over to carrying passengers too. Sometimes they took passengers in the same planes with the mail and sometimes they had two sets of planes, the big ones to carry passengers in and these small one-engine planes to carry the mail.

"Flying the mail could be sort of rough sometimes, *that's* the truth. They used to call the run over the Allegheny Mountains the 'Graveyard Run' because so many of the boys came down there. The weather was rotten there and a lot of the flying was at night, which made it that much more dangerous.

"Fortunately, cracking up didn't kill you every time. Some of the boys would crash but they would be okay, and if the plane didn't burn they would just fish out the mail bag and hike to a train station or somewhere and send it along that way.

"If you didn't crack up, sometimes you had to bail out because you would run out of fuel when you were lost. So you wore a parachute. I never had to jump myself, but they told about one boy who did, and he got tangled in some tree limbs and got banged up. But the funny thing was, his plane came down and landed itself fine without him. He should of ridden her down, but how could he know?

"I'll tell you one thing that *did* happen to me. I remember I was up over Philadelphia one time and I got caught in a storm like I'd never seen before. I flew into some clouds that I didn't want to be in and before I knew it I got hit by an updraft—bam!—that took me up a couple thousand feet. There wasn't a thing I could do about it, it just carried me up there. Then as soon as I leveled her off—bam!—a downdraft knocked me down even faster than I'd gone up. And it flipped me over. I mean, the next thing I knew, I was upside down and I'd lost control.

"I didn't know what the hell to do. I sure as hell didn't want to jump because I couldn't see the ground—I didn't know how high up I was or which way was down even, and I thought if I *did* jump the 'chute might not open up in time. So there was nothing for me to do but just hang on. So that's what I did. I just rode along until finally the plane fell out into the clear air under the storm. Then I could right the plane and go on.

"See, we were totally on our own. The mail planes just had the one person on board, the pilot. There was room for a couple of passengers in some of them but we hardly ever had any. We didn't *want* passengers on the mail flights, to tell you the truth. One of the boys got killed one time because he had a passenger. He got into some trouble and likely wanted to bail out, but passengers 'most always refused to jump. So he rode the plane down, to stay with his passenger, and they both got killed.

"I was pretty green when I started out and I thought I knew how to fly as well as the next man. But after that experience in that storm, I decided I better get some sense. I decided maybe I better try to learn the techniques the more experienced pilots used, because I'm not crapping you, anything could happen and you had to know how to react.

"There was this other time when I was flying from Pittsburgh to Harrisburg and the weather was fine. I didn't have a single problem. You could see your way pretty well as long as the moon was shining, and it was a good full one that night. So I was just sitting up there at five thousand feet singing to myself or whatever. And then all at once the engine quit.

"I switched gas tanks and I did this and I did that, but I couldn't get that engine back. So I had to do something in kind of a hurry because I was coming down. Well, I had these parachute flares with me, so I threw them over the side one at a time. That way I could see where the ground was and get some light on the subject. So I followed the flares down and I got under the last one and I landed at a farm.

"That's just the way it was back then, pretty wild and woolly. I used to joke about this girlfriend I had that my wife didn't know about. What

I meant was Lady Luck. But I knew your luck could run out so you had to try to learn how to really fly.

"I tried like hell to learn it. I studied how the other boys operated and I wasn't shy about asking them questions. And after a while I believe I did learn something about it. Enough so I didn't get killed anyway."

The first airmail pilots flew exposed to the elements, in cockpits that were open to the wind and rain. They had no choice. They had few instruments other than their senses, so they couldn't accept barriers between themselves and the sky. The wind on a man's cheeks told him whether he was flying straight or yawing to one side. The scents borne on the air helped him navigate—he learned to differentiate the distinctive odors of various mills and factories along his routes. He listened to the thrum of his propeller and to the concussive rumble of his engine, judging from these cues whether any problems were developing in his plane's mechanical innards. And if he was flying a biplane, he listened for changes in the sound of the air whistling through the guy wires: He had been told that if he approached a stall, the air would play the descending melody of "Nearer My God to Thee."

Each sense was important; each had to be attended to. Even senses located in relatively obtuse portions of the anatomy—the rump, for example—could convey useful information. "Flying by the seat of your pants" wasn't a description of carelessness in those days. The phrase had a technical, critically urgent meaning. If a pilot felt himself sliding across his seat while executing a turn, he knew that the plane was slipping sideways through the air; he had to improve his coordination of the rudder and ailerons. Or if he pulled back on the stick and the seat came up firmly, he knew the plane had plenty of lift and was well above stall speed. But if, conversely, the seat rose hesitantly, he knew the plane was mushing through the air—he had to get the plane's nose down or push the throttle forward to increase his speed.

Pilots tried to achieve an exquisite sensitivity to their aircraft and to the sky itself. They wanted to develop the subtle intuition called air sense: the fine attunement that would enable them—as far as their minds and senses were capable of it—to feel at home in the sky. They consulted the dials on their instrument panels for whatever information they could glean there, but most of their attention was focused outside the cockpit. There weren't many dials on the panels, in any case. Some early mail planes had only three instruments: an airspeed indicator, an altimeter, and a magnetic compass. Pilots found them helpful but not absolutely essential.

As the 1920s advanced, however, more informative instruments began appearing in cockpits. Gyroscopically stabilized compasses gave better guidance than the old-fashioned magnetic compasses. Rate-of-climb gauges told pilots how fast their planes ascended or descended. Turn-and-bank gauges told how fast the planes turned and whether they slipped sideways while turning. The most valuable new gadget was the artificial horizon, a gimballed sphere with a line painted on it to represent the earth's horizon. When a plane maneuvered, a gyroscope held this line steady. Thus, if darkness or clouds prevented a pilot from seeing the horizon outside his windshield, he could maintain his orientation in space by keeping his eye on the painted line.

The new instruments revolutionized the character of flight. They let pilots test their air sense and compensate for its deficiencies. If a pilot thought he might be coming down too fast during a landing approach, he could consult the rate-of-climb gauge to find out. If he thought he wasn't coordinating rudder and ailerons well enough during turns—if he felt that telltale slippage under his rump—he could consult the turn-and-bank gauge. By flying "on instruments," he could *know* what was going on, not guess. He gained far greater control over his aircraft.

The mail pilots didn't abandon air sense in favor of instrument flying. Air sense remained important to them, just as it remains important to pilots today. But, gradually, the mail pilots learned to put more faith in the data presented on the dials than in the conclusions they drew from their senses. They disciplined themselves to check the dials continually during each flight, and if there was a conflict between the dials and their senses, they disciplined themselves to go with the dials. It was hard, it ran contrary to natural impulse, but they knew it was necessary. They had seen too many of their buddies crash when trying to fly on air sense alone. During the early 1920s, the mortality rate among mail pilots was so high that few of the men survived for more than five years after taking the job.

The fundamental problem with air sense is that true adaptation to the sky calls for skills that lie beyond human capabilities. Millions of years of conditioning have prepared us for life under the sky, not in it: We possess neither the senses nor the intuitions that the sky requires. There are birds—sooty terns—that take their first flight when they are hatchlings and do not alight again for three years. They dwell wholly in the sky for those years, flying ceaselessly, eating on the wing, sleeping on the wing. They are meant for the sky in a way we can never be. But except for the extreme length of their flights, sooty terns aren't unique among birds. All birds are incomparably better fliers than the most skilled human pilot can dream of becoming.

Think of an ordinary sparrow sweeping low over your lawn, then sailing up, rising above the branch outside your window. Cupping and backpedaling the air with its wings as it emerges above the branch, it hangs a moment, stopped in midair. Then it stretches out its feet, grasps the branch, and there, so easily, it comes to rest. You could visit air shows for the rest of your life and never see a demonstration of flying skill to equal that. Or consider the birds' best-kept secret, their ability to migrate thousands of miles, navigating with what is—to us—uncanny accuracy. Flying by night as well as day, under clouds as well as through clear skies, traversing oceans, winging across continents, they return each year to the precise location (sometimes to the same branch in the same tree) where they last nested. How do they do it? We don't know. Researchers speculate that birds are born with magnetized materials in their brains—built-in compasses; or that birds have an innate knowledge of the positions of the stars, which they use for celestial navigation; or that birds' eyes, sensitive to portions of the electromagnetic spectrum in which we are blind, somehow convert the sun's rays into polarized directional markings in the sky. But we don't know. We lack whatever senses the birds call upon.

Glider pilots sometimes find themselves riding a thermal with birds. Spiraling upward inside an ascending column of warm air, the pilots look out their canopies to see broad-winged birds—hawks or condors—rising inside the same column. Sometimes a bird will sit in the wind just beyond a glider's wingtip. It's a wonderful moment, man and bird flying as companions in the sky; and for that moment, the man can experience something approximating true birdlike flight. But the approximation is crude. The man flies within a vehicle whereas the bird *is* its vehicle; its nerves stretch down the length of its wings, sensing and manipulating the air directly. No human flier will ever know how that feels. And yet many pilots told me that attempting to gain oneness with the vehicle is central to a pilot's function. If a pilot remains mentally separate from his aircraft, they said, his reactions will be too slow, his perceptions too opaque. A pilot cannot let himself feel that he, sitting inside a complex machine, is operating controls that, through a system of cables and hydraulic boosts, shift the angle of the hinged control surfaces out there on the wings and stabilizers. That's too ponderous, too abstract. A pilot must come to feel that in some manner his arms *do* stretch out along the wings, that when he turns, it is himself that turns, not the machine: *His* arms catch the wind, *his* body banks and changes course. He must try to experience the invisible flow of air over his wings, to comprehend his movement within the all-but-impalpable medium of the sky.

Not easy. We lack some of the senses the task requires, and—an equally severe handicap—the senses we do possess tend to go out of whack once we leave the ground. Our eyes, for example, are prone to a dysfunction called open field myopia. When we climb a few hundred feet up into the air, there are no nearby objects to help us judge distances, so our eyes lose depth perception—they tend to focus on a spot six feet ahead. In effect, they stop seeing.

Our other senses are similarly affected by conditions in the sky, which can leave us dangerously disoriented. Like Timothy Smithfield inside a thunderstorm, we may not even be able to differentiate up from down. There's a story about an English fighter pilot who used this human failing to his advantage during World War I. While flying through scattered clouds, he spotted a German fighter plane just a hundred yards or so away. His machine guns were jammed—he was defenseless. But, thinking quickly, he turned directly toward the German and then rolled his plane over so that he was inverted. Seeing him, the German pilot became disoriented; he couldn't tell which plane was bottom-up, his or the Englishman's. He guessed wrong. He rolled over to match his adversary's attitude, whereupon he stalled and crashed.

By the mid-1930s, flying and instrument flying had become virtually synonymous, and pilots came indoors. Cockpits were enclosed, cutting the pilots off from the elements. No more rain in the face or sleet down the collar. No more steering by smell or by testing the pressure of the wind on your cheek. Now pilots sat in small, heated cubicles behind panels loaded with delicately calibrated gadgets. It was a great improvement, but it was also an admission of defeat. Flight was transformed from a primarily physical to a primarily mental process. Pilots no longer tried to imitate the natural ease and exuberance of the birds; they concentrated on interpreting the movements of small needles across the faces of small circular dials.

Last year, my father told me that he has always considered flying to be essentially a mental exercise. Air sense had been subordinated to instrument flying more than a decade before he became a student pilot.

"When I was learning to fly," he said, "I quickly caught on that it was a thinking game. I don't mean that you had to be brilliant to do it. I've known some pretty dumb pilots. But the main impression I had during my first lessons was that I was suspended in the air inside this machine. I remember being surprised that there wasn't much sensation of speed. I didn't feel like I was soaring and swooping around—nothing like that. I felt stationary, really, and my job was to adjust the controls to get the machine into whatever attitude the instructor wanted.

"They still teach flying pretty much the same way. They start you off flying 'visual flight rules'—you only fly when there's good visibility, and the point is to get a feel for how airplanes handle. But then when you graduate to 'instrument flight rules,' you're supposed to go almost completely by the instruments. Making the transition can be tough. In a way, instrument flying contradicts the things you learned before. You don't totally ignore the feel of the airplane, but to a large extent that's what you're supposed to do. You're taught to believe the instruments.

"Flying was a science by the time I started. You moved the controls in a certain way and the plane responded in a certain way. The fun part was the amount of skill involved. A good instrument pilot could keep the needles pegged exactly where he wanted them. That's what we aimed for as students. The way I thought of it was, you visualized the position you wanted the airplane to be in, then you moved the controls to put it there. Basically, it was just a question of getting the needles to go to the right places."

I said I thought his description sounded radically different from most people's notions about flight. "It's different from mine, for sure," I said. Since boyhood, I'd had dreams in which I could fly—literally, bodily fly. The dreams never involved machinery. Generally they were levitation dreams. I described them to my father: how, standing in a meadow, I would catch a breeze on my body and rise into the air; I would glide above the ground effortlessly, sailing through gentle turns and climbs.

As far as I knew, I said, everybody had such dreams occasionally. I asked my father if he'd had them. He said yes, but not for a long time now. "If I dream about flying anymore," he said, "I'm always flying an airplane, not flying under my own power.

"The planes aren't necessarily realistic, though. I remember a dream where I was flying this weird metal wing. The thing didn't have a fuselage, it was just a wing, and I was sitting on top of it in a straight-back chair. I was flying it just by thinking about what I wanted it to do. I was doing a hell of a good job of it, too—the thing flew really well. But I kept having trouble with the chair. It kept sliding around on top of the wing, and that annoyed me. I felt like I should be skillful enough to control the chair as well as the wing."

The revolution that began with the development of new instruments in the 1920s reached its completion with the development of radio navigation systems in the '30s.

Two systems were devised. Pan Am came up with a long-range direction finder for use on its overseas flights, while domestic U.S. airlines outfitted their planes with "radio range" receivers. These were special radios designed to pick up the signals broadcast by a network of transmitting stations built along the major continental air routes. By following the signals, pilots could fly above the clouds or through fog and still find their way—they no longer needed to fly contact.

Radio-range signals made for dull listening. When a pilot was securely on course, all he heard in his earphones was a monotone hum. When he drifted off course, he heard a Morse code letter: an A (dit-dah) if he had drifted to one side, an N (dah-dit) if he had drifted to the other. Navigating was a matter of tuning in the station you wanted to fly toward and then approaching it by staying inside the narrow slice of sky—pilots called it a leg—where you heard the hum. (The term "leg" led to a certain amount of pilot humor. Several pilots told me leg anecdotes. An example: There was a radio range station in Mercer, Pennsylvania, not far from the town of Sharon. TWA had a particularly attractive hostess named Mercer, so when TWA pilots were flying above Pennsylvania they enjoyed getting on the radio to announce that they were working their way up Mercer's leg. Then, after they passed the station, they would get back on the air to report, "Mercer's behind me. Now I'm over Sharon." They would end the transmission with a loud sigh.)

Radio navigation got dicey in severe weather. The range stations broadcast on low frequencies, which meant storms could obliterate their signals. Lightning overwhelmed the signals with violent bursts of white noise. Heavy rain deflected the signals. Sleet splintered them, creating multiple phantom signals that swung side to side. Pilots sat with bulky earphones clamped to their heads, listening to a mad cacophony of squawks, pops, and squeals, and tried to detect somewhere within that chaos the humming that could guide them to the next station.

Landings could get dicey, too, especially if there was an undercast. Radio-range signals were not accurate enough to guide you to the precise spot in the sky where you should begin your landing descent. At best, they would lead you to the general vicinity of the airport, after which you were on your own. Newark Airport provided the classic example. In the 1930s, Newark was the busiest airport in the nation, but it did not have its own range station. The nearest station was in New Brunswick, several miles away. What should you do, then, if you found yourself above New Brunswick and clouds obscured your view of the ground? How could you find the airport in Newark?

Each airline had its own procedures. Retired TWA pilots told me they worked out this technique: While flying toward New Brunswick, they would radio the dispatchers in the TWA office at Newark. The dispatchers in turn would telephone Pam Setton, the wife of TWA captain Hal Setton. The Settons' house happened to be located under one of the New Brunswick legs. "So you flew along that leg," the pilots said, "and Pam leaned out her window to listen for your plane. When she heard you directly overhead, she gave the word to the dispatchers and they told you to start your turn. You banked around then and started down into the clouds. You wouldn't see a thing, but you would hold your heading and mind your descent rate, and if Pam Setton's hearing hadn't gotten worse since your last trip, the airport would appear smack in front of you when you dropped below the clouds. So you would come on in to land."

Bill Frandt, a former Eastern Airlines pilot, told me a radio-range story that, to my mind, serves as a fitting coda for the earliest days of airline flying. It's the story of the evening when Dick Merrill landed without meaning to.

Merrill was Eastern's most celebrated pilot, a fabled character from the airmail days. He was famous for flying his mail runs through weather that kept all the other pilots on the ground. And he was a colorful guy. Sometimes he flew the mail with his pet lion on board. Sometimes he flew twenty feet above the ground, where he said there were no headwinds. Sometimes in midsummer he flew in his swimming trunks, so the heat wouldn't bother him.

I wish I could have met Merrill—nearly every Eastern pilot I talked to had yarns to spin about him. They said that if any man embodied old-time, rough-and-ready flying, it was Merrill. I'd have loved to hear him reminisce. But Merrill died a few years before I began traveling around the country talking with fliers. The closest I could come to meeting him was to seek out some of his former crewmates, guys who had flown with him when he switched from the mail runs to passenger flights. That's why I looked up Bill Frandt. I knew Bill had been with Merrill on the evening of the unplanned landing (several retired Eastern pilots had referred to the episode), so I phoned him and asked if we could get together. Then, one winter afternoon in 1985, I visited him at his farmhouse in eastern Pennsylvania.

"Merrill was quite a guy," Bill said. "He was a gambler, he liked to go to the track a lot. And he hung around with show people. He married a movie star, you know [a Jean Harlow look-alike named, appropriately, Toby Wing]. But he was a good captain to fly with, he treated you okay.

"Now about this one flight. You need to understand that most of the time nothing especially exciting happened. The flights were uneventful. You would fly along and pick up the range signals fine and everything would be the way we wanted it. So this one flight was unusual."

It was a December evening in 1934. The weather was poor, but nothing to worry about by Merrill's standards: some snow, maybe a little chop. Merrill had flown through plenty worse, and in any case he prided himself on never cancelling a flight.

"I was his copilot and we were coming up from Charleston to Newark in a DC-2. We flew along and everything was fine for a while until we got into the weather. Then we couldn't see much and the radio faded out. We couldn't pick up any signals. Merrill had told me to work the radio while he flew, but when we hit the weather, I couldn't get anything. The weather was a mess."

The white of the sky and the white of the ground slid together: The plane swam through an indistinct blur of water vapor and eddying snowflakes. Slowly this white blur turned gray and then black as the night came on.

Pressing his earphones against his ears, Bill kept trying to detect an A or N, but without luck. He didn't fare much better with the company radio, either. There was no centralized air traffic control system in the mid-1930s; each airline operated its own radio centers, manned by dispatchers. When Bill dialed Eastern's frequency and asked for the Newark weather, all he got in reply was a cannonade of pops and whistles interspersed with a few almost-English phrases. "Metuchen," he thought he heard, and "three." He reported this to Merrill, who interpreted it as permission to descend to three thousand feet over Metuchen, a New Jersey town where legs from the Allentown and New Brunswick range stations intersected. So Merrill reduced power and started down. They weren't headed toward Metuchen, though. Merrill and Bill didn't realize that the winds, blowing far harder than expected, had shoved their plane northwest of its intended course. Instead of lying ahead of them, Metuchen was to their south.

As the plane descended, a new cannonade began. Sharp thuds suddenly sounded on the aluminum walls of the fuselage, loud rattling thwacks. Both men grabbed their flashlights, tugged open their side windows, and peered out.

"We were picking up ice," Bill said. "A real good coating of it."

Ugly, milk-white hoar ice was accumulating on the wings. The ice could weigh the plane down, or, worse, alter the effective shape of the airfoils, destroying their lift. The thudding sounds were produced by chunks of ice being flung off the propellers. The pilots increased the carburetor heating in the engines and activated the deicing boots on the front edges of the wings: long, hollow rubber tubes. Pulses of air blown into the tubes forced them to expand and contract, breaking off the layers of ice outside.

"We gave the props a shot of alcohol, too," Bill added. "We had a control that sent alcohol onto the propellers to melt off the ice there."

The plane reached three thousand feet, but it was still inside the storm, and Bill's radio reception had deteriorated further as the plane came down. Even the company frequency was entirely filled with static now. Merrill decelerated to less than a hundred miles an hour and descended further, hoping to get under the clouds so he could see the ground. With the radio out, he had no alternative but to fly contact. He took the plane down to two thousand feet, then to fifteen hundred. But the ground stayed hidden.

"By this time," Bill said, "we didn't know where the heck we were. Merrill thought fifteen hundred feet was plenty of altitude, though, and it would have been if we were over central New Jersey like he thought. He didn't realize that we had gone up toward New York where there are mountains."

Pushing back his useless earphones to say something to Merrill, Bill heard a whispering scrape travel along the belly of the plane—a quick, whisklike shiver racing under their seats. It came and went in an instant. Then it was repeated. Then it was augmented: more whisks, followed by heavier scratches, and then loud splintering cracks. The plane shook itself and, after seeming to pause in midair, lurched downward.

Merrill comprehended the situation immediately, Bill said. He pulled off the power and hauled back on the yoke. The sounds beneath them rose to a crescendo of breakage, then ceased. The plane had landed, ripping a downward-slanting path through tree limbs and shrubbery on a wooded mountainside in New York State, fifty miles north of Newark.

Merrill, Bill, and their eight passengers scrambled out of the plane. No one had been badly hurt. A few folks had a scratch or two, Bill said, but that was all. The plane seemed to be essentially intact also.

"One of the engines was on fire," Bill said, "but we threw mud and snow on it, and it went out.

"Then we built a fire to try to keep warm. We gathered wood and lit it, but then somebody made the mistake of tossing some pillows on the fire. They burned all right, but I can still smell the stink of those feathers."

A search party found them within a couple of hours and took them down the mountain to a small town where cars were waiting to drive them to Newark.

"I'm sure Merrill was embarrassed by the way the flight ended," Bill said, "but he didn't let on any. He just took things in stride. He acted pretty much the way he always did."

The night was still young when they reached Newark. So Merrill bid his passengers farewell and drove into Manhattan. He hooked up with some of his pals at a nightclub, pretty much the way he always did.

The DC-2 was never removed from the mountain. "It would have been too expensive to try to drag it out of there," Bill said. "After a while, somebody asked if they could buy it to use for a hunting cabin, and the company said sure. They took off the engines and left the rest of it where it was."

Presumably the plane is still there, crouching in the woods somewhere in the Catskill Mountains. Engineless, scratched and bent, an incongruous sheet-metal hunting cabin.

The Brotherhood

A S A KID, I WATCHED A LOT OF TV SHOWS ABOUT (YOU GUESSED IT) PILOTS—AIRPLANE PILOTS AND SPACESHIP PILOTS; THEY WERE INTERCHANGEABLE AS FAR AS I WAS CONCERNED. There was *Sky King,* a show about a modern-day rancher who, more or less inexplicably, rode an airplane instead of a horse when chasing bad guys. There was *Captain Midnight,* about an aerial commando who waged a relentless crusade against injustice by flying rocket planes from a secret mountaintop base. There was *Captain Video and His Video Rangers,* about a twenty-first-century inventor who whizzed around the universe in a handtooled spaceship.

Each of the shows followed the standard formula for popular adventure serials. The central character in each was an implausibly perfect hero, a guy with nerves of steel, fists of iron, and—hidden but accessible—a heart as big as anything. He was such a paragon, there was no way you could identify with him. All you could do was stand back and admire him from a distance. So to offset this separation between hero and viewer, the shows always included a secondary character, a sidekick who had recognizable human flaws. On *Sky King,* it was the rancher's nephew, Clipper; on *Captain Midnight,* it was Ichabod, a rocket mechanic; on *Captain Video,* it was the Ranger, the Captain's teenage adjutant. The sidekick offered comic relief from the icy perfection of the hero, and he provided an opportunity for the viewer to project himself into the action. The sidekick was comically imperfect, just like you. His defects were irritating (in half the episodes, he blundered into some kind of trouble from which the hero had to rescue him), but you didn't mind. You could identify with him, which meant you could tag along behind the hero and, to some extent, share in the hero's glory.

Most of the books I read conformed to the same formula, although sometimes they gave it a twist. I read all the Tom Swift Jr. adventures *(Tom Swift and His Flying Lab, Tom Swift and His Rocket Ship, Tom Swift and His Atomic Earth Blaster).* Tom Jr. was the son of the original Tom Swift, the scientific genius who starred in a series of adventures that my father had read. Now, in the new books, Tom Jr. worked alongside his father, assisting him on the patented line of world-beating inventions that were marketed by Swift Enterprises. Tom Jr. was his father's sidekick, but he in turn had a sidekick of his own, the books' representative flawed mortal, Bud. What made this Short Chain of Being interesting was that Tom Jr. sometimes rose above himself, threatening to displace his father at the top. Every so often we saw that, although he remained loyal to his dad, Tom Jr. was more forceful than the old man and, perhaps, brainier:

Before starting the ascent, Tom flipped on the audiogyrex, which he had designed to eliminate the elevator sensation of rapid rising. Then, gripping the throttle, Tom poured atomic power into the jet lifters. As the crescendo of the sound increased to a frightening roar, the Flying Lab began to rise. In a matter of seconds it was shooting skyward.

"We're air-borne!" Bud cried jubilantly. "Oh, brother, did we leave old Earth in a hurry!"

At two thousand feet Tom eased off on the lifters. The

mammoth craft stood still in the air, as if supported by an invisible giant's hand.

"Dad, we've done it!" Tom exclaimed, gazing down at the cheering throng far below them.

"We have, son!" came the excited reply over the intercom. "Your invention is another great step in scientific advancement."

(Tom Swift and His Flying Lab)

My conversations with pilots during the last three years brought these old shows and books back to mind. The themes of equality and subordination often entered the conversations. Many pilots told me stories about the unequal relationship between captains and copilots, and about the tensions this inequality produced.

A retired TWA captain, Russell James, gave me the following account of a trip he took to Albuquerque in 1947, soon after being hired as a copilot: "I was flying that day for one of our senior captains," he said, "which meant that I was basically just sitting there watching *him* fly. I didn't have much to do except for working out how long it would take us to reach various points along the route.

" 'How long till we get to such-and-such?' the captain would ask me. So I would fool with this little navigation calculator the company had issued to us, and when I'd worked out the answer I'd say, 'I make it fourteen minutes.'

" 'Naw,' he'd say. 'Thirteen.' And then we'd fly along, and sure enough, he was right, it took thirteen minutes.

"So then he told me to work out the time to the next checkpoint, and I was determined to get it right this time, so I really bore down. And when I was absolutely sure I had the right answer, I gave it to him: 'Sixteen minutes.'

" 'Nope,' he said. "Seventeen." And he was right this time, too.

"He was working out the times better in his head than I could do it with the calculator. He had flown that route about a zillion times and he knew it took two minutes to get from this farm to that highway, and three minutes from the highway to the next town, and so forth, all the way across country.

"So we kept that up for a while until he had out-calculated the calculator four or five times. Then he held out his hand.

" 'Give me that thing,' he said. And he grabbed the calculator out of my lap, slid his window open, and tossed it out. 'There,' he said. 'Now just sit still until we get to Albuquerque.' "

The lesson Russell learned that day had less to do with navigation than with the subservience demanded of copilots. It was a lesson every copilot had to learn. Nearly all the fliers I spoke with said the years they spent as copilots were tough. They took airline jobs because they wanted to fly airplanes, they said. They wanted to get their hands on the controls and steer the planes through the sky. They wanted to be in charge. But that was exactly what, as copilots, they were not.

Copilots were apprentices. During the 1920s, some airlines told applicants for copiloting jobs that they would not receive salaries: If the applicants were lucky enough to be hired, they would enjoy the inestimable privilege of sitting next to honest-to-god airline captains in the cockpits of giant, spanking-new flying machines. Did they really expect to receive a boon like that and get paid for it too?

During the early 1930s, a wave of liberality swept through the airlines, after which most copilots received at least a modicum of pay for their work. But the work itself remained demeaning. Copilots served as baggage handlers, and ticket agents, and flight attendants, and worse. They loaded cargo aboard the planes, then led the passengers out from the terminal, showed them to their seats on board, and punched their tickets. After takeoff, they handed out box lunches and cups of coffee. And at the end of the day, they unloaded baggage and emptied out the "honey buckets," the chamber pots carried on some planes for the passengers' use.

Captains had little sympathy for the apprentices. There were *some* good captains, large-spirited men who befriended their copilots. But, if the tales I heard are true, such captains were uncommon. Most captains held themselves aloof—some so much so that they refused even to speak to copilots, except when issuing orders. A long day of flying—several takeoffs and landings, leg after leg—would pass in brusque silence.

Sometimes the silent treatment extended to layovers as well. Crew accommodations were spartan in the '30s. When a captain and copilot ended their day at an airport far from home, they were often assigned to share a bunkroom located in the rear of a hangar. At best, they might be given a small lodging allowance—enough to let them go Dutch on a double room in a cheap hotel downtown. Either way, they would wind up spending a fair amount of time together in fairly intimate circumstances. Occasionally this served to bridge the gulf between captains and copilots. It wasn't easy for a captain to maintain his hauteur when he had to brush his teeth and change his underwear with a copilot present. But some captains managed the feat.

John Otley was another flier who, like Russell James, told me about the tribulations he endured as a copilot. John went to work for TWA in 1936, in the days of the Ford trimotor and the DC-2. "Flying copilot with some of the captains we had then got frustrating," John said to me. "They didn't want us to touch a thing in that cockpit unless they gave us a definite, direct order. And of course the only things they would order us to do were the things that they didn't want to do themselves, all the busywork that had nothing to do with flying. Do you think they would actually let us fly the airplane? They would *not.*"

One thing the captains certainly didn't want to do themselves was to raise the landing gear on the DC-2. The gear wasn't motorized. A member of the crew had to pump it up manually, using nothing except a long wooden handle and arm power. The crewman selected for the task was invariably the copilot. The moment the plane rose from the runway, he began pumping away, trying to retract the wheels in four or five vigorous strokes of the handle. It was hard—the handle was extremely stiff, like a Nautilus machine calibrated for Arnold Schwarzenegger. And sometimes sadistic captains ran the calibration up an additional notch or two. When they wanted to punish their copilots for some infraction or other, they would make steep takeoff climbs, so that centrifugal force pulled the gear outward. It was just about impossible to raise the gear then.

John said that despite everything, he admired the captains. He'd had almost no flying experience prior to being hired, so he was impressed by the skills the captains displayed. And they weren't all sadists.

"I would think to myself, 'God, but they're smart,' " John told me. "They would make these precise, three-point landings, or they would land in crosswinds as neatly as if there was no wind blowing. They could do just about anything with an airplane, it seemed to me.

"But they wouldn't tell me *how* they did the things they did. Even when they gave me an order, they wouldn't tell me how to follow it. There was an auxiliary radio behind the copilot's seat, and every so often they would tell me, 'John, check that radio.' But they never told me how to do it, so I didn't know a thing about it."

John said that during his first three years as a copilot, he received virtually no flight training from the captains. In theory, captains were supposed to instruct their copilots, converting apprentices into fully qualified airmen. But in practice, the captains slapped away the hands of any copilot who had the temerity to touch the controls.

"I didn't complain, though," John said. "They treated me like that, but they treated the other copilots like that too. It's just how things were."

So John kept his peace. But then one day matters suddenly came to a crisis.

"The chief pilot called me in," John said. "He told me that the company was getting ready to check out a bunch of copilots to make them captains, and I was one of them. He said he would take me up for a check flight next Tuesday and if I did all right, he would promote me.

"That excited me quite a lot, naturally, but I was also pretty worried because I knew I hadn't been taught the things a captain was supposed to know.

"Tuesday morning, the chief pilot and I took off and we did some air work—the normal stuff, turn left, turn right, approach a stall, fiddle around with the radio range. And I did pretty well, though I'd never done some of this stuff before. Like approaching a stall—the only reason I knew how to do that was because I had read up on it.

"But I did pretty well until it came time to do some landings. I hadn't ever done a landing in a DC-2, none of the pilots had ever let me. So I had a hell of a time. I couldn't land that son of a bitch to save myself. My downfall was that the book said to maintain a minimum speed—I forget what it was, maybe one hundred miles an hour. So I tried to hold that speed, but it was too fast. I couldn't get the plane down before we shot past the runway.

"After I'd missed about three landings, the chief pilot turned to me and said, 'John, what the hell's the matter with you?' And I said, 'Well, sir, I'm trying to do my best. The book says to hold it at such-and-such a speed.' And he said, 'Oh, the hell with the book! Get us lined up with the runway and let me show you.' So I flew back to the field and then he brought the plane down at about fifty-five, sixty miles an hour, and he landed us like a duck plopping down out of the air. Then he said, 'All right, we'll try this again tomorrow morning and if you can't improve, you are *out.*'

"Then we went into his office and he sat me down. He said to me, 'How much flying time have you had in the last six months? How many landings have you made?' So that's when I told him. I hadn't told anybody up till then, but in my three years with the airline I had gotten a total of four and a half hours of flying time. That's all. And *that* was really just time when the pilots let me hold the damned yoke for a few minutes because they were busy with something else. I'd never done a landing. Not one.

"You can believe me, he was stupefied! He said, 'Are you telling me the truth?' And when I said I was, he told his secretary to start phoning the pilots. He said, 'Tell them I want to see them here first thing in the morning. And I want you to be here, too, John.'

"He didn't know the pilots hadn't been giving the copilots their training, you see. So the next morning he went around the room and asked all the pilots how much flying time *he* had given *them* when *they* were coming up. Then he told them how little time they had given to me.

"That broke the ice. It didn't make me the most popular copilot in the world, you can believe that, but after that meeting the pilots did start to give more flying time to me and the other boys."

In almost every instance, the stories I heard about the relationship between captains and copilots made the captains out to be heavies. It was the same no matter what period the stories came from, the 1930s or the 1980s. Captains were unreasonable S.O.B.s, copilots their innocent victims. Captains were arrogant and headstrong; copilots were justifiably resentful. Captains bad, copilots good.

The stories were delivered with backspin and body English. The men who told the stories complained about the harsh treatment they'd received from S.O.B. captains, but they also seemed proud that they had borne up under the harshness, and I thought they more than half admired the old S.O.B.s who had been so hard on them. Most of the storytellers were former copilots who had persevered through their apprenticeship to win promotion to captain's rank. I assumed this accounted for the humor in their stories—after they were promoted, they had started to smile about things that hadn't seemed funny to them before. Maybe they'd even come to look at things more or less as the old S.O.B.s had. They couldn't bring themselves to forgive the S.O.B.s altogether, but perhaps they started to perceive some justice in the S.O.B.s' highhandedness. Keeping upstart copilots away from the controls struck them differently after they became captains themselves.

I wondered how the storytellers had comported themselves as captains. According to the logic implicit in their stories, they should have turned into heavies when they were promoted. (I once heard a riddle: If all babies are cute, where do all the ugly adults come from? Same logic here. If all copilots are swell fellows, where do all the nasty captains come from?) I studied the storytellers, trying to decide which of them would make a convincing heavy, but it was hard to say. I was meeting them when they were off duty or, in some cases, after they had retired. I wasn't able to observe them in action, issuing orders inside a cockpit. So I was left to speculate. But then I got at least partial confirmation of my suspicions. I met a retired captain—I'll call him Sam—who told me about the afflictions he'd endured as a copilot. He convinced me. I thought for sure Sam had been a sterling young fellow who'd had the misfortune to serve under some of the nastiest captains in airline history. But a few months after meeting Sam, I met a captain who is still flying the line, and he told me about some of the rotten, hard-assed captains *he'd* served under. One of them was Sam.

I can believe that being promoted to captain could turn a sterling fellow into an S.O.B. Captaincy has to be seductive. You wake up in the morning, and you're just yourself—you're ordinary. But then you put on your blue suit with the gold stripes, and you drive to an airport where people address you as "Sir," and you get into a cockpit where your word is law . . . . You experience an extreme version of a transformation that many men long for. I have several friends, men with good jobs in various professions, who treat going to work each morning as an escape. At home, they have to deal with the wife and the kids, personal obligations, moral confusion, mortality. Not so at work. The office is a simpler, more orderly arena, a place where there are clear-cut goals and clear-cut standards of success. Identity is no puzzle there: It's conferred by the position a man wins in the corporate hierarchy. Personal worth is precisely equivalent to clout, i.e., salary, i.e., job title. When you walk through the office door each morning, you assume the role that goes with your title, then immerse yourself in the simple, ego-aggrandizing game of climbing the corporate ladder.

Conditions are the same for airline captains, I think, except that for them the escape is more complete. They don't just leave home each morning—they leave the whole damned planet. They enter a microcosmic, high-altitude society occupied by only a few other carefully selected men. The cockpit is the most exclusive of societies. And within it, one man, the captain, occupies a place of unchallenged supremacy. He's It. He steers a stupendously powerful machine into the distance, leaving behind ordinary concerns and routines. When he's flying, the scope of his concerns becomes limited to the small world of the cockpit, and there he is the master. There he can think as well of himself as he pleases.

During one of my recent trips to visit my father, I told him some of the captain/copilot stories I'd heard, then I asked him about captains he'd flown with when he was a copilot. I said self-importance seemed to be an occupational hazard for airline captains. Had many of the captains he'd flown with pretended to be God's gift to aviation? My father looked at me quizzically, and for a moment I thought I'd made him angry.

"The majority of the captains I flew with were all right," he said. "They treated their copilots well enough, I guess. They let us fly the plane some. They didn't try to lord it over us.

"There was also a small minority of *excellent* captains, guys who were so super-competent that they didn't have anything to prove. They treated us really well, so I don't think anybody resented them. In fact, most of us looked forward to flying with them. We wanted to perform well for them, to show them what we could do. It was competitive in a way, but a good way. If you're worth anything as a pilot, you want to excel. And if you're flying with a guy who's known for being first-rate, you want to prove that you belong up there with him.

"I remember one flight I had with a captain I respected a lot. At one point he left the cockpit for a while and left me flying the plane, and not long after he left some ice started building up on the wings. It built up faster than I had ever seen before, and I decided I needed to descend fast, get the plane down into some warmer air. So that's what I did—I took us down from, I don't remember, maybe twenty thousand feet to fifteen thousand—down to an altitude where the ice melted off.

"When the captain came back to the cockpit, he asked me why I hadn't pushed the throttles forward and held our altitude in spite of the ice. I told him I could just tell from the way the plane was handling that we had to descend. I think he accepted my explanation. At any rate, he sat down and didn't criticize me or ask me any more questions. But I don't know to this day what he really thought. I didn't ask him—I didn't want to take the chance of finding out that he thought I'd done the wrong thing. That would have been crushing.

"My point is, there were some good captains we looked up to.

"But as for captains who rode their crews too hard, I agree, there were some of them too. Mainly I thought they were guys who were promoted to captain too soon, before they had really learned how to *be* a captain. Most of them could fly the airplane moderately well, but they had no idea how to get along with a crew. You know, crews got pretty big. On international flights, there was the copilot, a relief pilot [who spelled either the captain or the copilot during rest periods], the flight engineer, a navigator, a radio man, and the hostesses. It was a big group, so to do his job right the captain had to be a good manager. But a lot of them were no good at it at all. They were unreasonable and arbitrary—they acted like they had a God-given right to command. They made themselves easy to hate."

The tight expression gradually left my father's face.

"Maybe this is the best way to describe it. Did I ever tell you about Ron Burke? He became a copilot about the same time I did, so he flew under most of the same captains. He pulled a stunt one time that expressed the way we all felt.

"It was on a flight Ron made with Stewart Wallace. Wallace was not one of our most popular captains, to put it mildly. He's probably the kind of captain you're talking about. *He* thought he was God's gift to aviation, I believe.

"Well, anyway, Wallace was treating Ron fairly well during most of the flight, I guess, letting Ron fly some of the legs. But eventually he decided he should assert his authority some. He never let a trip go by without doing it one way or another. He wanted you to remember who was who in his cockpit. So during one of Ron's legs he said, 'Now, Ron, you're doing a pretty good job of flying the airplane, but like most copilots you're fouling up the landings. If you luck out and get the main landing gear onto the runway all right, you screw up the whole deal when the nose wheel touches down—you let it hit the runway *much* too hard.

" 'Now you go ahead and bring us in at this next airport, but as soon as the main gear touches the runway, I'll take over and show you how to set down the nose wheel light as a feather.'

"Ron said 'Okay,' and he didn't show any reaction. But he was annoyed, as anybody would be, because he knew that he'd been making perfectly good landings. So he decided to show Wallace up. Now, the thing you need to know—Ron might have been about the strongest man in the world. Honestly. He was a weight lifter and he'd won all kinds of competitions. He was one hundred percent muscle.

"So, on the approach to the airport, Ron started adjusting the elevator trim tabs [small control surfaces on the tail], doing it secretly so Wallace wouldn't notice anything. He trimmed the plane so that it wanted to pitch forward onto its nose. But at the same time he also pulled back on the yoke to hold the plane level. The strain would have pulled an ordinary man's arms out by the roots. There must have been tremendous forward pressure on the yoke, but Ron sat there holding the plane level with no apparent effort, and Wallace never suspected a thing.

"Ron flew the plane down to the runway as if everything was normal, and he let the main gear settle gently onto the runway. Then Wallace said, 'Okay, I've got it,' and he took hold of his yoke. Ron said, 'It's all yours,' and he let go.

"As soon as Ron removed his hands, the front of the plane flipped down like it weighed a thousand tons. Wallace couldn't do a thing with it—the yoke yanked him forward and the nose wheel slammed into the runway so hard, it damned near dug a hole in the concrete.

"That was Wallace's 'feather-light' landing."

Two types of documents throw light on cockpit relationships during the years when my father was a copilot, the late 1940s and early '50s. The first document was wholly informal: Copilots kept secret notebooks in which they recorded information about the captains and their flying techniques. Until jet airliners were introduced during the late '50s, captains were permitted to conduct their flights pretty much any way they wanted, and copilots were expected to conform to each captain's preferences. This meant the copilots had to learn several styles of flying, not just one officially prescribed style. They had to remember whether Captain X liked steep climbs after takeoff or whether he preferred to level out and build up some airspeed before climbing. They had to know whether X liked fast landings with the wing flaps up or more leisurely descents with the flaps fully extended. They had to comply with each of X's preferences, no matter what their own preferences might have been or what Captains Y and Z might insist on during *their* flights. So to sort things out, copilots kept notebooks in which they listed each captain's requirements. They carried the books in their flight bags and furtively used them to bone up whenever they were reassigned from one captain to another.

The other document was both official and ironclad: the seniority list. The day a pilot joined an airline, he got a seniority number, and thereafter that number controlled his career. He couldn't get the best flights, or receive a posting at the most desirable airports, or be promoted from copilot to captain until his number allowed it. He would move forward one slot on the seniority list each time any pilot who was senior to him left the company. But if everybody ahead of him stayed healthy and nobody was fired, he might be trapped at the bottom of the list for a long, long time.

The list divided the copilots from the captains—they were clustered on opposite sides of the numerical divide. This intensified the resentment copilots felt. They spent many hours studying the list, calculating when they would be able to cross the divide. How much longer would the most senior captains hang on? How many copilots would the company call up for the next round of promotions? How long till *my* number comes up?

The list was divisive, but it also represented a bond of sorts. It embodied the hierarchy that all pilots—captains and copilots alike— aimed to climb. And they all climbed it together, in lockstep. There was, for the most part, no opportunity to accelerate your own climb by demonstrating extraordinary job skills. An especially able captain might win designation as a check pilot (a captain who judges other captains' competence), or he might be offered the chance to become a chief pilot (the desk jockey who orchestrates crew operations at a particular airport). But most captains didn't aspire to these roles. They wanted to do the only thing that really interested them, the same thing their copilots wanted: to fly airplanes. In this sense, there was an underlying camaraderie among captains and copilots. They may have considered each other to be rivals, but they had no meaningful way to act out their rivalry. They would all ride the seniority list upward at precisely the same pace. For better or worse, they were all in it together.

The camaraderie, such as it was, helps account for a phrase I heard various pilots use: "the flying fraternity." Some of the same pilots who told me about jealousies between captains and copilots also told me that pilots looked on each other as brothers. They said that pilots recognized themselves in each other, seeing the same interests and dispositions, the same aptitudes and talents. "Pilots are a breed apart," one captain said to me. "I don't have many other friends besides pilots. With other people, what can I talk about? We don't have much in common. But as soon as I meet a pilot, I know what his life is like and he knows what mine is like, more or less. We're connected."

(The counterpart to "flying fraternity" was another term I heard pilots use: "ground people." It was a put-down, usually spoken with mock pity. Anyone who wasn't a pilot was a ground person, an unfortunate who lacked the qualifications for flight. Most of the pilots who referred to ground people in my presence gave me a wink or some other sign implying that present company was excepted, but I understood that they were merely being polite.)

Actually, the concept of a brotherhood among fliers was sharply limited. Not only were ground people excluded, but most pilots were too. Because of the seniority list, pilots rarely quit one airline to take a job with another. Each line had its own list, so to take a new job a pilot would have had to give up his place on one list to start again at the bottom of a different list. That was too great a price to pay. As a result, most pilots spent their entire careers with one airline, and they came to identify strongly with that line and with the other men who flew on it. The same conditions that created rivalries among individual pilots also bound the pilots together in units of group pride.

When I visited pilots' homes, I was struck by the airline insignias that were displayed in various ways—paintings, models, plaques. Men affirmed their pride in their airline through these displays. I never saw a painting of a Continental Airlines plane in a United pilot's home, or a model of a Delta Airlines plane in an Northwest pilot's home. But the insignia of each man's own airline was often exhibited prominently. If there was such a thing as a fraternity of fliers, I gathered, it was a decentralized fraternity consisting of many local chapters, and the brothers gave their loyalty to the locals.

Besides looking at insignias, I also took any opportunity I could to study the contents of pilots' bookshelves. Not all of the homes contained book collections, but some did, and in these a high percentage of the titles dealt with aviation. Several pilots owned histories of the airline they worked for (*Eagle:* American Airlines; *The Only Way to Fly:* Western Airlines; *An American Saga:* Pan Am; *Howard Hughes' Airline:* TWA). Some also owned large yearbook-like volumes printed privately for the pilots of a particular airline, containing descriptions of the various planes the line had used and photos of all the line's pilots, past and present. And there were novels. Some of the pilots had large collections of aviation novels—*Island in the Sky, Last Plane Out, Seekers of the Sky, Runway Zero-Eight, Wings.*

In one captain's home, I spotted a novel I hadn't seen before, *Band of Brothers.* I hunted for a copy during the following weeks, and finally found one in a used book store. It turned out to be a mystery-adventure about five airline pilots who unite to free a fellow pilot from unjust imprisonment in China. A strange book. But the image it presents of pilots is familiar: loners who, when the chips are down, are able to rise above themselves to perform acts of heroism. Variants of the same image can be found in almost all novels and movies about aviation. It's become a cultural stereotype. Reading *Band of Brothers,* I wondered how the image has affected real pilots. It sure affected me when I was a boy, but the guys who became pilots must have taken it differently, finding it attractive instead of intimidating. I wondered how conscious they were of the image, and how much—consciously or otherwise—they wanted to fill it. I wondered whether, contrary to *Band of Brothers,* the image might have been the real source of rivalry among pilots: Each pilot wanted to fill the image, and each resented any other pilot's claim that he filled it better.

I met a retired captain who owned a large collection of books and also VCR movies. He said that he'd been reading about flight all his life. He mentioned aviation magazines he'd read as a kid—*Air Youth Horizons, G-8 and His Battle Aces*—and then, running his forefinger along a row of VCR tapes, he named the aviation movies that had meant the most to him when he was growing up. He said that after seeing Errol Flynn in *The Dawn Patrol,* he left the movie house knowing that he wanted to become a pilot. *The Dawn Patrol* is a tale of World War I fighter pilots who realize that war is senseless—and who realize that the pilots on the other side are just like themselves—but who go up anyway each morning to engage the enemy. "I still think it's the best movie ever," the captain said. "I still watch it every so often." He slipped the tape into his VCR and invited me to watch a few scenes with him.

Last year, my father told me that he knew next to nothing about the seniority system when he became a TWA copilot. The consequence, he said, was that he made a crucial mistake five minutes after being hired. The chief pilot told him that he could either join a group of new copilots who would begin their orientation classes the next morning or he could wait three weeks and join a different group then. A three-week vacation sounded good. My father was fresh out of the Army and TWA was offering him the job he'd hoped for. Why not celebrate? So he opted for the holiday.

That decision reverberated throughout the rest of his career. During the three weeks he waited, eighty other new copilots began their airline training ahead of him, receiving lower numbers on the TWA seniority list. Without knowing it, he had traded away his chance for quick advancement. He said he'd expected to make captain in a couple of years at most, but because of his error, climbing the seniority list took far longer than that. In the end, he had to wait nearly a decade before his number came up.

"And then," he said, "when I finally got the chance to upgrade, I ran into a hell of a situation."

The procedures for upgrading had changed since the days when a captain-candidate was given a single check flight. By the mid-1950s, my father said, the candidate took two weeks of classroom work followed by two weeks of training flights and then a month of probationary flights out on the line. The candidate operated as a captain during his month of probation, sitting in the lefthand seat of the cockpit and making all the decisions a captain normally makes. But instead of flying with regular copilots in the righthand seat, he was accompanied by check pilots who where there to evaluate his performance and, if need be, ground him. He flew with progressively more senior check pilots as the month went along, until for the last flight of the month—called the final line check—the chief pilot himself sat in.

"Captain training was supposed to be a stressful time," my father said. "It was up or out—if you didn't make the grade, you couldn't go back to being copilot. You were fired. So the training was stressful. But I thoroughly enjoyed it. I was absolutely confident. Maybe that was one benefit of staying a copilot as long as I did—I was *sure* that I was ready to move to the left seat.

"But then on my final line check, I thought everything was going to fall apart for me. There was never any real chance that I would be fired, but the flight turned out to be strange enough to make me wonder.

"I was checking out in a Martin 4-0-4 [a short-range, two-engine airliner introduced in 1950] and the flight was a typical series of short hops from one airport to the next. The chief pilot who was with me was named Donches. I didn't know him well, but from everything I'd heard, I knew he was a no-nonsense kind of guy.

"Everything went fine until we made a stop in Baltimore. When we taxied out to take off again, I saw that our auto-feather wasn't working. This was a new gadget that would automatically feather a propeller if an engine broke down, and the rule was that a 4-0-4 wasn't allowed to take off if the auto-feather was out of commission. But TWA didn't have any maintenance facilities in Baltimore, so getting the repairs done there meant rounding up some mechanics from another airline, which would be a bother.

"The plane was light, we didn't have many passengers—there was no question that it would have been safe to take off and fly down to Washington where TWA did have mechanics. I didn't know how Donches would react, though, if I suggested that, so I was determined to go strictly by the book. So when I saw we had a problem with the auto-feather, I said, 'Captain Donches, we're going to have to go back to the gate and get this fixed.'

" 'Well, damn it,' he said, 'it's only fifteen minutes down to Washington.'

"I said I knew that, but the book said we had to get the problem fixed before taking off. I said, 'If you want to authorize me to fly down to Washington, I'll fly down to Washington. But if the decision is left up to me, I'm going to stay here and get it fixed. I'm on my final line check. What the hell else can I do?' I told him I knew it didn't make any sense, but I was supposed to follow the rules. So he said, 'Well, shit, okay.' "

So my father turned the plane around and went back to the terminal. He found a mechanic, and after an hour or two the auto-feather was mended.

"Donches was none too happy about the delay," my father said. "I'd shown him that I knew the rules, which should have counted for something, but he certainly didn't look pleased. So I knew I was in for kind of a rough day after that. It looked like Donches was going to be unhappy if I did what I was supposed to, and I was *sure* he would lower the boom on me if I fouled up. So it was one of those damned-if-you-do, damned-if-you-don't deals."

They flew on to Cleveland. After landing, my father, Donches, and the hostess waited for their passengers to disembark, then they walked together across the flight apron to the terminal. It was hot. An oversized July sun was pouring heat like syrup over the airport. Wavering currents of hot air rose from the concrete under their feet.

"We had four hours to kill before we took off again," my father said, "and Donches still looked put out. His expression hadn't changed since we left Washington. So the prospect of sitting around in the terminal with him for the next four hours didn't really appeal to me. I figured he would ask me questions or something—give me an oral exam.

"I tried to think of some other way to pass the time, and I came up with one. I asked Donches and the hostess if they wanted to go swimming. Donches looked at me like I'd lost my mind. He said no, he didn't have any urge to go swimming. But of course the hostess said, 'Yeah, I'd like to go.' So I rented a car from Hertz and we drove out to Lake Erie.

"We spent a couple of hours there while Donches waited at the airport. I don't know what he did during that time, but at least he wasn't grilling me.

"We had a swim, and I guess we ate some lunch, and then we started back to the airport. We had given ourselves plenty of time to get back, but I should have realized how my luck was running. On our way back from the lake, we got tied up in some traffic.

"We weren't exactly late when they finally pulled up in front of the terminal, but we had cut it close. I pulled over to let the hostess out before I returned the car. She hopped out and hurried into the lobby. She was going to change from her bathing suit into her uniform and then get out to the plane. Only she got arrested. There were some odd laws back then. I had never heard of this one and neither had she, but it turns out you weren't supposed to run around at an airport in your bathing suit.

"Well, she got pretty upset. I returned the car and changed my clothes, and when I came into the lobby there she was, crying, with a policeman on one side of her and Donches on the other side.

"The looks Donches had given me before were nothing compared to the ones he gave me now. All I had to do to become a captain was to fly us to St. Louis and then Kansas City without driving Donches to violence, but we were both starting to wonder if I was going to manage it."

The forces of the law released the hostess. Then, when all the crew members were properly attired, the next leg of the trip began. My father took off for St. Louis.

The sky closed in as he proceeded southwest. Bulbous clouds formed in the distance and marched toward the plane: thunderheads. So much for any hopes of giving Donches a pleasant ride. My father began steering between the clouds, trying to avoid the worst sections of the storm. Still, the turbulent air tossed the plane, rocking it uncomfortably.

"The hostess came up into the cockpit every so often," my father said. "She wanted to talk some more about getting arrested. And for good measure, she complained about the bumpy flight. I felt like telling her, 'Not today, please. Don't carry on like that today.' But of course I couldn't say anything."

Eventually the hostess would leave, and Donches would settle back in his seat, and my father would think that perhaps everything would calm down now. But then she would come back.

"The final straw was when she arrived one more time and announced that a passenger in row six was getting ready to have a baby. I looked over at Donches and he looked over at me, and he had this *weary* expression on his face. He had to be asking himself what in the hell else could go wrong on this flight. He must have wondered if I was jinxed, if all my flights were going to turn out like this. 'All right,' he said finally, 'you're supposed to be a captain. Go on back there and decide what you're going to do now.'

"So I turned the plane over to Donches and went back to ask the passenger how she was holding up. 'I'm not having any pains yet,' she said, 'but I think they're coming.' I thought, *'Please* hang on, lady. I don't want to have to make an unscheduled landing in Fort Wayne or somewhere, I just *know* how much Donches would enjoy that.' "

That was the moment, I think, when my father imagined everything falling apart. A bizarre scene must have flicked through his mind. They would land in Fort Wayne, and while Captain Donches and Copilot Rawlings sat immobile in the cockpit, an ambulance would jangle to the side of the plane and the lady would be carried onto it, and then it would race loudly away. And when the hubbub had quieted, Captain Donches would turn and stare at Copilot Rawlings, and Copilot Rawlings would know what was expected. An airline couldn't carry a jinxed captain on its payroll—it couldn't put up with problems like these on flight after flight. So Copilot Rawlings would unpin the wings from above his breast pocket and silently hand them over. Then he would return home, in disgrace, his flying career finished. He would get a job digging ditches somewhere, or maybe he would drive a bread truck for a living.

"Well, the passenger restrained herself, so we flew on to St. Louis and dropped her off. And then we went to Kansas City with no further adventures.

"So we got off the airplane in Kansas City and went upstairs to the operations center, and Donches wasn't being very talkative. He hadn't said anything to me, in fact, since that false alarm about the baby. He signed some papers in the office, then he picked up his bag and acted like he was getting ready to leave.

"When he got to the door, I stopped him. I said, 'Hey, Captain Donches, that was my final line check. Do you have any comments?'

"He looked at me a moment, and then he said, 'This was the goddamnedest day I've had in quite some time. But you pass, all right.'"

I don't think my father ever told me that story before. But as I listened, the memory of a related event came back to me. I remembered the evening when he first came home a captain.

He walked through our front door carrying a pizza and a carton of ice cream and wearing a broad smile. We had a party. I was young, but I understood why everyone was so happy. My father had gotten a new set of stripes to put on his sleeves. He had gotten a raise and would be his own boss from now on. And I would be able to tell all my friends that my dad's name was *Captain* Rawlings now.

I shared in the celebration, and later, when I went to bed, I dreamed that I would grow up to be my father's copilot: We would be buddies and go everywhere together.

Taboos

"T HE CAPTAIN WAS ASLEEP IN HIS SEAT," A FORMER CO-
PILOT SAID TO ME, "SO I WAS FLYING. And, see, the stewardess that evening was my girlfriend, so I had her up there sitting
on my lap a little bit while I flew.

"After a while, the captain woke up and looked over at us. We didn't
know how he was going to react. But he just glanced at me and then
at her, and then he said to her, 'He's a sweet boy, isn't he, honey?'
and he went back to sleep."

Whenever I repeat this story to my friends, they concentrate on the
part I find least interesting. "Asleep?" they say, ignoring the lap issue.
"The captain was *asleep?*"

I understand their concern, of course. As passengers, we do like to
believe that the captain commanding our flight is alert and ready, eyes
ceaselessly scanning the horizon, hands firmly clasping the yoke. But
sometimes, I've learned, he isn't. Among the piloting expressions I've
picked up is the slur "He's a three-percenter." Pilots apply it to any
of their colleagues who is incompetent. A guy who falls asleep in flight,

or who consistently muffs his landings, or who can't seem to master new procedures and equipment as they come on line.

Pilots estimate the number of incompetents in their ranks at just three percent. The estimate may be a bit optimistic. Recently my father told me about various screw-up pilots he's either known personally or heard about through the airline grapevine. He told me about a captain who, while his plane was far from shore above the Atlantic, got into an argument with his copilot. Evidently the captain thought the copilot was being insubordinate, so he yanked the landing gear handle, lowering the gear.

"He was trying to show that this was *his* airplane," my father said, "and that he could damn well do whatever he wanted with it. But later the company explained to him that there were *some* things he couldn't do, and lowering the gear at cruise altitude was one of them. A lot of passengers had complained after the flight ended. They'd been scared out of their wits when these loud sounds started coming from under the plane while they were out there over the ocean. They didn't know it was the gear coming down—they didn't know *what* was happening. They probably thought the bottom of the plane was falling apart."

My father also told me about a captain who decided to catch some shut-eye in the middle of a long overseas flight. While he slept, the copilot dug out a pack of cards and began playing poker with the navigator. (All the crewmen on this flight seem to have been three-percenters.) The copilot and navigator became so engrossed in their game, they neglected to hold the plane on course. The plane drifted unsupervised for an hour or more while the shut-eye and poker continued. When the crew finally turned their attention to their duties again, they discovered that they were thoroughly lost. In the end, they barely managed to reach an emergency landing field before running out of fuel.

I don't know what a true tabulation of incompetent pilots would reveal. "Three-percenter" may not be simply an optimistic underestimate; it smacks of a cover-up. If I were to judge from the number of stories pilots told me about irresponsible behavior among their colleagues, I'd be tempted to speak of thirty-percenters. But that would probably overshoot the truth as much as three percent undershoots— the pilots were telling me entertaining stories, not contributing data for a scientific survey. I suspect the answer is that a high percentage of young pilots are inclined toward a hotshot, Smilin' Jack kind of irresponsibility, and it becomes the task of the military and the airlines to either discipline these wild ones or weed them out. When I told one of my friends about the captain who slept while his copilot nuzzled a stewardess, she responded with the usual shock. *"Asleep?"* But then she said, well, really, it didn't surprise her. She said she'd gone to a college that, among its other programs, had an aviation curriculum. There were two sets of notoriously unruly students on campus, she said: the jocks and the aviation students. "They were the guys the girls had to look out for," she said.

In 1962, some three-percenters made headlines. During the course of Congressional hearings on airline safety, compromising photos were put on display: pilots dozing at the controls of airliners, or reading paperback novels in the cockpit, or holding stewardesses on their laps. Disgruntled flight engineers had taken the pictures using hidden cameras.

Newspapers gave the hearings big play. I remember coming home from school in the afternoons and taking the *Long Island Press* up to my bedroom where I would scan the national news section, looking for the latest installment of the scandal. Mainly I was looking for those red-hot photos.

The scandal didn't disturb me. I didn't connect it with my father. I assumed that he and the other *real* pilots were nothing like the jerks in the news stories. I don't recall whether the papers used the term "three-percenter," but I instinctively accepted the three-percenter defense. I assumed that only a few misfits acted the way the news stories described. To be honest, though, I didn't devote much effort to deciding what I thought about the scandal. As I say, mainly I just wanted to see the photos. Looking for pictures of stewardesses in pilots' laps gave me something of the same charge I got from thumbing through *Playboy,* the other publication that I sometimes smuggled up to my bedroom. In 1962, the sexual revolution was still several years distant and the women's movement was (to me, anyway) unimaginable. My notions of female sexuality came from the air-brushed photos in *Playboy* and from the movies made by sex goddesses like Marilyn Monroe and Jayne Mansfield. The swivel-hipped dream bimbos in the magazines and movies bore no resemblance to any woman or girl I'd ever met, but I hadn't yet drawn the obvious conclusion from this fact. I assumed that the world really did contain dream bimbos and that all normal men yearned for a crack at them.

Playboy probably never ran an article about stewardesses. I don't remember seeing one, and I can't imagine that any airline would have retained a stewardess who peeled for Hefner's cameramen. Still, there was a widespread belief in the '60s that stewardesses and centerfolds were very nearly the same. Everybody knew that stews were curvaceous young things who sashayed through an airplane offering more than food and drink—my friends knew it, I knew it, the media knew it. (In 1967, two stewardesses would write a bestseller titled in accordance with our supposed knowledge. *Coffee Tea or Me?* would sell over a million copies.) If a passenger was lucky, he could score with a stew—everybody knew that, too—but he would have to compete with the pilots for the privilege. Presumably, pilots and stews couldn't keep their hands off each other. Their flights were movable orgies. It was as though the airlines said to their pilots, "Here, fly these planes to far-off cities for a week or two. And oh, by the way, there are several attractive young ladies in the back of each plane. Take care of them when you're laying over in Miami or Paris or Rio."

During the last three years, I've asked various pilots to tell me how much of this mythology was true. How much action was there, really, between pilots and stewardesses? (I considered asking my father, but I chickened out. I tried to sidle up to the subject once or twice. I dropped some hints and alluded to some things other pilots had told me, but my father didn't respond, and I realized that I really didn't want him to. Each time I approached the subject with him, I felt myself becoming thirteen years old again. I got tongue-tied and embarrassed, and I had a recurrence of the discomfort I experienced during the official father–son sex lecture he gave me when I was thirteen. I was getting ready to go off to a coed summer camp, and—at my mother's insistence, he made plain—my father sat me down one evening in the living room for a talk. I don't remember everything he said. It was pretty much like the lectures that fathers have always given their sons, I suppose: Love comes first, then marriage, *then* sex. Just one detail stands out in my memory. My father said that one day when he was a teenager, he'd heard some of his friends admiring a pretty girl, making comments about her that he assumed were dirty. Among other things, they called her "nubile." He liked the sound of that; it evoked exciting images. Only later did he look up the word and discover that it meant marriageable.)

Most of the pilots disliked my question. Some refused to answer. Others told me not to be stupid: They said that affairs between pilots and stewardesses were probably less common than affairs between executives and their secretaries. "You see a girl on one flight," one captain said, "and then you may never see her again. Her schedule and yours probably won't ever mesh again. It's not like seeing the same girls around an office day after day."

But other pilots found the question flattering. They obviously enjoyed the mythology and wanted to endorse it. They developed an air of macho boastfulness, the kind I was acquainted with from locker rooms. One pilot told me about the "Mile High Club." He said pilots would invite new stewardesses back into an airliner's cargo hold for an initiation into stratospheric sex. Another pilot told me about the bunks on Lockheed Constellations. "For flights to Europe," he said, "we carried extra crew members because the flights lasted so long. Each [pilot] flew the plane for a certain amount of time, and then he got a rest break in this bunk that was set up behind the cockpit. The hostesses worked the same way—all of them got rest breaks too, using the same bunk. It was a double-wide bunk, with a divider board between the two sides. Sometimes when it was time for your break, one of the hostesses would be there with you. The board was removable. Usually it stayed in place, but not always." A third pilot told me about "stew zoos," apartments shared by several stewardesses. "If you got invited to a party at a 'zoo,' " he said, "you had a time, all right. Some of the girls thought certain things were expected of them, and some were quite willing to oblige." Several pilots told me a hoary airline joke: Pilots are interested in only three things: Sex, seniority, and salary, in that order.

The first flight attendants, hired in 1928, were men. Little if any consideration was given to hiring women. Despite the accomplishments of "aviatrixes" such as Harriet Quimby and Amelia Earhart, air travel was generally thought to be too arduous for the frail female constitution. Flight was for men. (TAT employed Earhart, briefly, but her main assignment was merely to pose for publicity photos in train stations and airport terminals.)

The airlines would sell tickets to women—they would sell to almost anyone bold enough to swap cash for a seat in a plane. But the arrangements on many of the planes, particularly the lavatory facilities, indicated how ill-prepared the airlines were to accommodate women. Some planes operated by Standard Airlines, for example, had no toilets as such: The passengers were expected to use tin cans. When, infrequently, a woman bought a ticket for a flight on Standard, she was told that if she needed to relieve herself, the pilot would land near a gas station.

Aviation was a male preserve. After the occupation of flight attendant had been established, however, executives at Boeing Air Transport decided to run an experiment. They calculated that hiring attractive young women to wait on passengers might be a shrewd marketing move. It would attract more (male) passengers. It might also help persuade the public that flying was safer than it seemed. If delicate young ladies could withstand the hazards of air travel day after day, what strapping male was going to admit that he was afraid to ride in a plane? Even potential female passengers might be heartened to give air travel a try. Boeing began using stewardesses in 1930, and ticket sales improved so much that several other airlines soon hired stewardesses or hostesses of their own. In most instances, registered nurses were given preference for the jobs. (Whether or not flying was safe, it was undeniably rough—passengers would be grateful for a little medical aid after a few hours of bucking and heaving.) But possession of an R.N. degree was just one of the criteria airlines used in the selection process, and sometimes it was waived. One airline is said to have recruited an entire stewardess class not from a nursing school but from a chorus line.

Pilots had obvious reasons to welcome the stewardesses aboard. The romance of flight took on a whole new dimension when women joined airline crews. (*Literary Digest* picked up on this almost immediately. In 1936, the *Digest* speculated that matings between lovely stewardesses and virile pilots would give rise to "a race of superior Americans.") Copilots, especially, were glad to see the stewardesses arrive, relieving them of the menial cabin chores they had been burdened with previously. Besides, copilots were young and generally unmarried, advantages they could put to good use during layovers. Captains had to rely on rank and maturity to attract the stewardesses, but copilots could make more sincere (or sincere-seeming) propositions.

The arrival of stewardesses was a good deal even for pilots who wanted nothing more from a layover than a relaxing, solo sleep. Stewardesses were serving girls. Their job was to make flights more comfortable not only for the passengers but for the cockpit crewmen also. Pilots could punch a call button at any time, and an appealing young woman would appear to take orders for food or drink. Few men would object to such an arrangement. In many cultures, men pay high fees to join clubs where they can receive treatment of this kind from wenches or geishas or Bunnies. Pilots got it free.

To my surprise, though, I learned that some pilots did object. There were some who felt that women didn't belong on airplanes in any capacity, no matter how subordinate. A retired pilot told me a story illustrating the point.

"I used to fly with a captain who didn't like having hostesses around," he told me. "Louis Hayes. He used to say that as far as he was concerned, they were nothing but a pain in the rear. He never would say why he felt like that, exactly, but I've got an idea. I know that one time after he landed a flight somewhere, the hostess came forward with a form that she was supposed to fill out. She was supposed to write down how much fuel he wanted put in the tanks, then she would give the form to the ground personnel. So she asked Lou how much gas he wanted, and he said 'Tell them full tanks.' The hostess scribbled something down and left. But later, when Lou taxied out for takeoff, he saw that the tanks were still half-empty. He got angry and called her up to the cockpit.

" 'What did you write on that form?' he asked her.

" 'Exactly what you told me,' she said. 'I wrote, "No thanks." '

"Lou decided that clinched it, I guess. Hostesses were pains in the rear. I thought he was off base, myself. I was *glad* when we hired hostesses. It meant that as a copilot I didn't have to wait on the passengers anymore. But that's how he saw it, and a number of the captains agreed with him. They liked women as well as the next man, on the ground, but they didn't want them in airplanes. That annoyed them. I think they felt it took some of the specialness out of flying."

Some pilots went beyond annoyance. They became abusive. My father told me about a captain who was notorious for mistreating the stewardesses on his flights. (This was as close as my father and I came to discussing airline sex. Making one of my half-hearted attempts to raise the subject, I said I'd always figured that pilots and stewardesses got on well together, but I'd heard some stories that suggested a battle of the sexes had raged aboard the planes. My father nodded and said he knew at least one pilot who fought with stews.)

"One time on a DC-3 flight," my father said, "this guy rang for the hostess. He wanted her to bring him some coffee. But when she didn't come fast enough, he started cursing. He turned around and looked through the window in the door leading to the cabin, and he could see that she was standing in the aisle waiting on a passenger. 'Damn her,' he said, and he kicked the rudder pedal. The plane swerved hard, which threw her off her feet.

"Another time, he called a hostess up front and while he was talking to her, he reached his hand down toward her legs. I think it was innocent this time—he was really reaching for something he'd dropped on the floor, a paper or something. But this gal must have had experiences with him before because as soon as she saw his hand moving toward her, she took the Coke bottle she was carrying and belted him over the head with it."

Some psychologists say that for men, dreams of flight represent a desire for sexual conquest: Flight is an assertion of will, an ecstatic act of mastery and release. This, I think, helps explain the sexual imagery found in much of the literature about aviation. In *Fate Is the Hunter,* former airline pilot Ernest Gann gives this description of the moments immediately following a near-crash:

> At last we had the airplane in hand. For now we could feel
> the controls; there was give—as sudden and wonderful a
> feeling as only a resilient woman could provide. We breathed.
> We luxuriated in the sensuous feeling of command and
> control. During those awful moments we had been little boys,

although we struggled like men. Our need was speed, which for these moments of time was better than love.

Guy Murchie, who had been an air navigator, uses similar language in *Song of the Sky* to describe straight and level flight through the clouds (the pitot tubes he refers to are probes that jut from the front of a plane):

> . . . Every now and then I think I sense a maidenly wile in the way some passing nimbus form waves at us as we thunder by—our four engines cooling roaring.
>
> A few of these buoyant wisps of cloud will only tentatively sway aside to let us pass, so awed are they by our slipstream, half turning to gaze wistfully after our virile hulk until we leave their view. And some cling to each other self-consciously—now giving way to timorous mirth, now raining a silent tear.
>
> For through their sky we play the dominant, the active role. We are their hero, their goer of the go. And as the plow lusts after the gentle body of earth, so our flashing propeller blades yearn for their tender mists, whirling apart the coy veils of cloud. Our airspeed pitot tubes and loop antennae are the antlers and pistils of the sky—our phallic fuselage with its powerful driving action into the passive softness of the cloud as wonderful a symbol of ravishment as can be known.

Ravishment. Some pilots I met described flight as the process of boring holes in the sky. Others talked about loving their airplanes. To praise the plane he'd loved best, one captain said, "The Electra was a real pilot's airplane. It was fast, responsive, just a pleasure to fly. It had very short wings, so we always called it the flying whore, because it had no visible means of support."

Language like this makes flight out to be a quintessentially masculine activity. A pilot conquers the sky just as he would like to conquer women. He subscribes to traditional sexual distinctions. Men are goers of the go, heroes; women are passive recipients of male action. Men desire women for their sexual charms and despise them for those same charms. I have a TWA route schedule printed in the 1940s. On the back is a drawing of an idealized stewardess: a buxom, leggy, blonde bombshell. When I showed the drawing recently to a retired Eastern Airlines captain, he told me that Eastern's president, Eddie Rickenbacker, had refused to hire stewardesses. Rickenbacker told his pilots that they "made enough money to afford their own pussy."

Not all pilots were Rickenbacker-style male chauvinists—I don't want to paint them all with one brush. Some pilots treated stewardesses with respect, I'm sure. Some were glad to have them around and behaved courteously with them. I imagine, too, that some of the pilots who behaved antagonistically toward stewardesses were not necessarily sexists. In some instances, they may have been the same captains who mistreated copilots: captains who wanted to preserve the exclusivity of their small society from any intruders, male or female. All this having been said, however, there's no escaping the conclusion that many pilots were extreme, unapologetic sexists. The captain who told me about Rickenbacker grimaced when he finished speaking, but then he laughed and slapped his leg. Clearly, he expected me to enjoy the story.

More than any other American males, pilots can live out an enduring American male fantasy. They can pick up and move on. In fact, it's what they're paid to do. They are forever heading out the door for distant destinations, with no apparent limits placed on their movements. The sky is wide open, and pilots are—or they can convince themselves that they are—free. The upshot is that for many of them, the American male clichés about women have special force. Women tie you down. They try to trap you, hem you in, ground you. They break your heart and, if they can manage it, your balls. So you have your way with them when the opportunity arises, then you get out. Ravish and leave. It's the *Playboy* approach, the attitude that Rickenbacker's comment exemplifies, the attitude that I thought I admired when I was a teenager.

Several retired pilots told me about pranks they pulled on stewardesses. None of the men seemed embarrassed by what they were saying. They seemed to think the pranks had been normal boy/girl byplay. Four separate pilots told me, for example, about a prank involving the automatic direction finder (ADF), a navigational device that pointed a compasslike needle at any radio station selected by the crew. To have fun with a new stewardess, pilots would tune a plane's ADF to a station that the plane had already passed. Then they would turn off the ADF, summon the stewardess to the cockpit, and tell her that the big dial on the pedestal in front of her was a virgin detector. So then they would switch the ADF on and laugh as the needle swung around to point at her. Every time I heard the story, though, the punch line was, "Then the stew said, 'I hate to tell you, captain, but that contraption is broken.'"

Like many of the pranks, this one was overtly sexual, and it was intended to make the victim look foolish. But the punch line rescues it. The stewardess gives as well as she gets. She responds playfully, perhaps flirtatiously—in effect, she taunts the pilots after they taunt her. There's sexual tension in the exchange, but perhaps not much more than is often present when young men and women are in each other's company. Change the ADF to some other gadget and transfer the scene from a cockpit to a college fraternity house: The same behavior, by males and females, is easy to imagine. It strikes me as basically adolescent: crude, but not intentionally abusive.

But other pranks that I heard about were less innocuous. If they had been pulled in the 1980s rather than in earlier decades, they would be branded sexual harassment. The stewardesses had to get used to the pilots who ran "girdle checks" on them, coming up behind them and suddenly rubbing their hands across their midriffs and thighs. They had to get used to "leg and fanny grabbers" (a term I heard one pilot use) or "the guys with the hands" (another pilot's phrase). They had to get used to the pilots who walked up and down cabin aisles during meal service, squeezing past the stewardesses repeatedly, or who summoned newly hired stewardesses to the cockpit and told them that their duties included coming up every half hour to throw those switches—those small ones in the corner—the ones the women could reach only by stretching across the pilots, pressing themselves against the pilots' arms or shoulders.

There were also pranks of a third sort, acts of open hostility, intended to be as offensive as possible. Retired pilot Harry Barkley told me this story:

"A captain and his copilot went into the coffee shop at one of the airports and ordered tomato soup to take out. Then they snuck the soup back out to the cockpit with them.

"After they took off, the captain rang for the stewardess, to set up the joke. He let on like he was getting airsick and told her to bring him one of the barf containers we carried for the passengers.

"After she brought it to him and left again, they poured the soup into it and broke up some crackers and stirred them in, and you know how that looks. Then a few minutes after that, the captain rang for her again, and this time when she came in he made out like he had just lost his lunch. He held the container where she could see into it while he wiped his mouth with his other hand.

"He pretended that he was embarrassed about getting sick, and the copilot pretended to laugh at him. So the captain said, 'Goddamn you, drink this!' And he handed the container to the copilot. The copilot said 'Aye aye, sir' and took a big swallow.

"The stewardess just about fainted."

I met Harry in Minneapolis, where he was attending a gathering of retired pilots and their wives. After I spoke with him, I spoke privately with his wife Sally, who had been a stewardess in the late 1940s. Sitting with her on a couch in a quiet corner of the hotel lobby, I asked

Sally how she and the other stewardesses had felt about the pilots' behavior toward them.

"We didn't think of it as harassment," she said. "Too naive, I guess.

"We were trained that the most important person on that airplane was the captain. He was the king. We were supposed to take care of our passengers, but making sure the captain was comfortable was even more important. The captain came first, then the copilot, and *then* the passengers.

"If the crew wanted us to make them special meals or fix their coffee a certain way, we would do it. We would do whatever we could, within limits. The girls on one airline were supposed to give the guys back-rubs after the plane landed. We didn't have to go that far, but we did everything else we could think of to make the flight a good one.

"We got along *nicely* most of the time. There were romances, but I mean that in a good way. It was fun to be young and flying around, seeing the world. I think the guys felt the same way we did about that. Some of them were really nice to us, too. Some of the copilots would come back if we got overworked and help us out sometimes—help pass out the food or whatever.

"But, well, for example, sometimes the guys *did* go a little too far. There was this one captain who used to grab all the girls on the leg, hard. None of us could get him to stop it. I think he did it mostly just to scare us, but whatever his reason was, we wanted him to cut it out. We couldn't think of what to do about it, though, until one time one of the girls took her garter and pushed thumbtacks through it with the points sticking out. That did the trick. The next time he grabbed her leg, believe you me, that was the last time."

In the late 1970s, U.S. airlines began hiring female pilots. Opposition from male pilots was all but unanimous. Allowing women to fly airplanes was incomparably worse than letting them potter around in the back of the planes doing women's work. It violated some of the most basic premises in the male pilots' view of their occupation and of themselves. The men thought of their jobs as demanding, masculine work, and they took their ability to fill those jobs as a confirmation of manhood. The last thing they wanted was proof that females could handle their jobs as well as they.

Several pilots raised the topic with me. Usually when I conducted interviews, it was up to me to guide the discussion. The pilots hardly ever volunteered information that went beyond my questions; they confined themselves to the subjects I brought up. But occasionally they deviated from this pattern. Sometimes they had something pressing on their minds, and then they didn't hesitate to let me know about it. The subject of women fliers was the foremost example. On several occasions, with no prompting from me, pilots started talking about women fliers, and the anger they felt was immediately apparent in their faces and language. They minced no words. They detested the hiring of women for cockpit jobs. They thought it was wrong in every way: biologically, socially, morally.

They used several lines of argument. Women are too weak for the job, they claimed. How could a woman keep control of a huge airliner in an emergency, when an engine goes out, say, or the rudder controls jam? Would *I* want to be a passenger in that situation, with a ninety-five-pound woman flying the plane? Or think about this, they said: Women should not take jobs from men. There are few enough jobs left in the world worth having. Do women want to take over in this field too? Then who in the hell is going to raise the kids? That's what women are for, several of the men argued: Society will collapse in chaos if no one brings up the kids properly.

Mostly, the men seemed to think it was obscene for a woman to put on a man's uniform and comport herself like a man. Why would she want to do that? As one pilot said to me, "It makes you wonder what's inside that uniform, doesn't it?"

The men spoke with such vehemence, I decided I should seek out some women pilots and ask them to tell me their side of the dispute. So I wrote to Bonnie Tiburzi, an American Airlines copilot who has written of her airline experiences in a book titled *Takeoff!* I asked her whether she could give me the names of women pilots who might be willing to meet with me. She wrote back to say that she didn't want to give out any names, but she added that she had made copies of my letter and passed it along to some of her colleagues with the suggestion that they contact me. During the next few weeks, I received messages from several of the women, including one who lived near my home, Gail Finnegan.

I visited Gail in the spring of 1986. We sat at her kitchen table and she told me about herself. She said that after graduating from college, she became a high school teacher. But in the early 1970s, wanting a change from classroom routines, she quit. She would travel around, she decided: see the world. So she signed on as a flight attendant at TWA.

Stewardess work was boring, Gail said. She quickly grew tired of pushing carts up and down airliner aisles, serving meals and drinks to an endless succession of passengers. She was glad that she'd taken the job, though. She'd thought of it as a stopgap, something to fill the time while she looked around for a more permanent career, and it had achieved that purpose. Watching the pilots had inspired her. Their work appeared to be challenging and responsible—she realized it was precisely what she had been looking for. No U.S. airline had female pilots on its payroll, but Gail didn't see why that should stop her. She began taking flying lessons in her spare time, aiming to earn a pilot's license.

When she told her friends at TWA—other flight attendants and some of the pilots—about her ambition, they tried to talk her out of it. Especially the men. They argued that she was just setting herself up for disappointment. They told her that airlines weren't going to hire women for cockpit jobs; the prejudice against it was too strong. And, anyway, women couldn't handle the work. She was fooling herself.

Gail listened to them. These were her friends, she reminded herself, and they seemed sincere. So she changed her plans. She continued taking flying lessons, but she lowered her sights from the airlines to other sorts of flying careers. Maybe she could become a flight instructor, she thought, teaching others how to fly private planes.

Then one day she heard that Frontier Airlines had hired a woman as a copilot. And shortly after that, Gail learned that American Airlines had hired someone named Bonnie Tiburzi to fly for them as a flight engineer. Gail said this news gave her the encouragement she needed. She completed her training and filed an application with TWA to become a flight engineer. In 1978, her application was accepted. She could move forward from the galley.

Her reception up front was not cordial, Gail told me. I could imagine. Here was this female—worse, a small female; worse yet, a pretty *stew* taking a seat among the men. The pilots couldn't believe it. Some of them were openly hostile. They wanted her gone. *Get the hell out of here.* Even the pilots who wished her well seemed confused by her presence. Was she competent? How were they supposed to treat her? She wasn't one of the guys, obviously, but she wasn't exactly one of the girls anymore, either.

Gail said the men constantly scrutinized her while she did her work, as if they expected her to foul up—they seemed to think they would have to push her aside at any moment and take over for her. And on nearly half her flights, she said, there was some sort of hassle, some rudeness or subtle attack. It got so bad that she found herself looking forward to the flights when the men were merely cold; their unfriendliness was painful, but it was better than the way they treated her the rest of the time.

She had to make several adjustments. Getting used to the T&A photos was the least difficult. She didn't think the men put the photos there to embarrass her. It just seemed to be a normal part of airline life, that you would open a cockpit panel and there would be a photo of a nude woman, something from *Playboy* or something raunchier. The pictures seemed to be part of the ordinary cockpit furnishings.

The hardest adjustment was learning to cope with the efforts some men made to trip her up and prove that she was inept. Gail told me that one time, after she had been promoted to copilot, she landed a 707 in Shannon, Ireland, and while the plane was still on the runway, she received instructions to turn the plane around. "Right here?" Gail asked the captain. "Shouldn't we go to the end of the runway first?" The captain told her to turn the plane where it stood. She began the turn but soon realized that there wasn't enough room. She hit the brakes, leaving the plane sitting crossways on the runway. The captain seemed to be waiting for that. "Here, I'll help you," he said, a trace of triumph in his voice. He gunned the engines on the outboard wing and stood on the inboard brakes. He got the plane turned, but one of the tires was ruined in the process. It had to be replaced. Gail told me she felt guilty about that for years. She had put an airplane in a position where it was damaged, one of the worst sins an airline pilot can commit. She considered it a serious blot on her record. But long after the episode, she met another pilot who had been aboard the plane that day. He told her it had been a setup. The captain had been hoping to ambush her since the trip began, and this had been his opportunity. He had known perfectly well that there wasn't room to turn the plane, but he ordered Gail to make the turn anyway, and then he blamed her when the maneuver failed.

That was one of Gail's unhappiest experiences on the airline. It went far beyond the sort of hazing captains often inflicted on copilots. This captain hadn't merely been hostile—he had been determined to defeat her, to drive her out of the profession. I couldn't conceive of a captain treating a male copilot the same way. Gail and I talked it over. She said only a small percentage of the captains were out-and-out sexists. For every woman-hater, there were several good guys. But she said the sexists could make her job miserable when they worked at it.

She gave me another instance, a trip she took while she was still a flight engineer. The captain and the copilot on this flight both had it in for her. They tried to teach her what she was going to have to put up with as an interloper in a man's profession. The funny thing, Gail told me, was that these guys really seemed to think they were doing her a favor. Or they pretended that they did, at least. They said, "This is what it's going to be like for you up here in the cockpit. You'd better get used to it."

At one stop early in the flight, the men—both of whom were middle aged—went into the terminal and bought large bags of popcorn. Then, when they had returned to the plane and taken off again, they began pelting her with the corn, flipping kernels over their shoulders at her or turning around to zing them at her directly. Strange behavior, Gail thought, childish stuff. She tried to be a good sport about it, though. No harm was being done.

But the men intensified the lesson as they went along. They returned from the terminal at another airport with some cigars. After the next takeoff, they lit up and started puffing intently, filling the cockpit with nauseating fumes. Gail asked them to stop; this humor was less endurable. But they refused. "C'mon, Gail, be a sport," they said. "Look, we even brought one of your brand." They handed her a tampon.

The dumbest thing the men did was to interfere with Gail's radio communications. Her responsibilities as flight engineer included reporting the plane's position periodically to air traffic control. The men used the cockpit interphone to break in. Pretending to be the controllers, they muttered obscenities to her and made lewd suggestions. Gail told me that she didn't catch on right away. She couldn't believe that the controllers would talk to her like that, she said, but she found it still harder to believe that her crewmates would do so.

By the end of the flight, the men were in great spirits. They'd had a blast. And they seemed to think that Gail should have enjoyed herself, too. They claimed to be surprised when she told them what she thought of them. "Christ, Gail," they answered, "you'd better learn to put up with a certain amount of razzing if you expect to get by in this business."

Gail did get by. She never had another flight quite like that one, and she told me that over the years the attitude of male pilots generally improved. The guys seemed to adapt to the gradual influx of women fliers. Gail established cordial working relations with those men who were willing to accept her as a colleague, and she held her own against the ones who wished she would disappear. She remained a pilot. By the time I met her, Gail had left TWA, but she hadn't quit flying. She'd gone to another airline where, having risen to the rank of captain, she flew 747s, the largest airliners ever built.

War Flights

L AST YEAR, I VISITED THE NATIONAL AIR AND SPACE MU-
SEUM IN WASHINGTON, D.C. It had changed tremendously
since my last visit more than twenty-five years earlier. Then, it had
been called the National Air Museum, and its collection consisted of
some antique aircraft kept in a quonset hut near a side door of the
Smithsonian Institution. There were also a few missiles. I have a photo
I took of one of them: an Atlas ICBM looming above a small boy, a
friend of mine. I remember that after I took the picture, my friend
walked off to look at the Smithsonian's displays of Colonial American
artifacts. I went into the quonset hut.

Today the Air and Space Museum is housed in a huge, multigallery
structure of marble and glass near the Capitol Building. It is the most
popular museum in America. Wandering through it, I was equally
fascinated by the flying machines on display—aircraft and space vehicles—and by the crowds of people who had come to gaze at them. We
have said something about ourselves as a nation by creating this
museum and putting it on the Washington Mall. Other museums stand
with the Air and Space on the Mall—museums of art, natural history,

American history—but they are different in kind from the Air and Space. They deal with large fields of human knowledge and activity; their focus is diffuse. The Air and Space, by contrast, is devoted to a single subject, one that by implication must have special meaning to the American public: flight.

The curators of the Air and Space obviously had a message in mind when they laid out their floor plan. The central gallery contains the Wright brothers' first airplane, Lindbergh's *Spirit of St. Louis,* Chuck Yeager's X-1, John Glenn's Mercury capsule, and the Apollo capsule that carried Armstrong, Aldrin, and Collins to the moon. The history of flight is presented here as a triumphal progress, mankind's upward movement from the soil into the sky and through the sky toward the stars. Standing in the central gallery, looking at these machines, it's easy to believe that flight is a noble enterprise, an expression of mankind's highest yearnings. And it's easy to congratulate ourselves for being the nation that has undertaken so many of the pioneering efforts in this enterprise. Flight is an American success story.

The two halls flanking the central gallery reinforce the message. They contain mail planes, airliners, research planes, NASA space launchers, lunar modules. Nearly all the flying machines in these halls, in other words, are civilian vehicles used for peaceful, constructive purposes. They heighten the impression that flight is an essentially idealistic activity, a reflection of what we like to call the American spirit.

There's truth in this message, but it's only a partial truth. When you move into some of the peripheral display areas at the museum, you see different types of flying machines. There are fighters, bombers, nuclear missiles. In fact, some of the museum's most elaborate exhibits deal with war. In one side room, there's a reconstruction of a World War I airfield, with a fighter doing a victory roll above a downed opponent. In another room, you stand in front of a eighty-foot-wide mural depicting a formation of B-17 Flying Fortresses: It's a head-on view, what a Luftwaffe fighter pilot would have seen as he attacked the formation. A third room contains a simulation of the bridge of a nuclear-powered aircraft carrier. You can stand at the con and watch Navy warplanes being catapulted into the air: heading out to bomb Hanoi, perhaps, or Libya.

From its start, aviation has been involved with warfare. The main impetus behind the search for techniques to make planes go faster, higher, and farther has been military need. The Wright brothers' first customer was the U.S. Army, and for most subsequent aircraft manufacturers financial success has depended on meeting the military's demands for ever more efficient war planes. The two greatest periods of aeronautical innovation came during the world wars, when nations contended for control of the skies. Space travel proceeded from the same motive. The U.S. and U.S.S.R. created powerful launch vehicles for military, not scientific, purposes. The first man to fly into space, Yuri Gagarin, rode a modified ICBM. The first American in orbit, John Glenn, did the same.

For pilots, the urge to fly has almost always implied a desire to be a combat ace. In one of his books, Lindbergh describes the first test flight he took aboard the *Spirit of St. Louis.* He had every reason to handle the *Spirit* cautiously—the plane had never been in the air before, no one knew how airworthy it would prove to be. But after taking off and performing a few tests, Lindbergh spotted a Navy fighter nearby, and he couldn't resist. He banked toward the fighter and engaged it in a mock dogfight. Years later, during World War II, Lindbergh volunteered for assignment to a fighter squadron. He was rejected because of his age and his participation in the America First movement, but he managed to get sent to the Pacific theater of war as a consultant to fighter manufacturers, and while there he participated—illegally—in a number of combat missions.

The great majority of airline pilots come out of the military. Like my father, they got their flight training while in the service, then they made the move to civil aviation. My father told me recently that airline pilots generally think of themselves as falling into one of two categories: former military fliers and fliers who missed out on military service. The guys with military backgrounds consider themselves a cut above the "draft dodgers," my father said, and the ones with combat records have the most prestige of all. "Actually," he said, "you could say there are three categories that count. Did you fly in World War II, Korea, or Vietnam?"

I asked most of the airline pilots I met to tell me about their experiences in the military. I particularly wanted to hear about World War II, the war my father had been in, and bombing missions, the sort of combat he had seen. I wanted to comprehend what such combat had been like. I knew that the images I'd had as a boy—slambang, nonstop action; exultation and heroics—came mainly from the war comics I read, not from anything the pilots might actually have gone through.

A former B-29 pilot, Jim Summers, gave me the account that stays most forcefully in my mind. Other pilots, including my father, told me war stories that had more drama. But the things Jim said struck me as expressing most clearly the eerily disconnected nature of war in the sky.

"The brass told us we were the biggest factor winning the war," he said. "I didn't entirely believe it. We were making strategic raids on Japan, but frankly the Navy probably could have beaten the Japanese without the Air Force getting involved. I remember flying over the Navy's invasion fleet off Iwo Jima, and it was gigantic. Obviously the Japs couldn't stand up against it.

"But it was good for our morale to hear how important we were, even if it wasn't totally true.

"You couldn't pay me enough now to get me to do some of the things we did then. We were young and cocky. Most of us started out firmly convinced that we weren't going to get killed. Some other guys might, but not us. We did crazy stuff. The air base on Guam had runways that went right to the edge of a cliff that looked out over the ocean. Sometimes when we took off, we had the planes so heavily loaded that they would go off the end of the runway and then sink down toward the water. We'd have to keep going a few hundred yards before we could get up enough speed to start climbing. I wouldn't make a takeoff like that now for any amount of money, but we didn't know any better. We just thought that was how it was done.

"We got scared sometimes, there's no doubt about that. There was no way to avoid it. But the thing is, it came and it went. You just had to go through short periods of it, then it was past. The average mission, we would take off, plug in the autopilot, and then basically just take it easy all the way from Guam to Japan. It was pretty relaxed. We wouldn't start getting anxious until we got close to the coast.

"Flying inbound was something. Most of our missions were at night, and if we were following behind other bombers that had gone in before us, we could see the fires from their bombs. We could be a hundred miles or more out over the ocean, and there would be a glow on the horizon from the fires.

"Ironically, we couldn't see that well when we got in closer. Over the target, we would be flying through smoke—we couldn't see much of anything. And I'll tell you, the air inside that smoke was fierce, from the hot air currents rising. It was like the turbulence in a thunderstorm. It really knocked the planes around.

"That was one of the things that got your blood pressure up. Then there was flak. The Japanese would send up a curtain of flak—they would fill a part of the sky with antiaircraft fire and we had to fly through it. You flat out got scared then, I don't care who you were. You couldn't really maneuver to avoid the flak. You just had to bore ahead and hope you got out of range before the flak clobbered you.

"Getting caught in a searchlight was the worst thing. At most of the targets, there would be searchlights waving back and forth trying to find us. If a light caught you, then you were in *serious* trouble. After one light found you, the other ones would swing over too and then all the guns would zero in on you. I've seen a guy off to one side with fifteen searchlights on him and flak shells exploding all around him, and meantime we were sailing along without any of the guns paying the slightest attention to us.

"I guess we got holes in our plane on ten missions or so from flak. The way we thought of it was, if you can hear a shell burst, that's okay. Fragments will probably put some holes in your plane, but you'll probably survive. It's the shell you *don't* hear that'll kill you. If it explodes in your lap, you won't hear a thing.

"I saw some guys go down. That's a terrible sight. The strange thing is how slow it is. You'd think that a plane would drop fast after getting hit, but actually it takes a long time. It flutters down kind of like a leaf—it might take five minutes to reach the ground.

"Fortunately, we didn't run into much fighter opposition. That was the big difference between what we had to face and what the guys faced in Europe. The Germans sent up hundreds of fighters—it could be murder. But we didn't have it that bad. The most I ever saw was a handful of fighters, and usually it would only be one or two. One of them hit us in the wing one time. He hit a fuel tank. But it didn't catch fire, so we were all right.

"Once you get past the searchlights and the flak, the excitement is basically over. The Jap gunners concentrated on the planes approaching the target, not the ones that had already made it and were turning home. So we would drop our bombs and get out of there.

"If we were lucky, nobody in the crew had been hurt, so we would put the autopilot back on and head back for base, and the flight back would be uneventful."

World War II bomber pilots wreaked more destruction than any other warriors in history. Carrying several tons of explosives per plane, they flew in immense formations, wave upon wave of bombers making coordinated attacks against targets deep inside enemy territory. All told, the American and British air forces dropped nearly three million tons of bombs on Europe during the war, leveling factories, refineries, shipyards, railway facilities, and other targets. Many thousands of Axis soldiers and sailors were killed. In addition, vast numbers of civilians died. Estimates made after the war indicate that a half million German noncombatants lost their lives to the bombers.

The toll in Japan was worse. A single firebomb raid against Tokyo on March 9, 1945, killed more than eighty thousand civilians and wounded another forty thousand. One million Japanese were burned out of their homes that night. Similarly devastating raids were launched against other Japanese cities during the following months, culminating in the atomic bombings of Hiroshima and Nagasaki.

Strategic bombing increased the ruinous effects of war manyfold, but the pilots rarely had to confront these effects. "We flew to a point in the sky," one pilot said to me, "dropped our bombs, and flew back to base. It was clean and simple. We didn't think about what the bombs did to the people on the receiving end, particularly. We were hitting a place on the map, not people." Several pilots made corresponding statements to me. They said they didn't see human beings dying as bombs burst and buildings collapsed and fire spread across urban neighborhoods. They saw canisters falling toward the earth several miles below them, producing small flashes of light followed by blossoms of dust and smoke. Then they flew back to their bases where they slept in dry, semiprivate quarters, and had meals in well-provisioned cafeterias, and stood drinks for each other in officers clubs. Their war had an unreal quality. It wasn't like being a grunt, wallowing in muddy foxholes and tramping across the countryside lugging a heavy backpack. It wasn't like firing a rifle at a man whose face you saw, or ramming a bayonet into his gut, forcing sharpened steel into flesh.

Bomber duty was soft. But not too soft, pilots insisted to me. They seemed eager for me to understand. Pilots who had been based in Europe told me that during most of the war, a standard tour of duty was twenty-five combat missions. Make just twenty-five flights through enemy airspace and you could go home. But there was a catch, the pilots said. Their planes were big and slow—easy targets for enemy gunners. Only a third of the bomber pilots stationed in Europe completed their tours. The rest were killed, wounded, or forced down behind enemy lines. During some missions, as many as sixty bombers—each with ten crewmen aboard—were destroyed by fighters and flak. It was harrowing. And yet even on the worst missions, death remained an abstraction for most pilots—it happened far away. If a pilot got his plane back to base with no casualties among his crewmates, he could generally blot out awareness of the deaths that had occurred during the mission, especially the deaths that his own bombs had caused. "We didn't have time to worry about the Jerries," one pilot said to me. "They were doing real well looking out for themselves. We were busy trying to keep our own hides intact."

Military historians speak of something they call the morality of altitude. A man who might be incapable of taking a life in hand-to-hand combat can readily drop bombs on people from thousands of feet up. He knows his bombs may kill civilians, including women and children, but the knowledge isn't quite real to him because the unseen civilians don't seem quite real. This is awful to contemplate—the morality of altitude implies tragic limits to human sympathies and reason. But the anesthetic effect of altitude is undeniable. Flight is always an act of disengagement, a process of physical removal that lends itself to emotional detachment. Anyone who has ever sat at an airliner's window during a takeoff has noticed how individuals on the ground quickly shrink to pinpoints and then vanish as the plane rises. From cruising altitude, the lands below seem uninhabited—the world appears pristine and empty, a blank slate. Physical distance thus becomes psychological distance that enables bomber crews to believe their actions are moral. Dropping bombs into emptiness hardly seems like an act of violence.

Of course, the moral anesthetic supplied by altitude cannot be fully effective. No one actually believes that an unseen death is any less real than a death that occurs in plain view. But bomber pilots had to pretend to believe it—they had to supplement the detachment that is inherent in flight with an intentional, willed detachment. Curtis LeMay, who commanded the Eighth Air Force in World War II, describes the process this way in his book, *Mission with LeMay: My Story:*

You drop a load of bombs and, if you're cursed with any imagination at all, you have at least one quick horrid glimpse of a child lying in bed with a whole ton of masonry tumbling on top of him; or a three-year-old girl wailing for "Mutter . . . Mutter . . ." because she has been burned. Then you have to turn away from the picture if you intend to retain your sanity. And also if you intend to keep on doing the work your Nation expects of you.

The intentional detachment pilots sought took many forms. Often it served to distance the pilots from each other as well as from the enemy. George Latham, who piloted B-17s in Europe, told me that the men in his bomb group avoided close friendships with one another.

"The toughest raid I went on was against Oschersleben," he said. "Our group lost an awful lot of planes. I started out as the last plane in the squadron, but so many other planes got shot down, I would up flying on the wing of the lead plane.

"I've never seen a novel or a movie that was accurate about the war. They always have a scene where somebody gets shot down and all his buddies get to mourning him and toasting him and all that. But I *know* that's not true. My crew and I were missing one time for a couple of days—our plane was shot up and we had to make a landing at a British field. When we got back to our own field, half our clothes were gone. That's how much the guys mourned for us. 'They got shot down? Too bad. Let's see what they left behind.'

"You got to the point where you took it for granted that some of the guys weren't going to make it back from each mission. There were crews disappearing all the time and new ones transferring in to take their place. That's just the way it was.

"We didn't make close friends with each other. We made acquaintances, not friends. I don't know if it was conscious or subconscious, but we didn't have a real closeness. We kind of alienated everything and everybody—we held everything at arm's length.

"The movies always have another scene where somebody gets

killed and his best buddy starts yelling about how he wants to kill some Jerries for revenge. I never saw anything of the sort. You have a job to do, to get your bombs to the target come hell or high water. If a German fighter pilot tries to stop you, you'll go after him. But you're not antagonistic towards him as a person, it's what he can do to stop you. If that airplane is going to stop *your* airplane, then you've got to stop *it* first.

"It's a very impersonal war, in the air. The only German any of us had a personal hatred for was Hitler, because we felt like he had caused the war. We figured the other Germans were just doing what Hitler imposed on them, so he was the one we concentrated on.

"As a matter of fact, we didn't *see* any Germans. People in the cities, gunners in the flak batteries—they were too far away, we never laid eyes on them. Sometimes we would get a quick look at a Luftwaffe pilot when his fighter came near, but he was there one second and gone the next.

"There was no feeling of triumph when we reached the target. Mainly we were just glad to get rid of the damned bombs so we could get the hell home. Because we weren't through yet—we still had half the flight ahead of us, with probably as many fighters coming after us on the way back as on the way out.

"I suppose the only time we felt a little elation was after the first raid to Berlin. The Germans were bound and determined that we weren't going to go to Berlin, so when we did it, it felt pretty good. But even then there was no whooping and hollering. The main thing we felt was relief, like after any mission—we were just glad we had made it back.

"We were aware of what bombs can do, more or less. We would get passes to go into London every so often and we could see what the Luftwaffe had done there. Sometimes buzz bombs would fall on the city while we were there, too. I don't know how much it affected guys, though. It depended on the individual.

"*Some* guys couldn't help thinking about bomb damage. We had a few basket cases. We had a pilot who completed his tour of duty, but he was so gung ho, he volunteered to fly extra missions as a bombardier. He wasn't a very good bombardier, that wasn't his expertise, but he wanted to extend his tour that way.

"He lived to regret it. One time on the way to a target, he was calibrating his bombsight and he forgot to hold the trigger in, so the bombs fell prematurely. They flat obliterated a French town. When he got back from that mission, he got off his plane in tears. It just about ruined him. He really went down with those bombs and killed those people, I guess. In the back of his mind, he could see those people dying. He was a basket case after that. That was the last mission he went on."

The doctrine of strategic bombing was devised during the 1920s by military theorists such as William (Billy) Mitchell of the U.S. and Giulio Douhet of Italy. They argued that air power would be decisive in future wars. By striking cities deep behind the front lines, large bombing planes would simultaneously destroy an enemy's industries and terrify his civilian population, thus forcing a quick surrender. The doctrine was built on a paradox. Bombers would be sent against cities, which meant attacking civilians, a violation of the traditional rules of war. But Mitchell and Douhet calculated that the total number of casualties resulting from a few decisive bombing raids would be far lower than the toll produced by prolonged ground battles of the kind that had killed millions of young men in World War I. So as a straight mathematical proposition, Mitchell and Douhet claimed, air war would be more merciful.

Leaders of the U.S. Army Air Corps never fully reconciled themselves to the idea of launching "merciful" attacks against civilians, but at times they came close. An Air Corps training manual published in the mid-1920s endorsed the use of terror bombing. By the time World War II began, however, the Air Corps had backed away from this strategy in favor of an alternative plan called daylight precision bombing. Although bombers would still be sent against cities, sophisticated bombsights would be used to pinpoint militarily important targets—factories, military command posts, railroad yards—within the cities. Care would be taken to minimize the number of civilian casualties.

The Army tried to make precision bombing work during the first years of the war, but there were problems. The top-secret Norden bombsight, which was said to be able to put a bomb in a pickle barrel from twenty thousand feet, turned out to be much harder to use in combat than in training. Bursting flak shells and cartwheeling fighter planes distracted the bombardiers—they couldn't give their full attention to the intricate operations the Norden demanded. Foul weather also interfered. The skies over the midwestern U.S., where the bombardiers were trained, tended to be cloudless much of the year. European and Japanese skies were less obliging. Clouds and fog filled them for weeks on end, preventing effective bombing. When the weather was at its worst, raids were scrubbed: The bombers were grounded. On days when clearing was forecast, the bombers went out, but too often the weather deteriorated again before they reached their targets—the bombardiers were unable to find the assigned aiming points under the thick cloud cover.

These problems gradually weakened the Army's commitment to precision bombing. In the Pacific, daylight missions using conventional bombs dropped from high altitudes were replaced by low-altitude night raids using firebombs. Japanese cities consisted chiefly of wooden buildings packed along narrow, winding alleys. The Army decided to light these tinderboxes. In Europe, precision bombing remained official policy, but as the war lengthened an increasing number of nonprecision raids were flown. Bombers were sent out on days when the generals knew the targets would be invisible beneath heavy clouds. It was better to bomb inaccurately, the generals decided, than to leave the bombers on the ground. Then, early in 1945, a few raids were flown with the specific purpose of fomenting panic among the German civilian population. Allied headquarters had decided that the crucial moment of the war had arrived. With the Wehrmacht retreating on all fronts, Germany might collapse if it were subjected to a crushing series of air attacks. The idea seemed to be worth a try, anyway. Consequently, on February 3, 1945, nearly a thousand B-17s bombed Berlin through a layer of clouds. Twenty-five thousand civilians died. A week later, the British and American air forces launched a series of firebomb raids on Dresden. The firestorm they created was so all-consuming that no casualty count could be made. Conservative estimates place civilian deaths at thirty-five thousand. Other estimates go above one hundred fifty thousand.

I met a number of pilots who participated in firebomb attacks on cities. Bill Heller was one. I met him after reading a letter he had written to an aviation magazine. In the letter, he identified himself as a former Eighth Air Force squadron commander, and he said he had led one of the Dresden raids. I wrote to Bill at his home in California, and he agreed to meet with me.

These days, Bill is a bald man of medium height, with a bristling mustache and thick eyebrows. He's impressive—intelligent and forceful. He answered my questions with little hesitation. I soon came to understand that his war experiences were uncommon in several ways, but I thought this lent authority to his comments.

"I led the February 14th [1945] raid on Dresden," Bill told me. "I was commanding the 360th squadron, and it happened to be our turn to lead. The assignment to lead a mission rotated from squadron to squadron.

"I have no regrets concerning Dresden. None. NBC News interviewed me on the fortieth anniversary of the mission and that's exactly what I told them.

"It was god-awful, that's absolutely true. There was no part of that city that was spared. People don't realize what a firestorm of that magnitude is like. I visited Dresden many times after the war, so no one has to tell me. It was an inferno—the fires created winds that literally sucked all the oxygen out of the city. But that doesn't change the facts of the military situation as it was at that time. The Dresden mission was militarily necessary.

"When NBC interviewed me, they also interviewed a Royal Air Force bombardier. He stood up there and said, 'Had I known what we were doing, I would not have gone on the mission.' Who is he kidding? The Krauts had bombed London indiscriminately, killing women and children and old people. They were massacring innocent people all over Europe.

"If the Dresden missions hastened the end of the war by one month, they were worth it. I'm German; my family comes from Germany. But that's the way I feel to this day. These people were aiding and abetting our enemy, and if our missions shortened the war by one month, then they were worthwhile.

"Don't forget this. We didn't attack Europe in order to start a war, we attacked in order to end one. I'm different from some of our guys, perhaps, but I was glad every time I saw our bombs going down. I knew that every time we hit the Nazis, we were bringing the end of the war that much closer."

When I'd contacted Bill, I hadn't paused to consider that Heller is a German name. I'd wanted to talk to an American pilot who flew against Dresden—I didn't give any thought to family background. Now, when Bill stressed his German lineage, I was thrown off balance. I couldn't imagine how a German-American could have flown missions against Germany—any sort of missions, let alone firebomb missions. I thought it must have been traumatic for Bill; a moral crisis. But then I fastened on a phrase Bill had used: "We were hitting the Nazis." I asked him how much he and the other pilots had known, during the war, about Nazism.

"It was perfectly evident what kind of madmen the Nazis were," he said. "We had no proof of what the Nazis were doing to the Jews, if that's what you mean. But we had suspicions, there were rumors. You didn't have to be a genius to figure the Nazis out. And I'll tell you this, I flew a bomb evaluation mission after the war and I got to Dachau three days after it was liberated. The inmates were still there. They weren't physically able to move and there was nowhere else to put them. What I saw there . . ."

Bill spread his hands.

"I'm a German," he repeated. "I didn't have any personal antagonism toward the people we bombed. But I did what I had to do."

I asked Bill about the years he spent in Germany after the war. In his letter to the magazine, he had said that he worked as a pilot for the German national airline during the 1960s.

"Many of the men I flew with [on the airline] were former Luftwaffe pilots," he said. "We had some interesting conversations, believe me. I compared notes with men who had flown against me on a given mission. Two good friends of mine had been fighter pilots who went up against us on the famous second Schweinfurt raid. I told them what a horrible mission that had been for me, and they said it hadn't been great fun for them either. A huge number of men on both sides died on that mission.

"We got along very well. I don't believe it was because I was German, although speaking their language undoubtedly helped. At core, we were all pilots. We had all flown in combat. We were much alike."

I asked Bill whether, during the war, he had felt special pressures because of his German lineage. I wondered how such pressures might have affected his motivation to fight. Had anyone questioned his loyalty to America? Had he felt he needed to prove he was loyal?

To answer, Bill described several unpleasant incidents. He told me that other bomber pilots sometimes made ethnic jokes in his presence (at least, they did before he became squadron commander): "Hey, Kraut," they would call to him before a mission, "what do your buddies have in store for us today?"

He told me of a day when some roughnecks walked onto his father's lawn in Pennsylvania shouting, "The Hellers are dirty Nazis." Bill's father went outdoors and fought them.

He told me of a day when Air Force counterintelligence officers took him to London and, after injecting him with sodium pentothal, interrogated him.

"That made me a little angry," he said. "But not too much. I saw it as common sense on their part. Let's face it, there was information getting out to the Continent. Sometimes the Germans knew what target we were flying against, which let them prepare their defenses. So here I was with a German name—you can't blame the Air Force for making sure I was on the up and up.

"But I don't know that things were much different for me than for any of the other guys in the bomb group. The main thing was not to let extraneous matters get in our way. We had to concentrate on the job at hand.

"I used a little trick that worked for me. It was a fake, it was a facade, but it did what I needed. Before taking off on a mission, I would rub my hands and say, 'C'mon, let's get 'em!' And when we got to the Channel, I'd lean forward and say, 'Okay, where are the Germans? Bring 'em on! C'mon up here, you bastards!' I would psych myself up. The other guys thought I was nuts, but it worked.

"You couldn't let anything extraneous deter you. You steeled yourself, and you tried to keep your mind on the positive things. I was damned proud of the men in my squadron. They would go out on a mission, fly through hell and back, and be ready to go out again on the next mission. Their quiet courage was magnificent.

"Most of all, you had to remember why we were over there. I put it to you like this. If your wife was being attacked, you wouldn't hesitate to defend her. You would go for the bastard attacking her and you wouldn't give any quarter. You would do whatever was necessary to get him off her. That's what we did."

A week after meeting Bill Heller, I went to Long Island to talk with my father about the war. I couldn't recall precisely when we had last discussed the subject—it might have been during one of our sails together in the '60s, or it might have been further back, in the '50s when I often asked him to tell me about his crash landing. Memories of the war must have come back to him frequently in the years since, but if so, he'd kept them to himself. The subject of the war, like most subjects, had been swallowed in the silence that had grown between us. But now I asked him to tell me about the crash again—tell me again about being attacked by German fighters and bringing his bomber down on to that field in Belgium. I said I wanted to hear about all of his wartime experiences. I'd been so young when I last heard about them, I wasn't sure I had any of it straight anymore. I said I wanted to know what his Air Force service had meant to him.

He and his crew had been flying over north-central Germany, he said, when their B-17 developed mechanical problems. The supercharger on one of their engines failed, reducing the engine's power by half. Then a different engine gave out altogether when an oil line broke. So their plane fell back, unable to maintain its place in the formation.

They dumped their bombs and swung to the south, trying to join a stream of bombers that had already reached the target and had turned for England. But while they crossed the corridor of empty sky between their group and the returning bombers, a flight of Messerschmidts pounced them. The fighters made a nose pass, raking them with machine guns and twenty-millimeter cannons.

They threw their plane into a dive. "There was a layer of clouds below us," my father said. "If we could get down into the clouds, we might be able to lose the fighters."

The Messerschmidts didn't make a second pass. Instead, they swarmed around another crippled B-17 that was close by—they pumped shells into it until it reared up into a stall and then spun to the ground. "That gave us time to reach the clouds," my father said. "If it wasn't for that, I don't think we would have lasted.

"We roared down into the clouds, then pulled the nose up. But we were coming down so fast, we couldn't get leveled out until we had dropped all the way through the clouds. But that was okay. The clouds were between us and the fighters, that was the main thing.

"So then we took stock, to see how we had come through the attack." The bomber was in bad shape. Many of the controls were inoperative; the oxygen and vacuum systems were gone; part of the left wing had been shot away. Worse, two crew members were wounded. The fighters' shells had torn apart the nose compartment. The navigator and bombardier had both been hit.

"We set course for the west," my father said, "keeping low and trying to navigate with the [magnetic] compass and a small map." They worked out a procedure. They chose a heading, climbed into the clouds for a few minutes, then dropped back down for a quick glance at the ground. Check the map, adjust the heading, hide in the clouds again. They flew like that for an hour or more, until they were over Belgium.

Their spirits started to improve. They thought maybe they were going to get back to England after all—the North Sea was only a few miles ahead. But the cloud layer thinned out as they proceeded across Belgium. Eventually they were flying through a cloudless sky, with no hiding places left, and then as they approached Brussels another flight of fighters spotted them.

"These guys were Focke-Wulf 190s," my father said. "We had blundered right over a Luftwaffe airfield, and here they came. One of them got on our tail and let us have it."

The bomber shook as shells ripped into it. The rudder controls went, then one of the engines erupted in flames. "That was the end," my father said. "We had four wounded guys now, and the plane was on fire. We had to get down.

"I lowered and raised the landing gear, to signal that we were giving up, and the fighter quit shooting. I don't know if he was being a good sport or if he was just out of ammo, but anyway he quit shooting.

"There was a wheat field directly ahead of us. I can still see it. There was a tree line with a gap in it, and past the gap was a flat, smooth field. I thought, 'That's the place.' So I brought us down there."

My father's words poured out. This was my fourth visit to Long Island to talk with him about his flying career. He had grown increasingly receptive to my questions each time I visited. We had talked together more easily each time and felt more comfortable with each other. But something else also was operating now. Many of the pilots I had questioned about combat became voluble. Men who were at a loss for words when discussing other topics seemed to feel an urgency about relating their war experiences. Combat had been the most intense episode of their lives—the most terrible but also in many ways the most energizing—and I thought many of them were still working through their responses to it.

My father told me he helped the navigator and bombardier out of the plane, and then, after some farmers had led the wounded crewmen from the crash site, he ran to a small woods. "We saw a truckload of Germans coming," he said, "so the crew scattered. I didn't see most of the guys again until long after the war. The engineer and I ran together toward these woods, but then we split up too, so I was by myself."

He spent the night in the woods, a mile or two from the burned-out hulk of the bomber. The next morning before dawn, someone entered the woods—my father couldn't make out whether it was a soldier or a civilian, but a man, anyway, and he seemed to be searching, as if looking for the downed Americans. My father hid himself among the trees until the stranger left. Then, after the sun rose, he emerged from the woods and approached a farmhouse. There, a Belgian family gave him some clothes and a road map. Running their fingers over the map, they traced the path he should follow to reach France. He thanked them and began walking southwest.

He told me some of the things that happened to him during the next few weeks as he crossed France and made his way toward Spain. He said he generally avoided towns, but sometimes bypassing them was impossible—all the roads converged. Once, he said, he walked into a small town only to discover that German troops were garrisoned there. He couldn't explain why they didn't stop him. He tried to make himself inconspicuous, but he stood at least a head taller than most European men of the period. "I was just lucky these particular Germans weren't very inquisitive," he said.

Another time, he said, he boarded a train. He was dressed entirely in civilian clothing except for his army boots, which were wet due to a recent rain. After walking through one car of the train, he turned and saw that his footprints were clearly visible in the aisle, and the prints all bore the inscription that was stamped into the boot soles: U.S. Army, U.S. Army. He dried his boots and hurried into the next car. Later, when the train slowed on a curve, he hopped off.

As he described these events, we opened an atlas to work out the route he'd taken through France. Then he pulled down his Army flight log from a shelf, so I could read the notations he'd made about each of his missions. He also showed me various official documents he'd kept: enlistment papers; notification of selection for bomber training; notification of assignment to a combat unit in England.

"You know," he said, "I wanted to be a fighter pilot. Before Pearl Harbor, I had an idea that I wanted to join the Royal Canadian Air Force and fly fighters against the Germans. I thought fighters were where the 'glamour' was.

"After the Japanese attacked and I joined the Army, I still thought fighters were the thing. But you know how the Army operates. When my class graduated from primary training, the Army needed warm bodies in the bomber squadrons, so that's where we were all assigned. There might have been one or two exceptions, but not many—they shipped us all out for bomber school.

"It was all right. The B-17 was a great plane. It could take a stupendous beating and keep flying. Every crew that flew 17s fell in love with them, I think. Still, I would have liked to fly something quicker and more maneuverable. After I started flying 17s, my idea was that I was going to finish my twenty-five missions, then volunteer to fly the de Havilland Mosquito. That was a small two-engine plane that I thought was really slick. But of course my plan went by the boards after we got shot down. I couldn't go back to finish my missions. The Air Force wouldn't put you back on combat duty after you were shot down—they were afraid that if you got shot down again, the Germans would torture you to find out whatever you had learned about the underground.

"I don't know how I would have felt if I had completed my tour—I don't know if I would have volunteered for Mosquitoes the way I planned. I flew less than a dozen missions, so I never went through some of the things other guys in our bomb group did. Crews typically got more and more tense when they were getting near the end of their tours. They knew that the odds made finishing a tour almost impossible. We were losing six or seven percent of the planes on each mission, and if you multiply that out, it means nobody should still be alive after twenty-five missions. So every mission got harder than the one before. But I didn't complete enough missions to get the full impact of that.

"I remember when I first got to England, before I'd flown any missions, I was sitting in the mess hall one morning when our squadron's lead pilot sat down across from me. I was extremely impressed—I thought, 'Here's God having breakfast with me.' But I didn't know what to say to him. The answer is, I should have kept my mouth shut. But I didn't know any better, so I piped up and said, 'Gee, captain, sir. I sure am glad to meet you.' And then I said something brilliant like, 'I haven't been on any missions yet, but I sure am looking forward to it. I expect I'll be sort of nervous the first time out, but no doubt it gets easier later on.' Which was absolutely the wrong thing to say, as he let me know. He gave me this look of absolute contempt, which shut me up very effectively.

"A couple of days later, headquarters asked for a volunteer to fly tailgunner on this same captain's ship. They always wanted a pilot to sit in the tail of the lead ship—he would watch the formation and tell the captain how it was holding together. So I demonstrated how green I was again by sticking up my hand and saying I wanted to go.

"So that was my first mission. I remember it better than any of the others, except for my last mission of course. I remember we took off and rendezvoused with the other planes that would be in the formation, and I just thought it was wonderful. There were airplanes everywhere, milling around, trying to form up. I had a list of all the planes in our group and I checked them off and reported to the captain from time to time. I thought I was doing a hell of a good job. I was having a great time. I mean, I was *green.*

"Finally we were formed up and we headed off across the North Sea. We went to Bremen, and while we were coming up on the target, I saw flak for the first time. I thought, 'Yep, that's flak all right. I'd know it anywhere.' And I saw some Me-109s buzzing around. A couple of them made passes at our group, but they didn't do any real damage—they were concentrating on other parts of the formation. So I just enjoyed the hell out of that flight. I mean, I was just so happy to be there, it was just like in the movies. I thought, 'Goddamn, here I am in the Eighth Air Force. I'm on a mission. And those are some German fighters over there. And these are my machine guns. You know, I could fire these machine guns if I wanted to.'

"Everything impressed me. I was *extremely* impressed by how the crew handled themselves on the interphone. They were imperturbable. It would be, 'Uh, Left Waist Gun to Skipper.' 'Yes, Left Waist.' 'Skipper, I've got four bandits here at nine o'clock high.' 'Roger, Left Waist. Keep me advised.' They almost sounded bored by it all—they were totally calm. It was just great stuff.

"So we dropped our bombs and flew back over the North Sea. Then we let down over the English coast and came in a thousand feet above the base and made a formation landing. One plane after another peeled off and came in to land at thirty-second intervals. The captain brought our plane down like a feather and taxied in to the hard stand [i.e., the plane's parking and maintenance area] and swung the plane around and shut down the engines. And I was euphoric. I had a mission under my belt!

"But then here came a medical team racing up to our plane. I realized somebody in the crew had been wounded, and suddenly my mood evaporated. I crawled out of the hatch and ran around to the front of the plane, and there was a crowd of people carrying somebody out of the plane. I worked my way into them and I saw that it was the captain.

"I was crushed. I thought this was the worst thing that could possibly have happened. This terrific guy had been hurt. But then one of the gunners saw me and he said, 'Oh yeah, you're new, aren't you?'

"It turned out the captain wasn't hurt—this was how they always took him off the plane. He would fly a perfect mission, but then when he got back and turned off the engines, he would collapse. So they would haul him off to a rest home where he would recuperate, and then they would rouse him up after a few days and tell him it was time to go out and be a hero again.

"The thing was, I had no way of understanding what things were like for him. He'd flown a couple of dozen missions already, plus he had the extra pressure of leading the squadron, while I was a complete rookie. I was *such* a rookie that seeing him carried off the plane didn't really affect my attitude. I thought about it, but it didn't have much meaning to me. I was still glad to be in the Air Force. I was still eager to go out and win the war.

"The war never did become real to me, I guess, until the mission when we got shot down. When I looked up and saw the fighters coming straight at us—with the guns flashing on their wings, you know—that was the first time I was *sure* that somebody was shooting at me individually. Everything got very serious all of a sudden.

"I've wondered what my attitude would have been if I had racked up a lot of missions. Maybe the medics would have been carrying *me* off the plane eventually. But as it was, my war experiences were relatively light. I didn't get wounded or go through battle fatigue. I wasn't captured and stuck in a prison camp after we were shot down. I had a relatively easy time of it. I went into the war feeling basically invulnerable and I guess I came out feeling pretty much the same. I was still young and I hadn't seen that much combat action. I know that on the airline afterwards, I always assumed nothing too serious could go wrong. As long as there weren't any Messerschmidts barrelling straight at my windshield, I figured everything was fine."

Glory Days

T HERE WERE NO LIMITS TO TWA'S GRANDEUR—NONE I WAS AWARE OF WHEN I WAS A KID, ANYWAY. I remember getting excited one evening when, digging through the record collection in our living room, I found an album titled *TWA's The Night Before Christmas.* What an airline! It even put out its own Christmas records! I begged my mother to play the album for me. When she stopped laughing, she gave me a quick lesson in capitalization and the uses of apostrophes.

My loyalty to TWA obliged me to despise TWA's chief business rival, Pan Am. I ranked Pan Am with the other bad guys of my childhood, the Brooklyn Dodgers. My world contained good guys (the Yankees and TWA) and bad guys, and I was clear on which was which. I did make one concession to Pan Am, however. I was intrigued by a certain kind of plane Pan Am had operated in the past: flying boats. I'd only seen photographs—Pan Am retired the flying boats at the end of the 1940s—but what I saw intrigued me. Flying boats were airplanes that could take off and land on water. They had hulls grafted to their bellies; I thought they must be some kind of combination of airplane and yacht. I clipped out the photos I found, and, despite some mild qualms, I bought a plastic model of a Boeing 314, the last and largest of the Pan Am boats. I assembled the model, then put it on a shelf in my bedroom, amid a cluster of TWA planes and Air Force bombers.

In point of fact, the 314 was a more interesting aircraft than I understood. As the successor to such early flying boats as the *China Clipper*, it was the best long-range airliner in use at the start of World War II. For this reason, it was the plane that Allied statesmen, including both Roosevelt and Churchill, took when flying to transatlantic conferences. It was a big plane, a hundred feet long with a double-deck fuselage. The cockpit, crew quarters, and baggage compartments were on the upper deck, the passenger compartments on the lower. The wings were so large, they contained tunnels leading out to the engines. During ocean crossings, flight engineers could clamber out through the tunnels and, standing erect, perform maintenance work inside the engine nacelles.

The passenger accommodations were opulent. Rather than sitting in rows of assigned seats, the passengers could roam at will through seven compartments, one of which was earmarked specifically for promenading. At night, several of the compartments were converted to sleeping chambers with full-length beds. There were separate men's and women's dressing rooms, a galley and bar manned by stewards, and a deluxe "bridal" suite located near the tail. At mealtimes, the passengers gathered in a dining compartment where they ate at linen-covered tables set with china, crystal, and silver. A few passengers were selected during each meal to dine at the captain's table.

I've spoken recently with some retired Pan Am pilots who flew the 314. I told them about that lone Pan Am model on my bookshelf and asked what the real 314 had been like to fly. Bob Lynch was particularly forthcoming. "Of all the planes I've known," he said, "I probably liked the 314 best. There wasn't anything to compare to it. It had a lot of class.

"But it was a dog, too, in some ways."

Like all flying boats, the 314 was a compromise design, a hybrid intended to perform well both in the air and on the water. It couldn't. The 314's boatlike features hampered its performance in flight, while its planelike features reduced its seaworthiness. Bob said these problems were most evident during takeoffs and landings, the moments of transition from one environment to the other. A captain had to be alert when he tried to coax a 314 to rise. As the plane accelerated across the water, the wind could reach under a wing and tilt it up, threatening to capsize the plane. "Three men into the wing!" the captain would holler then, and that many crew members would rush to the end of the tunnel in the up-tilted wing, using their weight to help cantilever the plane back onto an even keel.

Landings were equally precarious. A 314's stately passage through the air could end shockingly if the hull hit the water wrong. "People think water is soft," Bob said, "but it isn't. If you don't come down on it carefully, you might as well be smacking down onto concrete.

"Smooth landings were wonderful. If you got everything right, you knifed down into the water, and there was this whishing sound as you skimmed the surface, and then the hull settled down—there was nothing to beat it. But a rough landing was something else. If we dropped onto a wave that was rising, we could damage the plane pretty badly, especially if we hit it head-on. So we had to be aware of what the waves were doing when we landed. We tried to come down in the same direction the waves were blowing, and we tried to time it so that we were behind a crest when we touched the water. Otherwise, it could make a hard landing on a runway feel like nothing.

"Don't misunderstand. I *liked* the 314. It was so big and ugly, you *had* to like it. But making it behave took some doing."

Bob fell quiet, trying to decide how to explain his affection for the 314.

"I don't suppose we ever flew much faster than a hundred-and-fifty miles an hour," he said after a moment. "The plane would drone along for hours. We would stay in the air ten, twenty hours at a time. And the primitive autopilot it had wasn't good for much—we had to fly the plane manually most of the time. It was exhausting. But that was also part of what made it special. There was a grandeur about it.

"You had to know what you were doing, to fly the plane well. It was so heavy, sometimes it took us several hours to climb to just a thousand feet. Even after we'd burned off a lot of fuel, we couldn't get very high. We went low and slow. And the controls were extremely sluggish. You would turn the wheel and nothing would happen. Then after a while, *slowly* the wings would start to tilt and the plane would come around to the new heading. Everything took forever. So you had to stay ahead of the plane; there was no such thing as making a quick maneuver.

"That just seemed normal to us, though. It was part of the challenge of flying that plane, to plan out each move well before you made it. You had to be steady. You had to make the plane behave better than it wanted to."

Several Pan Am pilots let me know they weren't entirely comfortable about talking to a TWAer's son. "Your dad flew for Teeny Weeny?" one retired Pan Am captain said, skeptically surveying me from head to foot. "Well, maybe I'll talk to you anyway."

Pan Am had been the bigger, more prestigious airline. During the era of the flying boats, it was the only U.S. airline authorized to fly overseas. It was, for most intents and purposes, the official U.S. flag line. TWA, by comparison, was a small domestic carrier, of no concern to globe-girdling Pan Am. But after World War II, competition developed between these mismatched companies when TWA got government permission to begin flying to Europe using new long-range land planes: DC-4s and Constellations. Retired pilots from both TWA and Pan Am told me about the contentious spirit that ensued on both lines.

Pan Am crews resented the inexperienced upstarts at TWA. They monitored radio transmissions from TWA flights, and if they heard something they considered stupid (the use of the wrong call letters for contacting a midocean weather ship, say), they would break in with a correction. TWA crews retaliated in the same spirit. Pan Am's motto was "The World's Most Experienced Airline." If a TWA pilot overheard a Pan Am crew radioing a report of an inflight problem—an engine failure or a navigational glitch—he would be sure to break in with the question, "What's the matter, Pan Am? Having another experience?" The rivalry also took more active forms. If a Pan Am DC-6 and a TWA Connie were due to depart from an airport at approximately the same time, the crews would likely jockey for precedence: One captain might pull his plane away from the gate a minute or two early, trying to reach the runway first; the other might take a "wrong" turn on a taxiway, to cut him off. It was like a rivalry between sports franchises. Pilots from the competing lines rarely met face to face— they didn't know each other as individuals. But because they wore opposing colors, they considered themselves to be opponents.

Residual tension from the rivalry affected my conversations with Pan Am pilots. The effects were covert, though. The Pan Amers asserted their pride indirectly, telling me a special sort of story from Pan Am's past. Most of the stories concerned foul-ups of one kind or another, almost as if the pilots were criticizing their airline. But I'd heard enough hangar flying by this time to take the stories as they were intended, I think. There was nothing derogatory about the stories. They were boasts, actually—inverted boasts about a period that Pan Am had dominated, an exciting period when Pan Am's crews experienced adventures no other pilots had shared. They were a form of coded one-upmanship.

"I'll tell you a story," a former 314 pilot said to me. "Under some wind conditions, you had to tow a seaplane away from the dock, you couldn't taxi it. Okay. So, one day, a crew had a boat tow them out and then they turned into the wind and started off across the bay, trying to take off. But they couldn't get up out of the water.

"They kept going for a couple of miles and the captain tried everything he could think of, rocking the yoke and so forth, trying to climb out of the water, but nothing worked. So finally they cut the engines and stopped.

"They were going to talk the situation over and decide what to do. They thought they would have to go back to the dock and unload some cargo to make the plane lighter. But while they sat there talking, the plane drifted around and they could see that the tow boat was still attached to them!

"They had started their takeoff run before the guys in the boat could release the tow line, and then the line got fouled, so the plane dragged the boat behind it. God, think what a ride that was for the guys in the boat. They must have been trying like anything to release that line, and you *know* they were praying that the damned plane wouldn't get into the air with them still hitched to it. That's no way to cross the ocean, dangling from the end of a rope."

"Here's a story for you," a former 314 flight engineer said to me. "In that time, engineers didn't just keep the equipment working when the plane was flying. The job was bigger than that. If anything busted, it was up to us to fix it after we landed.

"Well, we landed one time on Fisherman's Lake in Africa, and when we came down onto the water we hit a log or something that ripped a hole in the hull. The captain gunned the motors and got us over to the shore fast, so we wouldn't sink in the deep water. But then we had to work out how to patch the hole.

"It took some doing. The plane was sitting in, I don't know, four feet of water or thereabouts, and we had no way to haul it up onto the beach. We would have to repair it where it sat. I mean me and the other engineer on board.

"What we finally figured out was, we took some five-gallon tin cans and cut holes in them, and we fastened pieces of glass in the holes, and ran some hoses from an air pump to them, and there we had diving helmets. So then the two of us climbed down under the hull with these helmets on our heads and we fastened a metal plate over the hole. You know: We drilled holes, and bolted the plate on, and sealed around the edges.

"It wasn't a perfect job, but it seemed good enough. Admittedly, some water was still leaking in, but not enough to worry about. But the maintenance guys there at the lake thought we should do something more, so they poured concrete into the hull on the inside, to seal it from the inside. That didn't do a whole hell of a lot of good, it just added several thousand pounds to the weight that had to be dragged back to New York.

"But the plane made it back like that, hauling that plug of concrete. It went slower than ever, but it got back to New York eventually."

I took my first airplane ride before I was two years old. TWA transferred my father from Kansas City to the East Coast, where the company was gearing up for its competition with Pan Am. So my parents and I headed for the big time, flying as nonpaying passengers in a TWA Connie.

I don't remember that flight, naturally, but it set the tone for the rest of my boyhood. Beginning that day, I was to fly scores of times, always for free, always on TWA. It was a strange way to grow up. But in the '50s, it didn't seem so very strange. Those were boom times for the airlines. Pan Am, TWA, and the other lines retired their old aircraft—314s, DC-2s, DC-3s—in favor of newer, racier machines, and ticket sales soared. People's fear of flying had subsided; in a sweeping reversal from the prewar years, everybody wanted to fly now. The war had taught Americans to associate aviation with the nation's strength and, ultimately, with victory. FDR had called for the production of fifty thousand airplanes a year, an aerial armada that would crush the Axis. So the nation put its faith in air power. Aviation was the hope of the future, the technology that would carry us into a brighter age.

America's infatuation with aviation persisted and, if anything, grew after the war. The signs were everywhere. The Air Force, having been separated from the Army and made a coequal military branch, quickly became more equal than the other branches: During the '50s, it was given exclusive responsibility for packing America's Sunday Punch (as nuclear deterrence was called then). During the same decade, aviation stocks became the hottest issues on Wall Street. The airlines surpassed ship lines, railroads, and intercity bus lines in the number of passengers they carried annually. Books about aviation climbed bestseller charts, and aviation movies were big box office. Magazines like *Popular Mechanics* carried frequent articles about the private aircraft we would all soon buy as replacements for our outdated automobiles. Detroit responded by giving new cars names like Skylark and Thunderbird and attaching airplanelike tail fins to them. The more a car resembled an airplane, carmakers learned, the better it sold.

Many pilots have told me the '50s were great years for them. Their profession was accorded extraordinary prestige, which redounded to them as individuals. They were set apart and, often, lionized. When they walked through an airport terminal wearing their uniforms and carrying their flight bags, they saw heads turn toward them and heard voices fall. "When people saw that uniform," a retired American Airlines captain said to me, "they acted like you were some kind of celebrity or something. They made a fuss over you." A retired Eastern Airlines captain told me he learned not to stop for groceries or other supplies when driving home from a flight. "It got embarrassing," he said. "If I went into a store in my uniform, strangers would come up to me to ask what line I flew with and where I went. It was sort of flattering, but enough is enough. After it happened a few times, I made a point to go home and change before I went to the store."

I suspect the decade seemed particularly sweet to TWA pilots. Their airline had grown tremendously. A few years earlier, a TWA captain would have flown short, puddle-jumping flights, hauling small groups of passengers from one bush-league city to another. Now he was an international aircraft commander flying to London and Paris and Cairo in giant four-engine transports. His horizons had, in the most literal sense, expanded, and his responsibilities and authority had enlarged correspondingly. He undertook a sort of flying that was wholly new to him. A flight across the ocean wasn't a succession of up-and-down hops—you weren't constantly rising from one airport and then quickly preparing to descend at another, the way you did on most domestic flights. Ocean flying was both more demanding and more leisurely than that.

Several TWA pilots described ocean flying to me. It called for self-discipline more than anything else, they said. You sat for hours in the cockpit without a great deal going on. Autopilots had improved—you didn't need to keep your hands on the wheel every moment. Mainly you gathered information from your crew members and considered your options. From your flight engineer, you got reports on the condition of the engines and the amount of fuel remaining. From your navigator, you got half-hourly updates on your position. From your radio man, you got transcriptions of any weather reports or other messages he managed to snatch from the ether. You took all the data, weighed its implications, and thought through any changes you might need to make to ensure a successful trip—changes in altitude, speed, heading, engine setting. Often you wouldn't change anything; you stayed with your original flight plan. But just as often, you would make dozens of changes, continuously revising your plan as unexpected circumstances developed.

Every trip was different, the pilots said. Gremlins would clobber some piece of equipment that they'd never attacked before; or a passenger would get sick; or, almost certainly, you would hit different weather than the last time out—different winds, different storm patterns. If you ran into headwinds, you might decide to divert to Iceland or the Azores for more fuel. If you ran into icing conditions, you might descend, to find warmer air. If there were thunderstorms ahead, you might turn south or north, to fly around them. The decisions were up to you. There weren't many other planes out there; there wasn't any air traffic control. You assessed your situation and made your own choices.

Getting an airplane across the ocean was a challenge, the pilots said. Nothing to write home about—hundreds of other guys had flown the ocean before you, thousands more would do it after you. Still, each flight across was an achievement. When you had spent twelve hours or more nursing your fuel reserves and sidestepping storm cells, and then you descended through a murky cloud deck to set your plane down right on the runway numbers at London airport—then you knew you had accomplished something.

Some pilots told me they preferred flying the ocean during daylight hours. They enjoyed looking out at the cloud formations and the glinting patterns of light that the sun threw on the water below. Others said they liked flying at night. They said it was a kick to sit in a darkened cockpit with the engines purring and the dials glowing on the instrument panels—you sat there where you were warm and comfortable, and gazed out at a black sky that stretched away to infinity.

I asked my father what he remembers about the transatlantic trips he made during the '50s, and whether he preferred flying the ocean by the day or by night. He answered tangentially. "Everything is up when I'm in the cockpit," he said. "If it's night, I might be even more up than during the day because I have to push myself more if I'm tired. You learn not to let the clock dictate to you. I keep my watch set on Greenwich time, no matter where I am. When you cross time zones constantly, it doesn't make sense to try to stay on the local time.

"At night, over the ocean, there's an illusion that you're not moving at all. You're going hundreds of miles an hour, but you can't see it. There's nothing visible below you, and the stars aren't moving—there's a kind of timelessness about it.

"The thing you aim for is to be quietly alert. If there's an emergency, you have to move fast—shut down an engine that catches fire, or whatever. But usually it's not like that. You stay alert, you note what all the instruments show and what the weather's doing, and usually you have plenty of time to decide what steps to take. Really, that's what makes long flights interesting, keeping everything methodical and under control.

"I can't answer whether I liked flying best at day or at night. For me, whether I was tired before the flight or not, whether the sun was up or not, when I got into the cockpit I just felt ready. I always looked forward to it."

The '50s were high times for my father and other TWA pilots. But while things seemed to be going great guns, their airline suffered from a hidden problem throughout the decade. Eighty percent of TWA's stock was owned by reclusive billionaire Howard Hughes. Hughes was the prime architect of the airline's expansion. He was also the unwitting scoundrel who nearly drove the airline into bankruptcy.

Hughes loved aviation. As an amateur pilot during the 1930s, he had set several aviation speed records, including the record for round-the-world flight. Later, when he got tired of racing, he looked around for an airline he could buy—he thought operating one might be fun. Unfortunately for TWA, his eye lighted on it. During the late 1930s, he began picking up TWA stock. By 1940, he owned a controlling stake in the company.

Hughes wanted his airline to be the biggest, and he had the cash to pursue that objective. He bought a fleet of new planes for TWA and arranged to have them fly dozens of new routes, especially overseas routes. As a signal of his intentions, he changed the airline's name. When he took control, TWA was still known by its original name: Transcontinental and Western Air. But that sounded too provincial to Hughes, so in 1945 he registered a more grandiose (and semantically warped) substitute: Trans World Airline. He proposed to send his airliners everywhere.

Hughes had limitless ambitions, but he subverted them through his own bizarre behavior. He was arbitrary and unpredictable—an impossible boss. He was often negligent, leaving important decisions to his subordinates. But then at other times he asserted his will, insisting that even the smallest matters required his personal approval. For as long as this phase persisted, he would engross himself in questions like what color scheme to use in the cabins of TWA planes—and while he pondered such trivia, he postponed decisions on major issues for weeks or, in some instances, months.

His management style (if it can be called that) produced corporate paralysis. He rarely held face-to-face meetings with his corporate officers. Instead, he would summon the officers to the corridor outside his hotel room and, staying hidden inside the room, talk to them through the transom above his door. Or he would phone the officers late in the afternoon and keep them on the line until well past midnight. One TWA vice president learned to keep a Mason jar near his desk for use as an emergency urinal.

Hughes appropriated TWA aircraft for his private use, going off on "test flights" that looked suspiciously like joyrides. Sometimes he kept the planes for months on end. He evidently believed that he could do whatever he pleased with company assets. He insisted that TWA adjust its operations to suit his own convenience and the convenience of his retinue. If a starlet he was dating wanted a seat on a flight, she was to be accommodated even if this meant unseating a passenger who held a reservation. And if the starlet arrived late for the flight, so be it—the plane could not leave until she was aboard.

Hughes selected the aircraft TWA would operate, sometimes making his choices without consulting any of the airline's officers. At various times he ordered planes from almost every major manufacturer (although he refused to do much business with the largest of the lot, Douglas Aircraft—he and the president of Douglas were not on speaking terms). He contracted for Lockheed Constellations, Martin 2-0-2s and 4-0-4s, Boeing 707s, Convair 880s—a long, ill-conceived string of acquisitions. In the end, this is the habit that did him in.

During the late 1950s, Hughes could not decide what kinds of jetliners to buy. He put off the decision until most other U.S. airlines had already ordered jets. Then, realizing that he had damaged TWA's competitive position, he panicked and ordered so many Boeing 707s and Convair 880s that, despite his enormous financial resources, he couldn't cover the cost. He had to turn to Wall Street financiers for aid. None of them would touch the deal, though, as long as Hughes remained in control at TWA: They insisted that he sell the airline. Hughes resisted, looking for alternatives, but finally he had to accept the financiers' terms. So in 1960, TWA passed to new ownership.

Most of the retired TWA pilots I met winced if I mentioned Hughes. They were embarrassed to have been associated with him, despite the tenuous nature of the association. Most of them said they'd never clapped eyes on the guy, much less met him. They knew he owned the company, and they'd heard rumors about him. Some said they'd had flights that were postponed or diverted at his orders. But generally they said they'd had nothing to do with Hughes nor he with them. They didn't see him, they didn't think about him. They went about their jobs as if he didn't exist. I got the impression that Hughes lurked in the background at TWA like a half-loony rich uncle whose eccentricities a family tries to hush up.

But a few pilots gave me a somewhat different account. They said that once in a long while Hughes emerged from his seclusion, and then at least a small number of pilots had to contend with him in the flesh. A retired captain whom I'll call Dave Stoddard told me of one such episode. He said that, with no advance warning, he and two other captains were assigned to help Hughes improve his flying skills.

"One Sunday I got a phone call at home," Dave said, "and it was the office saying they wanted me to go out to Burbank, California. I said, 'What do you mean? I've got a flight to take out tomorrow.' But they said, 'No, Dave, you are going out to Burbank to help Howard Hughes get an air transport rating.'

"I was thunderstruck. This thing came totally out of the blue. I mean, ask yourself how you would react if you got a call like that without any warning. I thought, 'God almighty, why me?' I sure didn't want to tangle with Howard Hughes. I don't mean that he had a reputation for firing people, particularly. But he was unpredictable. I saw no benefit in bringing myself to his attention."

Dave argued for a reprieve, but the voice on the other end of the line was implacable. So the next day, Dave flew with two of his colleagues to California.

"I don't know to this day why Hughes wanted a transport rating," Dave said. "It's the license you need if you want to be an airline captain. I assumed Howard Hughes didn't want to fly on the line. I sure *hoped* he didn't, anyway. But whatever his reason was, he wanted to get his rating, and he ordered the company to send him some pilots to show him the ropes."

Arriving in Burbank, the three captains were met by a Hughes representative who took them to the Ambassador Hotel, where private rooms had been reserved for them. Large, fully stocked private rooms. Each captain found a bottle of scotch and a bottle of bourbon on his dresser, along with an ice bucket and glasses.

But the captains didn't have time for many drinks that evening. "After we checked in," Dave said, "we got a message that we would be picked up at seven in the next morning. So we went to sleep early, because we wanted to be sharp in the morning. None of us knew what in the world to expect."

When they assembled at the hotel entrance the next morning, they found a limousine waiting for them. They had seen bigger cars in the movies, maybe, but not in real life. They climbed in, though, and as they rode out to the airport they discussed what they should say to Mr. Hughes when they met him. "But that turned out to be a wasted effort," Dave said, "because when we got to the airport we found a Connie sitting there and a flight engineer waiting beside it, but there was no sign of Mr. Hughes. Nobody could tell us when to expect him, either. I heard later that that was how he was. He never got anywhere on time.

"So we cooled our heels a good long while."

They huddled, trying to decide how to proceed. By the look of things, Hughes wanted them to give him flying lessons in the Connie. But which of them would go first? None of them wanted the honor. They debated the point briefly, then drew matchsticks.

"And who do you think got the short one?" Dave asked me. "You're looking at him.

"Well, I went on over to the flight engineer and we got into the plane. We went to the cockpit and sat ourselves down there. I took the copilot's seat, figuring Hughes would want to play captain. Then we waited some more.

"Finally Hughes showed up. He came into the airplane and walked up the aisle, and I said hello to him, expecting him to smile or say hello like a normal person. But nothing doing. He got into the captain's seat and started fiddling with his belt, silent as a clam, and he never looked at me."

That was perhaps the one response Dave hadn't anticipated. Why drag a man halfway across the continent on a special assignment if you were going to ignore him when you got him there? Dave didn't know what to make of it. But he told himself to hang on, there was no point getting chesty with the boss. So, after Hughes had settled himself, Dave picked up the checklist and began reading it aloud. Standard procedure before taking off was for the copilot to read each item on the list—Navigation Lights: check; Ignition: off; Pitot Heaters: check; and so forth—while the captain confirmed that the specified controls were set properly. But Hughes wasn't playing. Dave read the first item and waited for Hughes to respond. Silence.

"Hughes didn't want anything to *do* with that checklist," Dave said. "It was like I was talking to myself. He just moved the controls a little, then without waiting for me to finish the list he started up the engines and taxied us out toward the runway.

"So the engineer and I quickly looked over everything to make sure the plane was ready, then we hung on to see what would happen next. We could see he was going to take off as soon as he hit that runway.

"Let me tell you, the *way* he took off was something. He only knew one way to do it, I guess, from his racing days. He pushed the throttles all the way forward and just *blasted* up into the air."

Hughes flew a short distance straight ahead, then he leveled out and turned to fly back past the airport. All the while, the engines were screaming wide open. Dave wondered if he should do something about it. Correct procedure was to use full power for takeoff, then throttle down for the climb, and throttle down further for level flight. But

Hughes didn't seem to know—or care, anyhow—about that. Dave thought maybe he should speak up. Was that the plan? Was he supposed to spot the flaws in Hughes's flying technique and offer corrections? He wasn't sure. Nobody had said. So instead of telling Hughes to adjust the throttles, Dave reached over and silently eased them back himself, hoping Hughes wouldn't take offense.

Hughes didn't seem to notice. He continued past the airport, then turned again and began descending. So, Dave surmised, Hughes intended to shoot landings—take off, circle the airport, land, then take off again and repeat the sequence. It was a standard routine for student fliers. Hughes didn't announce his intentions, but Dave could see how things were tending. Dave got ready to lower the wing flaps and landing gear.

"He brought us in to land, then," Dave said. "And we just *dove* onto the runway! He came down like he'd gone up, hell for leather. And as soon as the wheels touched down, he pushed the throttles to the wall again and we roared back into the air. I'm not joking, I was going crazy and so was the engineer. I never saw a man treat an airplane so rough. He didn't ask for flaps to be retracted, or the landing gear, or anything. And he never touched the radio. He didn't give a shit.

"We went around like that again, and the engine oil was starting to boil, and I decided I really had to do something. I mean, if I was supposed to teach him how to fly like an airline pilot, this sure wasn't it. So when we got on the ground again, I scraped together my courage and I said to him, 'Mr. Hughes, please pull over onto the taxi strip.'

"He didn't open his mouth or give any sign he'd heard me, but he did pull the plane over, and believe me I was kind of nervous. I told him to shut off engines one and two, and all the time I was thinking, 'What's going to happen to me now?' Because all this man had to do was lift one finger and I would be looking for work. He could have me fired just like *that.*

" 'Sir,' I said, 'I'd like to talk to you for a minute.'

" 'To get an air transport license, sir, you've got to abide by *some* rules and regulations. And this is one of them: We've *got* to follow this checklist.

" 'Now, I'll do everything I can to help out and be as informative as I can, but I'd like for us to follow the list, if that's all right. If you don't want to, I will read it and check all the controls myself. Anything you say. But at least one of us should check things over. Is that all right?'

"Well, he agreed that I could go down the checklist if I wanted to. That would be satisfactory to him. He wouldn't fool with it himself, but if I wanted to, he didn't seem to mind.

"So we got set to go again. I suggested we do something else besides landings, though. I wasn't eager to do more of them. I said, 'Sir, I'm satisfied with your landings. Why don't we go do some air work?' Which he agreed to. So the next time we took off, we went out a ways and I told him different maneuvers to try. He put us in a forty-five-degree bank, for instance, and he held it there, circling. And he did it nicely—he maintained his altitude and he kept his airspeed steady. He seemed to enjoy this kind of flying as much as shooting landings, in fact. I think he would *still* be in that turn if I had let him. I don't think he really cared what he did, as long as he could do it in an airplane."

Hughes knew how to fly, after a fashion. Dave could see that. But Dave could also see that Hughes was totally unpolished. If Hughes really wanted to learn to handle a plane like a pro, he would have to make some major adjustments—learn the rules of air safety, learn some common sense. But there wasn't much evidence that Hughes was willing to do that.

"This went on for five days," David said. "I would fly with him for a while, then the second pilot would replace me and fly with him, and then the third guy. Hughes sat in that plane all day long, flying the daylights out of it, with never much conversation. Mostly he stayed just as silent as he started out.

"He never warmed up to us. He seemed to appreciate what we were doing, because we kept going. But he sure didn't get to be friendly to us. We would come back to the hotel each evening, and there would be a new bottle of Black Label in each room and a new bottle of bourbon. That was his way of trying to thank us, I guess you could say. We stuck them in our suitcases so we would collect new ones the next day. One evening his assistant said, 'Mr. Hughes is grateful and he wants to be sure you boys have everything you want. If you'd like some female companionship or anything else, just let me know. Don't forget, you're on our expense account.'

"But Hughes's flying never really got proficient by airline standards. He improved in some ways. How could he miss, flying seven a.m. to seven p.m. with three airline captains to instruct him? And he was a good pilot, on the basics. He could control the airplane and make it do what he wanted. But underneath, his approach stayed the same, *rough*.

"I never found out whether he got his rating. We worked with him for the five days, and then we went home, and that was that. It was the last I saw of him, and I can't say I'm sorry."

I didn't know much about Hughes or his connection with TWA when I was a boy. If I had known, I probably would have considered it another point in TWA's favor. TWA gained a reputation during the '50s as the Hollywood airline. Hughes liked to provide free rides for Hollywood bigwigs such as Daryl Zanuck and Clark Gable—he thought it was good publicity for the airline. I knew about that, and I liked it. "The Hollywood Airline." But that was just about the extent of my knowledge concerning Hughes. My father never met Hughes and, as far as I can recall, he never talked about him. Sometimes my father mentioned various movie stars who turned up on his flights, but he didn't have much to say about them either. I don't know whether they were Hughes's cronies, and I doubt that my father knew. I suspect he was aware that the stars were aboard only because the hostesses told him. I can't imagine him going back into the cabin to meet a star. I remember my sisters and I asked him to get autographs from any actors or athletes who flew with him, but he refused. He said it would be demeaning.

There were never any stars on the flights I took. I flew enough for the odds to be good, but I suppose I just didn't hit the right flights. During the '50s and '60s, my mother, sisters, and I flew several times each year. We visited our relatives in Kansas City each summer and winter, and we frequently supplemented these trips with sightseeing vacations in other, more distant cities. We flew to San Francisco (Nob Hill, Yosemite), Los Angeles (Disneyland, Beverly Hills), Phoenix (the Grand Canyon), and London, Paris, Rome (museums and cathedrals, museums and cathedrals, museums and cathedrals). We became accustomed to traveling across the continent or the ocean; it came to seem unremarkable. Distance meant little to us. The planes obliterated distance, and TWA didn't bill us for the obliteration.

We carried an eight-millimeter movie camera along on most of our trips to document the sights we saw. The films we shot sit now in rows of carefully marked cans in my parents' basement. Occasionally when I've visited during the last three years I've taken out a few of the films and watched them. They intrigue me now; they trace the changing character of our travels. The earliest films reveal how we took nothing for granted at first—our trips still seemed special to us; we thought we were seeing marvels. During our first trip to Los Angeles, for example, we ran the camera almost nonstop: There are scenes of my mother and my sisters outside Grauman's Chinese Theater, and my sisters posing on the corner of Hollywood and Vine, and all of us taking rides at Disneyland, and me in my swim trunks, standing knee-deep in the Pacific.

The later films are less complete. As we traveled more, we became blasé, so these films have frequent gaps and quick cuts: In one scene, we are standing at the base of the Eiffel Tower; in the next, we are walking past the Colosseum. Several days have been left out, expunged from the record. Other scenes are indeterminate about location: We're at a beach, but where? On the Atlantic coast? The Pacific?

The Mediterranean? There are no clues. And suddenly the beach disappears, replaced by a street scene in an unidentified city.

I appreciate these disjointed, collage-like films the most, actually—they correspond with my memories. Taking vacations by air was disorienting. I liked the flying, but the time we spent on the ground between flights was unsettled. We left home and rode at hundreds of miles an hour to a place where the clocks all showed the wrong time and the scenery was all weird. (Palm trees in Phoenix: Who would have imagined that? Or the Hansel-and-Gretel straw roofs on the cottages outside London). There was no way to make a connection with any of it; it was just extremely weird stuff. So we wandered around for a couple of days in this outlandish place, and then we were snatched away into the sky again and the whole scene vanished as if somebody had thrown a switch.

The one constant in the films—an unintended framing device—is provided by the aviation footage I shot. I liked to carry our camera to the observation deck at any airport we passed through, to capture the rows of TWA planes standing at the gates. Then when we were airborne, I liked to shoot out the window, recording yet another view of an airliner's wing with vague patches of clouds below it and vaguer bits of country below the clouds. Each of our films seems to have a version of that scene—I took it over and over.

I tried to shoot the planes' interiors, also, but there wasn't enough light. I wish at least one of the films had a clear shot of the small compartment that was located near the front of a standard TWA Connie. Most passengers tried to avoid the compartment—it was less comfortable than the main cabin. But I liked riding up there. We often had the compartment to ourselves, so we would spread out, play cards (decks provided by the airline), and pretend this was a charter flight made solely for our sake.

One member of our family rarely shows up in the films. As I've said previously, my father hardly ever came with us on our trips. His absence is more evident to me now, looking at the films, than it was then. I remember missing him on the trips, but by and large I took his absence for granted. I understood that he couldn't very well come with us to Paris if he was scheduled to fly somewhere else that day. Still, I wanted him to be with us, and as I grew older my vague sense of dissatisfaction sometimes sharpened and I felt myself getting angry. I wondered why my father's schedule was so often out of sync with ours. Surely, I thought, he could have come with us more often if he really wanted to. My anger confused me, though—I didn't know what to do with it. So for the time being, I put it away.

I liked our trips to Kansas City better than our sightseeing tours. To me, KC wasn't a place so much as a set of pleasing associations. KC was where all of our relatives lived—both my mother's family and my father's. It was where I had been born. It was the center of the continent; America's heartland, as my aunts and uncles regularly told me. It was Mark Twain country: The city straddled the Missouri River, which fed into Twain's Mississippi. The local baseball team, the KC Blues, were a Yankee farm club; my grandfather and I went to the games, and he told me about seeing Mickey Mantle play when he was coming up. And KC was TWA's headquarters; I enjoyed watching the airliners come and go overhead, and I thought about my father doing the same when he was young.

A lot of time has passed, now, since I've been to KC. I don't suppose it's the same city any longer. But I still think about America's heartland—the city and the wide Midwest that surrounds it—and I imagine that I can discern clues there to the love that, in our different ways, my father and I both have for flight. It seems to me no accident that the Wright brothers, Charles Lindbergh, Amelia Earhart, and many other aviation pioneers came from the Midwest. The immense sky that arcs over the heartland's plains must have lured them into the air. Watching hawks ride the thermals in that immensity, they must have dreamed of riding like that too, and their Midwestern innocence must have made them believe that their dreams could be realized.

Innocence is a hallmark of the Midwest, I think. The settlers who came out onto the plains in horse-drawn wagons were innocents who dreamed of starting fresh in a new part of what they called the New

World. As if fresh starts were possible. As if this continent really were a new realm where the old problems and struggles could be forgotten, where the laws of nature themselves might prove more beneficent, more amenable to human desires. A man could come west, declare his independence on a plot of ground that became his property, and find fulfillment. That's what the settlers were looking for, and I think it's related to what fliers look for. We didn't find perfect liberation on the plains, but maybe we could find it by pushing farther west—or if not there, then by redirecting our aspiration: Go up, young man.

My grandfather, a lifelong Midwesterner, was a big Mark Twain fan. He owned a book called *The Family Mark Twain,* an anthology that included most of Twain's major works and several of the lesser ones. I used to read parts of it each summer. My favorite part was a short novel, *Tom Sawyer Abroad,* which tells what Tom, Huck, and Jim did after the end of *Huckleberry Finn.* It was terrific. The three of them became aeronauts—they flew across the Atlantic in a blimp. I read the novel over and over, imagining the delights of floating effortlessly through the sky the way Huck described:

> We was used to the balloon now and not afraid anymore, and
> didn't want to be anywheres else. Why, it seemed just like
> home; it 'most seemed as if I had been born and raised in it,
> and Jim and Tom said the same. And always I had had hateful
> people around me, a-nagging at me, and pestering of me, and
> scolding, and finding fault, and fussing and bothering, and
> sticking to me, and keeping after me, and making me do this,
> and making me do that and t'other, and always selecting out
> the things I didn't want to do, and then giving me Sam Hill
> because I shirked and done something else, and just
> aggravating the life out of a body all the time; but up here in
> the sky it was so still and sunshiny and lovely, and plenty to
> eat, and plenty to sleep, and strange things to see, and no
> nagging and no pestering, and no good people, and just
> holiday all the time.

I loved the novel, and I was relieved for Huck's sake. I hadn't liked the ending of *Huckleberry Finn,* where Huck said he was going to light out for the Indian territories. I couldn't see why he wanted to go into that wilderness of sagebrush and rattlesnakes. But here was another story, and it said that Huck didn't go out there after all. He found something much better instead. He learned to fly.

High Tech

O N JUNE 30, 1956, A TWA CONSTELLATION AND A UNITED AIRLINES DC-7 COLLIDED TWENTY-ONE THOUSAND FEET ABOVE THE GRAND CANYON. It was the first midair collision between airliners in U.S. history. All one hundred twenty-eight people aboard the planes died.

The collision led federal authorities to overhaul the nation's air traffic control system. In the 1950s, the skies above the U.S. were webbed by a hundred thousand miles of federally controlled airways— invisible aerial paths defined by the radio beams emanating from government-operated transmitters. Air traffic controllers were the airways' traffic cops. They directed the aircraft moving along the airways, and supervised takeoffs and landings at major airports. They had to work blind much of the time: They had few radar sets with which to track the planes they were supposed to control. Generally, when an airplane was more than a few miles from an airport, it was beyond radar coverage. To figure the plane's position, controllers consulted the last radio message received from the plane, manipulated slide rules to factor in the effects of wind and other weather conditions, then pushed a plastic marker across a tabletop map to indicate the course they believed the plane was following. There were no direct radio links between controllers and pilots. Instead, the men in the control centers and the men in the cockpits communicated by relaying messages through intermediaries, either airline dispatchers or Department of Commerce radio operators. Messages passed back and forth slowly, a time-consuming arrangement that precluded prompt, coordinated action during emergencies.

Because of these limitations, controllers exercised only a small degree of real control. Pilots remained, for the most part, their own masters. They were expected to follow the controllers' instructions whenever practical, but their own judgment and authority remained paramount. Indeed, they often operated outside the traffic control system, entirely free from supervision. Traffic controllers had authority only for those thin slices of sky that lay within the airways. The rest of the airspace over the U.S. was uncontrolled—if pilots elected to fly "off airways," they passed beyond the controllers' purview.

That was the situation when the Constellation and DC-7 rammed each other. The pilots of both planes were flying off airways. Their only protection against a collision was the care they exercised to scan the sky ahead, watching for other planes. (An air traffic controller working in Salt Lake City that morning noticed that the flight paths of the Connie and DC-7 would probably intersect over the Canyon, but he didn't attempt to send a message to the planes. He was busy working with several flights that were being made in controlled airspace. Issuing warnings to off-airways flights wasn't part of his job.)

Crash investigators weren't able to decide why the collision occurred, but they came up with a couple of possibilities. There were scattered clouds over Arizona on June 30—perhaps the clouds blocked the pilots' view of each other's planes. Or perhaps the pilots were conducting "Canyon tours," banking to let their passengers gaze down into the steep ravines below. In that case, the pilots' attention would have been focused on the ground, not on the sky around them.

Whichever explanation was correct, the collision was the worst aviation disaster up to that time, and it prompted several reforms that were phased in during the final years of the 1950s. Off-airways flying was banned. New, long-range radars were installed at traffic control centers, providing blanket coverage of the nation's airspace. Improved communications equipment was installed, eliminating the middlemen from ground-to-air communications. Most important, the controllers were given greatly increased jurisdiction: They began exercising continuous supervision over virtually all scheduled flights in the U.S., military as well as civilian. They became controllers in fact as well as in name.

For pilots, the consequences of the Grand Canyon collision were bitter. Much of the authority they had previously enjoyed was lost, transferred from their cockpits to radar control centers on the ground. Pilots wanted flying to be safe—as several of them said to me, "We sit in the front of the plane: We reach a crash scene first." But surrendering authority is surely not the solution most pilots would have selected. One retired captain expressed a view that I thought a majority of his colleagues probably shared: "Crash investigations are a slap in the face for pilots nearly every time. The easiest finding is 'pilot error.' If the investigators can't figure out what the hell really happened, they can always lay it on the pilots. Dead men can't defend themselves. Sometimes the pilots *are* at fault, but whether or not, the investigators usually say they are, and then they come out with a new batch of regulations aimed at the pilots. That's how bureaucrats operate. Find the easy answer, regardless of whether it's wrong, and then stick a paper solution on it. Take the Grand Canyon thing. 'Pilot error.' So bingo, they make a bunch of 'improvements.' But here's something to think about. The Canyon was the first collision. There's been a lot more since then. Whose fault were they if the whole point of traffic control was to prevent them?"

Pilots had scarcely begun adjusting to the changes in air traffic control when an even more profound change overtook them. On October 26,

1958, the first U.S. jetliner made its inaugural run, a Pan Am flight from New York to Paris. The jet age had arrived.

Pilots had been hearing for years that jet-powered airliners were coming, and many were eager to get their hands on one. The jets would be hot-damn marvels, able to streak nearly six hundred miles an hour at altitudes of up to forty thousand feet. The airlines distributed promotional material to their pilots, pamphlets and spec sheets published by jet manufacturers, and enthusiasm swelled.

But a sizable minority of the pilots had misgivings. The word going around was that jets were wholly different from previous types of planes, calling for wholly new cockpit skills. It was said that pilots upgrading to jets had to learn to fly all over again—the transition to jets was comparable to the shift from contact flying to instrument flying in the 1930s, entailing a basic alteration in flying technique.

The worries airline pilots felt were fed by reports coming out of the armed forces. Stories circulated about problems that Air Force crews had experienced when breaking in the first jet fighters and bombers. Some of the crews were said to have succumbed to "high-speed stress"—they'd been overloaded by the demands of trying to operate planes that flew at such blistering speeds. Others had gotten themselves into a frightening dilemma called "the coffin corner"—when flying at cruise speed, they'd found that they couldn't accelerate further, because that produced uncontrollable buffeting of the wings, and they couldn't decelerate, because that produced a stall.

Several of the retired airline pilots I met said stories like these created a good deal of anxiety. They told me they'd known some senior captains who were so spooked that they decided not to test themselves against the jets. Forsaking the higher salaries that jets offered, they stayed with piston planes; and when those planes were finally retired, they retired along with them.

The pilots who attempted the transition to jets were sometimes as anxious as the ones who opted out. They found that many of the rumors were true. Jets *were* different. To operate a jet properly, you had to rid yourself of any lingering impulse to fly by the seat of your pants; you had to concede the final victory of technology over air sense. Piston planes had allowed a little leeway. You didn't need to follow the instruments slavishly when you took off in a piston plane. You shoved the throttles forward, steered down the runway until you felt the plane become buoyant under you, and then climbed out at whatever angle suited you. There was a certain informality about it; you could make decisions based on your sensations and your personal preferences. None of that held true in a jet. Turbine engines were extremely powerful, but they reacted sluggishly to changes in throttle position, and they needed delicate handling. For these reasons, taking off in a jet meant accelerating to a precomputed speed, then lifting the plane's nose to a precomputed angle and climbing at precisely that angle. Your sensations and preferences were irrelevant. You didn't so much fly the airplane as you flew the numbers that had been laid down as law by the plane's designers.

There were marked differences, too, between landing a piston plane and landing a jet. If you approached the runway too low in a piston plane, you shoved the throttles forward and the plane responded instantly, climbing back to a safer altitude. If you were too high, you chopped the throttles, dropped to the altitude you wanted, and then poured on the gas again. Not so in a jet. There was scant margin for error or for variations of technique. You had to hold a jet at precisely the proper descent rate and precisely the proper airspeed. You had to nail the numbers.

The tightening of air traffic control combined with the strict requirements of jet flight put an end to the era when captains could develop their own flying styles. Individualism was out. Every pilot now had to fly like every other. A jet pilot's job was to put his plane where the controllers told him to, and to do it in strict compliance with prescribed jet procedures. The mark of good piloting now was scrupulous conformity.

There were compensations. Some pilots told me that they'd been stimulated by the new demands placed on them. They'd had to learn to fly with far greater precision than ever before; it called for tremendous discipline and skill, the pilots said. The money wasn't bad, either. Captains could double their incomes when they switched to jets—some of them began pulling down as much as doctors or lawyers. And flying jets could be fun, sort of. There was gratification to be had from operating such awesome machinery. When you cranked up the engines of a 707 or a DC-8, you unleashed a stupendous torrent of power. The air screamed and the ground shook—you made your presence felt.

Nevertheless, many pilots grew dissatisfied as the 1960s began. They believed that the best times were behind them. Technology was ascendant; the pilot's role was being eclipsed. I met several retired captains who spoke ruefully of the losses they thought they had suffered at the beginning of the '60s. They looked on the advent of jet flight as a crucial—and, in the main, a sad—turning point for the flying profession. It was a step down from the pinnacle.

Stanley Johnson looked on it that way. He had begun his career in Ford trimotors in the 1930s and ended it in Boeing 707s in the late 1960s, and like many pilots whose memories spanned those decades, he said he was of two minds about the progress he'd witnessed. There had been gains for pilots, he said, but the gains had often been offset by losses.

"Everything got standardized, standardized," he said. "When you're a passenger in a jet airplane, there's no way you can tell who is flying. All the pilots do it exactly the same. Back in our day, you could tell who was flying just by the way he did it. Each guy had his own technique. But not in the jets.

"I'm not saying it was wrong altogether. Some of the rules they put down about the jets made perfect sense. But some of it was propaganda, to my way of thinking. Jets were different, but maybe not as different as they were made out.

"Listen, one time I was taking off from London bound for New York in a 707, and we hit a bird. A seagull, I guess. A big bird, anyway. It smacked into the nose and cracked it and jammed the radar. That, and it wiped out the airspeed indicator on my side.

"Technically speaking, we should have turned back and landed. We didn't really need the radar, though—I knew the weather ahead was good. And we still had the copilot's airspeed [indicator]. We weren't really in bad shape, and my feeling always was that we got paid to make our flights, not to turn back unless it was absolutely necessary. So I decided to push ahead.

"It worked out fine. Mostly, it was an ordinary flight. I didn't report about hitting the bird until we were descending into New York. Then when I did, I let on like the bird hit us *then* instead of back in London.

"But when we came in to land, I said to the copilot, 'This is interesting, now.' I learned to fly in an old OX-5 biplane that didn't have any airspeed [indicator] to begin with. We learned to control the airplane by the attitude we held it at. You weren't supposed to be able to do that in a jet, but when we got set to land, I said to the copilot, 'I'm going to take it in the old way, and all I want you to do is keep an eye on the speed and sing out if I get too slow. But if I'm doing all right, just leave me alone.'

"So that's what I did. I flew it down and landed it that way, and you know, there wasn't the slightest problem. I just took her in, and let the nose down, and there we were.

"I thoroughly enjoyed it. For once I could fly a jet like a regular airplane. And when I asked the copilot, he said I'd held it right at twenty miles an hour over the book speed all the way down, which is pretty much what I was aiming for. I wasn't about to let the speed get too low, that'd be dangerous. So I aimed to come in just slightly fast, and he said I did it.

"I liked that. In fact, when I was lining up with the runway, I *knew* I had the thing in hand. We landed softer than normal, as a matter of fact.

"After that, I wasn't shy about telling people. I said, 'All this talk that you can't fly a 707 without airspeed is a lot of hooey. I don't necessarily recommend it, but it *can* be done.' "

Pilots are almost completely dependent on the products of high-tech research labs: They can fly only because an advanced technological society has given them appropriate machinery. This was as true for the Wright brothers as it is for today's astronauts. The Wrights achieved powered flight before anyone else because they went at it more scientifically. They were painstaking engineers who studied all the available literature on aerodynamics, made their own studies of bird flight, and then applied advanced engineering processes to resolve previously unanswered questions about lift, propulsion, and three-axis stability. One of their innovations was the use of a wind tunnel to test airfoil designs.

The association between flight and technological progress is so strong that pilots have often been pictured as representatives of mankind's bright, high-tech future. The Wrights, Lindbergh, John Glenn, and many other famous pilots have been acclaimed as harbingers of the future, and sometimes their anonymous fellow-pilots have been cast in the same role. In 1936, H. G. Wells created a feature film called *Things to Come.* The film depicts a devastating war that shatters civilization, hurling mankind backward into barbarism. But one small outpost of civilization survives: a band of scientist/aviators who call themselves the Airmen. Intent on lifting humanity out of the darkness, the Airmen fly around dropping "peace bombs" on their barbarian neighbors. The bombs contain an anesthetic gas. When the barbarians get a whiff, they are knocked senseless; when they wake up again, they see the error of their ways and become civilized. After the Airmen wipe out the last pockets of backwardness, they build a utopian society and set to work preparing the first manned flight to the moon.

Actual airmen do generally embrace technology. I spoke with a number of pilots who said they liked jets just fine; they denied that there had been any letdown when piston planes became outdated; or at most, they said, the letdown had been minor. Several of these pilots identified themselves as gadget freaks. They said one of the reasons they liked to fly was that cockpits were packed with gadgetry: elaborate navigational gear, radio equipment, flight instruments. They said that playing with all the dials and switches (and, increasingly in the 1980s, all the on-board computers) was like playing a marvelously intricate video game.

Pilots depend on technology, and most of them embrace it, and yet throughout aviation's brief history pilots have often been reluctant to accept the next stage of technological advancement. When air sense was subordinated to instrumentation, and when biplanes gave way to monoplanes, and when pressurization systems made high-altitude flight possible, and when jet aircraft were introduced, many pilots resisted the changes. They were uncertain whether they could keep up with the changes, and uncertain whether they wanted to. Technology had given them the freedom of the sky, but then they saw further technological progress placing restrictions on that freedom.

There's nothing mysterious about the pilots' ambivalence toward technology. Most of the rest of us share it. Sometimes we feel sure that technology is going to save us: We dream that we'll awake one morning and find ourselves well off and civilized, living in GM's City of Tomorrow. But that dream alternates with nightmares in which technology destroys us: The machines we've built to improve our lives turn on us—they become our masters rather than our servants; they harrow our spirit, foul our planet with pollution, assail us with nuclear fire. Sometimes behind the gleaming facade of the City of Tomorrow we catch glimpses of dark Satanic mills.

In the 1960s, a select group of pilots became the equivalent of Wells's Airmen. The Mercury astronauts were deified. Every time one of them was launched into space, the nation seemed to hold its breath. People clustered around TVs and radios, avidly following this next installment in the struggle to beat back the Russians and keep the sky safe for democracy. And when the flight ended, the victorious astronaut was taken to the White House where President Kennedy would give him a medal. Then there would be a national tour, and ticker tape parades, and splashy four-color coverage in *Life*.

I thought the astronauts were magnificent. I remember sneaking a tiny portable radio into one of my high school classes so that I could listen to the sixth Mercury astronaut, Gordon Cooper, blast off. I hid the radio under my shirt, then I sat at my desk pressing a small earplug into my left ear. When the countdown reached the final few seconds, I scribbled a commentary in my notebook for the kids sitting on either side of me: ". . . three, two, one. Ignition. Liftoff. Looks good. A-OK. A-OK."

Not everyone shared my regard for the space program, though. The editor of our school newspaper killed an article I submitted for the December issue one year. I thought it was an innocuous piece, one of a series of articles I had done about space. This one dealt with the military advantages the U.S. would get from establishing a base on the moon. (The moon was high ground: a perfect place to set up telescopes to spy on the Russians; also a good launch site for nuclear missiles.) The editor said he didn't think the subject suited the Christmas season.

I took the rejection fairly well. I was aware of the objections some people raised against the space program. The major sticking point was cost. People said we would be better off spending those billions of dollars on the inner cities or on education, not on schemes to fly to the moon. I didn't disagree, entirely. Despite the impression I created, I really wasn't much more in favor of bombing the earth from the moon than most of my classmates were. And I thought eliminating poverty sounded sort of nice. Then, too, my feelings about flight—all forms of flight, whether in space or inside the atmosphere—were undergoing a slow shift.

The reasons were largely unconscious. Starting at about age four-teen—at about the time when I might have become a student pilot: a quiet crisis for me—I tried to take myself in hand. "Grow up," I repeatedly told myself. It became a refrain for me. I quit buying model airplanes, and got rid of most of the models I'd collected over the years, and quit reading my father's aviation magazines. Eventually, I ducked out of some of the vacation flights my mother planned. I said I was bored with traveling around, taking in the sights. I said I'd rather stay home by myself. This was revolutionary, Roger asking *not* to fly. Once or twice, my mother gave in. She and my sisters went on the trips, leaving me to fend for myself at home.

My behavior during this period must have convinced my father that I didn't want to become a pilot. That must have been my intention. When my father and I were together, I made a show of indifference. I didn't ask him about his flights or anything else related to piloting. I acted as if I didn't care whether he had moved up to a new kind of plane or had secured a bid on some better routes. I implied that, as a matter of fact, airplanes bored me. I didn't really like to fly. I said I didn't like the continuous shriek of the engines, and I was annoyed by the thin, dry air that was blown into the cabins. There was something unnatural about it, something unpleasant about being so high, moving so fast in that artificial environment. I said maybe people really weren't cut out for flying.

I didn't believe half of what I said, and none of it squared with my arguments for space travel. But I wasn't trying to be reasonable.

Jet-age technology changed conditions for pilots on the ground as much as in the air. During the mid-1950s, airlines began using electronic flight simulators in their pilot-training programs. The first simulators were rudimentary devices, unable to mimic flight convincingly, but sophistication came quickly. By the early '60s, the airlines were able to rely on simulators to provide most of the re-education their pilots needed in order to qualify for jets.

Seen from the outside, a jet simulator was a large, nondescript metal box. Inside, it was a full-scale replica of a cockpit. When a pilot moved the controls, the gauges on the instrument panels gave the same readings they would give in flight. The pilot could take off, navigate to a distant airport, and land there, all while sitting in a mechanism that was earthbound. The illusion of flight was intensified by hydraulic jacks under the floor that imitated the motions of a real plane, causing the cockpit to pitch and roll while elaborate projection systems threw pitching, rolling views of the sky and earth onto the windshields.

Pilots who attempted the transition to jets generally had to spend dozens of hours conducting pseudoflights in simulators. It was a form of operant conditioning. Instructors seated behind the pilots used a special control panel to set up simulated flight conditions—adjusting the weight of the simulated airplane, and the mechanical condition of its engines, and the weather it was flying through—then they drilled the pilots in the proper procedures for coping with those conditions. If they caught a crew making an error, they could freeze the simulation, explain the error to them, then recycle to the beginning of the simulation and tell the crew to take another stab at it.

After simulators had proved their worth for piston-to-jet transition work, the airlines began requiring all of their pilots to pass two simulator sessions each year whether or not they were moving from one type of plane to another. The ostensible purpose was to let the pilots practice emergency procedures that were too dangerous to practice in real planes. But there was also another purpose. The instructors doubled as examiners. They kept an eye out for pilots whose skills had slipped, guys who were falling toward three-percenthood. If they found one and decided that his case was hopeless, they would lift his license.

Pilots didn't love simulators. I heard various pilots refer to them as "humiliators" and "electric torture chambers." Entering a simulator, pilots told me, was tantamount to handing your license to the instructors. Then you sat down and for several hours coped with one godawful in-flight emergency after another, calamity piled upon calamity. And at the end, when you'd been thoroughly wrung out, you stood up and asked the instructors if you could have your license back now please.

I observed a simulator session recently. One afternoon in February 1986, my father showed me around the TWA training center at

Kennedy Airport. It's a squat, windowless building located near the TWA hangar. We poked through classrooms (rows of tables facing lecterns; audio-visual equipment; oversize mock-ups of cockpit control panels), and pushed the buttons on self-test boxes hanging on corridor walls (multiple-choice questions about cockpit procedures: press button A, B, or C), and looked into a room where crews practice what to do in case of an "ocean landing" (an inflated life raft lay in the middle of the floor). Then we let ourselves into the three-story-tall enclosure that houses TWA's 747 simulator. We couldn't go into the simulator itself—it was being used—but we stood for a few minutes watching it bob on its hydraulic legs.

"I've spent a lot of hours in that contraption," my father said. "I suppose it's one of the oldest simulators still around. It's been here since we got our first 747s in the late '60s.

"I didn't mind simulator rides as much as some guys. I always kind of liked showing what I could do. There's more action packed into one hour in a simulator than you're likely to see during a year of real flying.

"But it can get tense because you know you're being graded. That's the real pressure—the fact that this is a test, not the amount of action.

"I was offered a job as a simulator instructor one time. I was tempted. But after thinking it over, I turned it down. I wanted to stay out on the line."

We closed the door and walked back toward the classrooms, getting ready to leave the center. But near the exit, we ran into a couple of instructors my father knew. We talked to them for a while, and I made an appointment to come back and interview them the next morning. I said I wanted to learn more about pilot-training procedures.

When I returned the following day, the instructors had a surprise for me. The best way to learn about training, they said, was to watch a simulator session. They introduced me to a crew who were getting ready to spend the day in the 747 simulator, and they offered to let me sit in. I hadn't anticipated an opportunity like this. It seemed unfair to the crew—besides trying to satisfy the instructors, they would have to work under the gaze of a stranger who would publish a record of their performance. But if they were willing, I certainly was. I shook hands with the crew members—Paul Brelland, captain; Stephen Haldane, copilot; and flight engineer Earl Thorez—then I trailed them and a pair of instructors into the simulator.

The crew sat in their normal positions at the front of the cockpit while the instructors and I took the observation seats behind them. The cockpit was dark, as if we would be making a night flight. The view out the window showed a black sky; a narrow band of luminescence representing the horizon; and, on the dark earth, the lighted surfaces of Kennedy's taxiways and runways.

I asked Paul afterward whether the instructors had consulted him about inviting me along. "Yes," he answered, "they cleared it with me. I probably would have objected a few years ago. The simulator is a pretty tense place. But this was my last simulator ride before I retire, so it didn't mean that much to me. Besides, I had been through the hoops so often, I guess I was pretty confident that I could handle whatever they threw at me."

They threw a lot. For four hours during that morning-turned-night, the instructors served up a scarifying assortment of emergencies, shutting down engines, knocking out generators and fuel pumps, sabotaging the plane's brakes, disabling essential flight instruments. In each instance, Paul and his crew exchanged quick, monotonal comments, reviewed checklists, and took the necessary measures.

Afterward, I asked Paul how well he knew Stephen and Earl. I thought crewmates who were acquainted with each other should be able to coordinate their actions more easily. "I don't know either of them very much," he said. "It's not supposed to make any difference. You often get put in the simulator with guys you never met before, just like on regular line flights. You don't have to know your crew. Everybody's supposed to follow the same procedures. We're supposed to be interchangeable."

In addition to mechanical malfunctions, the instructors arranged various weather problems to test the crew. During one landing approach, Paul was proceeding down the glideslope (a radio beam that marks the correct angle of descent) when the plane suddenly slowed and began falling. "Windshear," one of the instructors whispered to me—an abrupt downdraft had slapped the plane toward the ground.

Earl was leaning forward between the pilots, monitoring the instruments. "Airspeed, airspeed," he called, and Paul shoved the throttles forward. Red lights began blinking above the thrust gauges, warning that the engines were overheating. But this was the prescribed procedure for dealing with a windshear. The plane shuddered, caught itself, and began climbing.

Paul banked to the left, intending to circle around for another landing approach. Before he'd gone far into the circle, though, the instructors switched scenarios.

"The worst part is how they can pile the problems up on you," Paul said later. "In a real plane, they would have to go slower. They can give you a problem in a real plane, but when you solve it, they have to wait awhile before setting up the next situation. You have to fly the plane into the attitude they want before they can start, so you have some time to catch your breath. But in the simulator, you deal with one thing, then they give you something else right away."

The instructors interrupted Paul's circling climb. "Nice work on the windshear, Paul," they said. Then they fiddled with their control panel, and the view through the windshield flicked to a new scenario. The plane was no longer climbing but descending, coming down through an overcast. "New day, new problem," the instructors said.

We were in the simulator all morning. Then, after a short lunch break, we went back in for three additional hours. The session's toughest set of emergencies came immediately after lunch. Paul lined up with Kennedy's runway 13R and began a takeoff. We could hear the engines spooling up (the simulator had sound effects as well as visuals) and the jacks under the floor jostled us a bit to counterfeit the trundling of our tires across the concrete. The plane accelerated slowly because we were loaded to max weight: 775,000 pounds, almost four hundred tons.

"V-1," Stephen called after we had traveled several thousand feet down the runway. We had reached "velocity one," a critical juncture during a jet takeoff. The 747 was now moving too fast to stop safely on the runway. If any problems arose after V-1, Paul would have to continue accelerating and complete the takeoff regardless. So the instructors arranged a problem. A few seconds after Stephen spoke, the outboard engine on the right wing flamed out and the plane yawed sharply to the right, threatening to careen off the runway. Paul jammed his left rudder pedal down and steered us back toward the runway's centerline.

"You know they're going to give you that situation sometime during the day," Paul told me later. "It's one of the standard problems they throw at you, an engine failure during a max-weight takeoff. But you don't know whether it will be before V-1 or after V-1, which makes a tremendous difference. In one case you have to stop the plane, in the other you have to keep going. And you don't know whether it will be on the right wing or the left wing, which also changes how you have to react. So you try not to think about it. You just wait until something happens and then react automatically."

A fully loaded 747 rolls a long way when taking off with four good engines. Now that we were down to three engines, our roll would be that much longer—the plane scarcely had enough power to break free of the ground. The far end of the runway became visible, sliding toward us. I stared at it, and realized that I was holding my breath. I knew there was no danger of a crash—we weren't in a real plane. But the illusion was convincing. We were running out of runway. If we rammed a dike beyond the end of the runway, we would create one hell of a fireball. I wondered what sort of pyrotechnics the simulator would shoot off.

"V-R," Stephen said at last: rotation velocity. Paul pulled back on the yoke and the 747's nose lifted, pulling the nose wheels from the runway. We rode like that for a moment—nose high, tail low—until, reluctantly, the main wheels rose. ("Airborne!" I thought someone should exclaim. But no one did.)

Paul coaxed the plane through a shallow climb to eight hundred feet, high enough to clear any obstacles in our path, and leveled off. He drove straight ahead then, trying to build up enough speed to allow the wing flaps to be retracted. The plane was lethargic. Paul held it at eight hundred feet for more than five minutes, during which time the engines remained at full takeoff power. As they had during the windshear exercise, the thrust gauges protested. But once again, this was the prescribed procedure.

Gradually our airspeed increased, and Stephen raised the flaps in stages: ten degrees, five degrees, one degree. When the flaps were fully retracted, Paul pulled in the yoke once more, throttled back slightly, and began climbing. He intended to steer out over the ocean, dump fuel, then return to the airport and land. It wouldn't be safe to proceed with the flight on three engines, especially after they'd taken such a beating.

The fuel dumping went smoothly, but the instructors threw a wrinkle into the landing approach. They changed the weather. The clear sky filled with clouds, cutting off the view ahead. One of the instructors whispered to me that the bottom of the cloud deck was one hundred thirty feet above sea level, which meant Paul wouldn't be able to see anything out the windows until an instant before the wheels touched down.

Paul banked around to intercept the glideslope, then he cut power and headed downward. We followed the simulated electronic glideslope down toward the simulated invisible ground. I assumed the point of the exercise was to see if Paul could emerge from the clouds precisely where he should be, directly over the runway. But I was wrong. While we were still several hundred feet up, the flight director (an instrument that displays the attitude a plane must maintain to stay on course) broke down. Paul had to abort the landing. He pulled up and prepared to circle the airport for another try.

The instructors added more wrinkles during the climb. An alarm went off and a red translucent handle on the ceiling began glowing. Engine number three, the remaining engine on the right wing, had caught fire. Stephen and Earl attacked the fire while Paul flew the plane. Earl read out the instructions on the engine-fire checklist and Stephen performed the specified operations, shutting down engine three and triggering a fire extinguisher inside the engine. Then Stephen and Earl studied their instruments to see if the fire had gone out. It hadn't. So Earl counted off thirty seconds and Stephen triggered a second extinguisher. If this one didn't do the trick, Paul would have to accelerate, trying to use the plane's forward rush to blow the fire out.

Paul was spared that; the second extinguisher worked. But the plane was seriously crippled now. Paul had to nurse it back to the field on only two engines.

"That's one of the harder things they want us to do," Paul said to me later, "a two-engine-out landing. It's not so hard physically. The plane wants to yaw around toward the wing without any good engines, but you can hold it straight without too much difficulty. The big problem is the concentration required. You have to constantly monitor all the instruments to stay on top of everything. Everything is constantly changing. You're slowing down, letting out the flaps, putting down the landing gear. . . . Each event changes how the plane handles, and you have to readjust the control settings to keep up. So the concentration is the big factor, that's what can wear you out. A simulator doesn't handle exactly like the real thing, they can't get all the nuances exactly right, but it's close. When you're in there, you concentrate so hard that you almost forget that you're in a simulator. You really get wrapped up in what's going on."

Paul maneuvered the plane to the proper place in the sky, found the glideslope, and started down again. This time the flight director behaved itself, so the approach continued all the way to the runway surface.

As we descended, I studied Paul, trying to judge what he was feeling. But I couldn't read much in his bearing or gestures. He sat almost motionless, making barely perceptible adjustments of the controls. He may have been wrapped up in this simulated struggle with an unstable, crippled airplane—he may have felt as if he were contending with a real emergency in the air—but if so, he didn't let on. I was considerably more excited than he seemed to be. I leaned forward in my seat, trying to see over Paul's shoulder, to study the readings on the instruments. And every few moments I looked up to the windshield, looking for the first glimmerings of the runway lights.

Stephen called out the altitude when we reached a thousand feet, then he confirmed that the flaps and landing gear were down. A few moments later a horn tooted, signaling that we were at five hundred feet. Then, in rapid sequence, we broke out of the clouds, the runway rose toward us, another horn sounded, Paul pulled up the nose and closed the throttles, and the wheels pressed down onto the concrete. We'd landed.

"Okay," the instructors said. "Nice landing, Paul."

Then they set up another scenario. New day, new problem.

There probably will not be many legendary jet pilots. Chuck Yeager springs to mind as an exception, but in fact he carried out most of his noteworthy flights in piston-powered fighters, becoming a combat ace during World War II, and in the rocket-powered X-1, breaking the sound barrier in 1947. He logged thousands of hours aboard jets during his career, but those flights added little to his reputation. Certainly among commercial pilots, the jet age has produced few legends. Several pilots told me stories about airline captains who, flying in the piston era, gained reputations for being larger and more colorful than life: Ed Musick, for example, or Dick Merrill. But I heard no such stories about captains who spent their entire careers in jets.

Jet procedures don't leave much scope for a pilot to make a name for himself. I was impressed by the skills Paul Brelland demonstrated in the simulator, but I knew he was executing maneuvers that he'd practiced many times, and I knew that all other airline captains were expected to acquit themselves in precisely the same manner. "What you saw," Paul said to me after we left the simulator, "was an old dog performing old tricks. If you watched ten different pilots, one would perform pretty much like the next." Paul was being too modest, downplaying his own abilities. But his modesty had an objective basis: During the simulated flight that I watched, he carefully conducted himself by the rules. Repeatedly he and his crewmates reached for checklists to confirm the procedures they should follow to resolve various emergencies. They weren't supposed to rely on their memories to come up with the right procedures, and they assuredly weren't supposed to improvise. They were supposed to follow their checklists. This wasn't always possible, of course. If a particular emergency called for instant action, as when an engine died during takeoff, they had to remember what they should do and then do it fast, without pausing to read a document first. But in any situation that allowed sufficient time, they were supposed to disregard whatever they thought they remembered and follow the appropriate checklist instead. The premise underlying their training was that air-safety experts had foreseen all the problems that an airline crew might conceivably face. The crew's role was to recognize each problem as it arose, recognize what checklist applied to it, and faithfully follow the experts' prescriptions as enumerated on the list.

Jet pilots aren't clones—they can't be as perfectly interchangeable as the airlines might like them to be. Inevitably, some handle airplanes better than others. Some are smarter, some are better coordinated, some are more self-disciplined. But the range of variation among them is far smaller than was permitted among piston-era airmen. Training is stricter now, standards are more rigorously enforced. That's good; it means flying has gotten safer. I'd rather fly with Paul Brelland in a 747 than with Dick Merrill in a DC-2—there's less chance that I'll wind up on a snowy mountainside fifty miles from the nearest airport. From the pilots' perspective, though, the improvement in air safety has come with a stiff price. Not only must jet pilots operate within tight constraints, but they must accept some strange reversals. Their most memorable flights are likely to occur on the ground, inside simulators, rather than in the air. And the mastery they strive to achieve during their flights (the real ones as well as the mock ones) is less a demonstration of exceptional skills than a concerted effort to avoid looking bad.

Nearly the only way a pilot can distinguish himself now is negative. If a jet pilot commits an extraordinary blunder, it will be discussed throughout the piloting corps, and laughed over, until it becomes one of the standard items in the hangar-flying repertoire. The miscreant will never live it down. A number of jet pilots told me about blunders their colleagues had committed. They seemed to enjoy telling these stories almost as much their predecessors enjoyed telling the old legends (Connies flying under bridges, seaplanes dragging towboats across the water). But there was a difference. There was no hint of admiration in the jet pilots' voices when they talked about jet-age errors. The statute of limitations hadn't expired on these errors—that was part of the difference, I thought. More than that, though, jet pilots seemed to judge each other by a sterner set of criteria than they applied to their predecessors. Having absorbed the lesson that today no deviation from prescribed procedures is acceptable, they cut each other no slack. I thought their instructors would have been proud.

The most entertaining jet story I heard concerned a captain who, despite the beefed-up training for jet crews, had failed to master some of the fine points concerning the controls in his airplane. One day in the early 1960s, the story goes, he and his crew were sitting in the cockpit of a 707, getting ready for a flight. All the passengers were on board; everything was set. But before starting the engines, the captain pointed to one of the switches above his head and asked the copilot, "Do you know what this switch is for? I've been flying these damn planes for three years now, and I don't." Then he reached up and flipped the switch. And back in the cabin, all the passengers' oxygen masks dropped from the ceiling. Bedlam. The flight attendants had to scurry around reassuring the passengers, and a maintenance crew had to be summoned to roll up the masks and stuff them back into the overhead compartments. The rolling and stuffing took about half an hour. Finally, when the masks were all back in place, the maintenance foreman entered the cockpit and said, "Well, captain, we've got you all set to go. But you know, I'm going to have to write this up. What happened? How did the masks come loose?" The captain shook his head and shrugged. "Christ," he answered, "I don't know. All I did was this." He reached up and flipped the switch again.

If a pilot had screwed up like this in a Ford trimotor, I imagine his fellow pilots would have considered him something of a card. *That son of a gun,* I hear them saying, *he doesn't even bother learning what all the controls are for. He just climbs into some new airplane, cranks her up, and goes.* They would have liked his style. But because this captain made his mistake in a jet, he paid with his good name. Every pilot who told me the story said the captain had become a laughingstock.

The ambivalence pilots feel concerning technology is related to another set of mixed feelings. Pilots are of two minds about safety. The normal human instinct for self-preservation makes pilots want to end each flight with a safe return to the planet. They know that flying is hazardous—their training leaves them with no doubts about that—so they work to acquire skills that will minimize the hazards. At its most essential, that's what learning to fly means: It's learning how to get back to the ground in one piece. But no matter how much they may want to survive or how seriously they may take their passengers' survival, pilots inevitably have other, deeper motives than safety. Flesh-and-blood mortals don't spend their lives venturing into an alien environment like the sky if they are cautious sorts, after all. The only foolproof way to avoid dying in a plane crash is to never go up in a plane, and by definition no pilot can make that choice. Deciding to become a pilot means accepting the possibility that someday an airplane might kill you.

Early pilots, especially, had to accept a significant degree of risk. Their planes were primitive, so their lives often ended abruptly. But to them danger seemed a fair tradeoff for the freedom they could achieve in flight. Mastering the sky meant mastering the sky's perils—that was the challenge, the adventure. Of course, they intended to survive the challenge if at all possible. But the very real chance that they might smash up wasn't a deterrent to them; it just made the challenge seem more worth taking.

Later pilots had less reason to accept risks. Technology reduced the perils of flight a little more each year until by the 1960s trips through the sky were no more dangerous (arguably less dangerous) than a drive in the family auto. Some risk remained. Jet engines were more reliable than piston engines, but they did sometimes fail; radar and computers improved air traffic control, but they could not totally eliminate midair collisions. Still, pilots who began flying in the '60s could go about it with a different set of expectations than previous generations of pilots had. Crashes were rare now; genuine, unsimulated emergencies were almost equally exceptional. Pilots could reasonably expect that most of their flights would pass without disruptions of any kind, and for this reason they became more conservative in their behavior on the rare occasion when a disruption did occur.

Sometimes when talking with pilots who had never flown any airliners except jets, I told them about Stanley Johnson's encounter with the seagull. Most of them seemed shocked that Stanley had elected to continue the flight despite the damage the bird had done. "That's the old-timers for you," one American Airlines copilot said. "A lot of them kept flying the old way after they got into jets. Not many guys would do something like that nowadays. If your plane gets damaged, you land, get it repaired. You don't push on."

The copilot shook his head and, simultaneously, smiled. "I don't suppose he was playing games," he said. "He probably thought his job was to make that flight, come hell or high water. I can respect that. But basically, that's an approach from the old days. The old guys used to do it like that because it was the only thing that let them get through—they kept going no matter what. But things are different now. We've got different priorities."

The differences between older pilots and younger ones may not be as sharp as the copilot implied, but I thought it was at least true that fliers who started in piston planes needed to change their thinking about risk when they moved to jets, and sometimes they may have found the adjustment difficult. Last year my father told me a couple of stories that bear on this point. He didn't tell the stories in order to prove any thesis concerning risk; he was simply recounting some events that he thought I might find interesting. But the stories reveal more than he intended, I think. Both deal with occasions when he, as a captain, had to decide whether to push on to his destination despite knowing that conditions at the airport where he wanted to land were potentially dangerous.

"All things being equal," he said, "you tried to get your passengers to the place that was written on their tickets. It was a point of pride for most pilots. But it meant you had to make some close calls. I wouldn't say you took chances, but you had to weigh the factors in your mind and decide what to do."

He told me about a landing he made one evening during the late 1950s, in a Connie. As he drew near LaGuardia Airport, he received a report that rain showers had made the runways there slick—planes were having trouble braking after they landed. He considered diverting to some other airport where conditions were better, but he decided against it.

"I knew what landing on a slick runway in a Connie could mean," he said. "A short time before this, I was deadheading on a Connie that landed at LaGuardia after a rain. I was dozing in the cabin, but when we touched down I became aware that we were sliding sideways. We slid up on the dike at the end of the runway. The pilot had ground-looped the plane—we wound up sitting almost backwards on the dike.

"That made an impression on me. But on my own flight, I checked things over in my mind—the direction of the wind, and how much of a load we were carrying, and so forth—and I was confident that we could land all right.

"Still, I came in cautiously. I alerted the crew. I said, 'I'm going to set this plane down right on the [front] end of the runway, and I'm going to put the nose down and test the brakes, and if I have any doubts at all about being able to stop, I'll pour on the power and we'll get out of there.'

"The key to landing on a wet runway is to put the plane down firmly, to prevent the wheels from hydroplaning. You want to shove the wheels down through the water so they get good traction. That's what I planned to do. I lined up with the runway, and floated in just above stall [speed], and put the plane down right on the end of the runway. Then I immediately got the nose down, hard, and I tried the brakes. And guess what? The airplane stopped on a dime.

"I felt humiliated. I mean, that was no soft landing by any means. I'd really thumped it down. I'd made a big production out of the whole deal and I didn't need to at all. The braking was fine.

"We *had* gotten into New York on schedule and I'd been right that we could land without any problem, so I felt good about that much at least. But that report about bad braking had been a totally false alarm."

I asked my father why he'd decided to land when the reported conditions there were unsafe. Why not divert to an airport where the runways were dry? He said he couldn't really explain it, he'd just had confidence that he could get the plane down in good shape. "But I'll tell you about a time when I made the opposite decision," he added.

He said that many years later he was approaching New York again, this time in a 747. He had taken off that morning from London, and while crossing the ocean he'd received weather reports indicating that a heavy snowstorm was moving northward through the Middle Atlantic states. As he came down over Nova Scotia, he learned that the storm had reached New York. His destination, Kennedy Airport, was still open, but the weather there was deteriorating so badly that some inbound pilots were electing to divert. My father continued toward New York, though. He said he didn't want to give up on Kennedy until he definitely had to.

"But then as we were descending into New York," he said, "the tower gave us an update and this time things sounded so bad that I told them, 'No thank you, that's not adequate. I'm going to Boston.'

I figured we could wait out the storm in Boston, then when things got better at Kennedy, go on in. I didn't think it should take very long.

"So I pulled up and headed back up toward Boston. And I'm glad I did, because the next plane after us accepted the conditions and tried to land at Kennedy, and he slid off the end of the runway. That closed the airport down for several hours."

My father flew to Logan Airport in Boston, where he landed and had his plane refueled. Then he and his passengers sat, waiting for Kennedy to reopen. My father knew the snowfall was thinning in New York, and he assumed the ground crews at Kennedy would clear away the downed plane soon.

"I didn't let the passengers get off in Boston," my father said. "I intended to get back over to Kennedy quickly, and I didn't want to have to round up everybody from inside the terminal. I thought we would get an 'all clear' from Kennedy before long."

But while they waited, the edge of the storm reached Boston. Snow started falling at Logan, covering the runways and the planes parked at the gates. "It wasn't sticking yet," my father said, "but it would soon, and then we would be trapped in Boston for the night, and I didn't want that. I was still determined to get this flight into New York."

So he taxied back out and took off. Then he dawdled, flying the 747 at its minimum allowable speed as he guided it across Connecticut, down over Long Island Sound, and diagonally across Long Island. He had taken on plenty of fuel. He figured that if he was patient, Kennedy would surely be open again by the time he reached it. But he was wrong. As he descended toward Kennedy for the second time this day, he got word that the airport would remain closed indefinitely.

So he switched plans again. He asked for clearance to go to Newark Airport. He thought most of his passengers would be reasonably satisfied if he deposited them in Newark—it was a lot closer to New York than Boston was, anyway. But after he made the request, he was told that Newark was saturated with planes that had diverted from

Kennedy: The traffic controllers said they wouldn't be able to squeeze him into Newark for a couple of hours yet.

"Everybody was getting exhausted by now," my father said, "and I realized it was time to toss in the towel on this one. I had the fuel to circle for a couple of hours, but I decided against it.

"In the end, we wound up going down to Philadelphia. The blizzard had already passed there and the runways had been cleared.

"I landed there and cancelled the rest of the flight, and we put all the people on buses up to New York. They weren't happy about it, but I had done my best for them.

"That was just the way it happened sometimes. Sometimes you couldn't get to your destination no matter how hard you tried."

The Code

THE FIRST FOUR PILOTS I INTERVIEWED WERE UNCOOP-
ERATIVE. They stonewalled, denying that they had anything interesting to tell me. They said their careers had been uneventful—
dull, really.

I knew they were lying. All four were retired captains who began
flying 'way back when, in Ford trimotors or DC-2s. I was sure they'd
slugged through thunderstorms, made forced landings, contended with
windmilling engines and static-blurred radios and rain-slicked runways.
They'd had adventures worth recounting. But they denied it. They said
their flights had all been pretty routine. They wished they could recall
some rip-roaring episodes to describe, but their memories were blank.

I understood why they held out on me. Pilots prize coolness above
any other trait. They want to remain unruffled, wholly in command of
themselves and the situation, no matter what is going on. Think of the
times you've heard pilots making P.A. announcements in flight. Their
voices were ice-water cool, pitched to assure you that everything was
going to be just fine. The words the pilots used were all but meaning-
less ("Welcome aboard; thanks for flying with us"), but the real point

of the announcements was carried in the subtext, in that comforting intonation: *You're perfectly safe,* it implied. *The men flying this plane are superbly competent. They are more than equal to any crises that might arise.* It's part of a pilot's job to allay his passengers' concerns. Normally, he can do this simply by choosing the right tone of voice. But if crises do arise—if an engine falls off or gaping cracks appear on a wing—he will add explicit deceptions over the subtext. "Folks," he'll say, keeping his voice as nonchalant as ever, "we've got a little problem here, but it's nothing to be concerned about. Just settle back and relax. . . ."

Pilots school themselves to be phlegmatic, to look on outbursts of emotion—excitement, fear, exultation, relief—as marks of failure. Even when there are no passengers present, they strive to be absolutely cool. I remember my father telling me, years ago, about a cockpit tape recording made during the last few minutes in the lives of a pair of test pilots. The pilots had intentionally put a new airliner into a stall, and then they found that they couldn't bring it out. The plane began falling tail-first toward the ground. My father told me that the tape, which was found later among the crash debris, showed that the pilots stayed calm as the plane dropped from the sky. "Well now," they said, "this is interesting. I wonder why we can't recover from this stall. Let's try Procedure 19. Doesn't that work? No? Then let's try Procedure 33." They quietly discussed their little problem and possible solutions to it until the moment of impact.

Pilots deny that an event is exciting while it is happening, and if they survive, they keep up the denials afterward. The first pilot who acknowledged to me that his career included a few memorable episodes was Arthur Davis, a retired TWA captain who'd started flying in the 1920s. Early in our conversation, he made the same disclaimer that I'd heard from other pilots: He had no tales to tell me. But he smiled when he said it, as if he didn't expect me to take the disclaimer literally. I thought he wanted me to doubt his word. So I stayed with Arthur through a long, largely quiet afternoon at his farmhouse in eastern Pennsylvania, and gradually as the afternoon ticked away, sure enough, his memory improved. He said that, come to think of it, one or two mildly interesting things *had* happened to him.

He told me, for instance, that an out-of-control airliner once creased his car's roof. He had been driving to LaGuardia Airport to take out a flight, he said. He had exited from the highway and was driving along the airport perimeter when a DC-4 crashed through a fence and came bounding toward him. The plane had been trying to take off—Arthur could see its propellers spinning and hear its engines howling—but something had gone wrong. Instead of climbing, the plane was hurtling along at ground level: a huge silver juggernaut of a thing, racing straight at him.

Arthur said he didn't have enough time to do anything except brace for the collision. One moment the plane was at the fence, the next it was just outside his car window. "I figured I was a goner," he said. But at the last split instant before it would have smashed into the car, the plane struck an embankment and ricocheted into the air. It passed inches above Arthur's head, dragging its belly across the roof of the car. There was a crunching scrape on the roof, then the plane was sliding across the grass on the far side of the road.

"If that embankment hadn't been there," Arthur said, "the plane would have squashed my car flat as a pancake."

I asked Arthur what he did after he knew he was safe. I assumed he'd gone home, taken off the rest of the day—or maybe the rest of the week. No, Arthur answered. He drove to the parking lot, checked in at the crew offices, and prepared for his flight. "That's what they were paying me to do," he said. He flew as scheduled.

Talking with Arthur helped prepare me for my subsequent meetings with other pilots. The story he told wasn't about flying, exactly—Arthur had been on the ground when the episode occurred, not in a cockpit. Nevertheless, it served me as a primer on the pilots' code. The point of the story was that Arthur hadn't gotten emotional about nearly being crushed to death. Emotions wouldn't have helped him—they would have been a hindrance, preventing him from proceeding with his job. Pilots, Arthur's story reminded me, would rather admit almost anything than that they are excitable.

Another lesson about the code was contained in the smile Arthur gave me. Arthur asserted that he had no stories to tell, and then, after a decent interval, he told a story. His disclaimer had been purely *pro forma*. Later, I found that the same held for many other pilots. They would say, "My career has been uneventful," but they were speaking in cipher. Crack the code, and the message that emerged was something quite different. In many cases, I learned, the message was "I'm a damned good flier. I've never lost control, never had an incident that would mar my record. Of course, circumstances have put me in some tight spots, but I've handled them awfully well. Want to hear about some of them?"

Occasionally I met pilots who couldn't take refuge in disclaimers. They'd handled certain tight spots so well that reports had reached the news media—they knew I knew that their careers had held moments of high interest. Still, the code made it hard for them to discuss those moments without evasion.

On December 4, 1965, Tom Carroll was the captain of a 707 jetliner that was involved in a midair collision. An Eastern Airlines Constellation hit the 707 from below, ripping away the outer third of its left wing. The 707 should have been uncontrollable, but Tom kept it airborne, flying it fifty miles to Kennedy Airport, where he made a successful landing. All of his passengers and crew survived without serious injury. (The occupants of the Connie fared less well. The Connie crash-landed on a hillside near the New York/Connecticut border. The captain and three passengers died.)

I wanted to meet Tom because his adventure had occurred in a jet. Months had passed since I'd spoken with Arthur Davis, and in that time I'd heard many stories about dramas that occurred aboard piston planes. But I'd heard almost nothing about jets. I counted on Tom to become the first jet pilot to break this silence for me.

Tom seemed glad to receive me when I arrived at his home in Connecticut. He said he knew my father slightly—they had been members of the same copilot training class in 1946. He said he'd be happy to tell me anything I wanted to know about the collision. Yet he was wary. My visit was obviously awkward for him. I'd come to hear about some piloting heroics; I wanted to hear how Tom managed to fly a jetliner that was missing a third of its wing. But Tom couldn't very well admit to being a hero—that would be an extreme violation of the code, boastfulness rather than cool denial. So he repeatedly led the conversation into other channels. Two or three times when we began speaking of the collision, Tom branched off to talk about some other episodes from his career instead. He told stories that he might have hesitated to tell normally, but on this day they served him as useful diversions, especially since he managed to twist them into jokes on himself.

He told me about a night flight he once made that switched from routine to bizarre in an eyeblink. He said he was flying a Martin 2-0-2 from Pittsburgh to New York, and shortly after the plane passed above Harrisburg, its electrical system failed, knocking out the lights, the radios, and most of the cockpit instruments.

Tom said he and his copilot had been flying blind already. Climbing out of Pittsburgh, they had risen through a layer of clouds that cut off their view of the land below. Then ice had begun forming on the windows. "Not too much ice," Tom said. "Just a coating." But enough so they couldn't see out.

And then, over Harrisburg, the electricity died. "I remember thinking," Tom said, " 'Good grief, this is getting to be kind of a bad night for us.'

"Actually, it wasn't as bad as it sounds. Some of the instruments weren't tied to the electric system, like the artificial horizon and the airspeed. They kept working, thank goodness, so we weren't totally helpless. My copilot held his flashlight on the control panel to help me see what was what. I would tell him which instrument I wanted to see and he would shine his flashlight on it. We could keep going well enough like that."

Tom tried to hold the plane on course as he proceeded east across Pennsylvania and then New Jersey. With no radios and no view of the ground, he couldn't be sure of his location, but he had flown this route often enough to make a pretty good guess. He timed his progress until he calculated that he was above Flatbush, on western Long Island. Then he turned southeast, aiming to fly out over the ocean. He knew he would have to get under the clouds in order to spot his destination, Idlewild Airport, but he didn't want to descend until he was sure there were no tall buildings below him. He didn't want to imitate the B-25 pilot who had descended over downtown New York a few years earlier and crashed into the Empire State Building.

When he figured there was nothing but water below, he reduced power and eased the plane down through the clouds. He emerged from the bottom of the clouds about eight hundred feet above the water, and fortunately the ice had melted off the windshield as the plane dropped into the warmer air, so now he could see out. So Tom banked around to the northwest, expecting to see the lights of New York on his left and the runway lights of Idlewild on his right.

"Wrong," Tom said, slapping the table and laughing. "There was nothing but black out there. Black sky, black ocean. If it *was* the ocean. Frankly, I couldn't decide where in the world we were. For all I knew, the wind had blown us up over Connecticut somewhere and we had come down over Long Island Sound, not the Atlantic. There wasn't any way to tell. All I knew was that I was lost."

Tom and the copilot craned their necks, searching for any spark of illumination that would help them get their bearings. Finally they spotted one, a small blinking light in the distance. Tom headed for it, and as he got near he recognized it as the beacon at Floyd Bennett Field, a naval air base a few miles west of Idlewild.

"That was a relief," Tom said. "That was about the prettiest light I ever saw."

He flew over the beacon, then swung east and flew toward Idlewild.

"All I had to do now," Tom said, "was get the attention of the guys in the control tower [at Idlewild]. I couldn't radio them, so I flew over the field, slow, at about two or three hundred feet. They noticed that, all right, and they figured out that we must have lost our electricity because they couldn't see any lights on us. So they flashed the lights on runway 31L, to tell me which runway to come down on.

"So I came around and landed on it. But here's what you won't believe. It was kind of a firm landing—I guess I was feeling pretty relieved, and maybe I was congratulating myself a little for getting to the airport okay. Anyhow, the fact is we hit the runway kind of hard, and you know what? All the electricity came back on! Really! I swear, bingo, all the lights and everything clicked back on just like that!

"I couldn't believe it! It gave me some explaining to do, that's for sure. I had to convince people that we had really had a problem. I think a few of them never *did* believe me. They thought it had all been some kind of stunt.

"I'm exaggerating. But really, it was funny."

After we'd exhausted most of the other topics available to us, I told Tom that I'd read some old press accounts of the collision and of the flight he made afterward to Kennedy in the crippled 707. Then, foolishly, I asked him how he had reacted when he was called a hero for saving his passengers' lives. Grimacing, Tom waved the question away. "He-ro," he said, drawing out the syllables with distaste.

Tom left the table—I thought the interview had ended—but he came back from the kitchen after a minute and sat again.

The collision occurred at eleven thousand feet, he said, near the New York/Connecticut border. He and his crew were preparing for their descent into New York. They were cruising on autopilot when suddenly the Connie appeared ahead of them.

"I remember we were just slightly above a cloud layer," Tom said, "and the horizon in front of us was empty, and then all of a sudden here came a Constellation up toward us. One second he wasn't there and the next second he was.

"I flicked off the autopilot and pulled on the wheel, starting a climb to the right. I thought we could climb away from the Constellation. But as soon as I started it, I could see it wasn't going to work. He was coming up too fast. So then I pushed the wheel forward, to try to dive under him. But by then it was too late. He hit us."

"How long did it take?" I asked. "From the time you saw him until the planes collided. . . ."

"Things went pretty fast," Tom said. "One thousand one, one thousand two, one thousand three, one thousand four, and smack." Tom slapped the table again.

"Was the impact violent?" I asked. "Did it knock you around hard?"

"I thought I'd wrenched my back," Tom said. "It was hard enough for that, anyway. Everything in the cockpit—our manuals, the charts, everything—was all over the place. I guess the cabin was the same—everything flew out of the overhead racks and out of people's hands. So, yes, we felt it all right."

During those first chaotic moments, Tom didn't know how much damage his plane had sustained. All he knew was that the plane was canted far over to the left—it had flipped nearly ninety degrees from horizontal and was threatening to fall from the sky. He had to get it back up. He hauled the control wheel in, cranking it hard to the right while he stamped with his full weight on the right rudder pedal.

"How did you figure out what to do?" I asked. "How did you know what control movements to make?"

"I just did what seemed right," Tom said. "The plane was pitched way over. I could feel it getting away. I just went on reflex to bring it back."

"Did the plane fight you?" I asked. I'd read that the collision had removed the 707's outboard aileron and ruptured the hydraulic lines. "Did the controls want to respond? Was the plane still shaking from the collision?"

Tom smiled. "No," he said, "the plane wasn't shaking. I was."

As he struggled to pull the plane up, Tom brushed against the throttles, knocking two of them out of alignment. He said his copilot readjusted them. "It was a team effort. We couldn't have made it otherwise. All I could do at that moment was hang on. I left everything else to my crew."

Reluctantly, the plane began to right itself. The left wing inched upward and the nose gradually rose toward its proper place on the horizon ahead. When the plane was level, Tom began adjusting the trim settings for the control surfaces on the wings and tail. If he could find the right settings, he could relax his pressure on the wheel and rudder pedals—the plane would maintain the attitude he set for it.

"I put in trim, trim, trim," he said. "I started to think I wouldn't be able to put in enough to hold it. But slowly I could feel it coming around, and finally it was all right, the plane was trimmed."

"How serious would it have been if you couldn't put in enough trim?" I asked, "What would you have done?"

"Oh, I don't know," he said. "The plane was either going to be flyable or it wasn't. Fortunately for us, it was flyable."

When the plane seemed to have stabilized, Tom looked out his side window and, for the first time, learned what had happened to the left wing. He saw that it had been clipped off less than a foot beyond the number one engine pod; and the air intake at the mouth of that engine was dented, as if it had been hit; and there was a deep dent on the leading edge of the wing inboard of the pod.

"We were *so* lucky," Tom said. "If we'd lost just a little more wing, we would have lost the [number one] engine, and then I don't think we could have pulled up. We needed all four engines."

"Was there a fire?" I asked. "Some of the passengers reported that the wing caught fire."

"No. Thank goodness, no. That would have been as bad as losing an engine. I don't even want to think about that. The collision ripped off the fuel tank out there at the end of the wing, but that tank was empty so late in the flight.

"Anyhow," Tom continued, "things settled down after that. We checked over the instruments, and the plane was in basically good shape. I told the people from Boeing later, 'You guys build a strong airplane. *Thank* you.' The hydraulics were out, which meant we would have to use back-up procedures to get the landing gear down and to lower the flaps. Other than that, though, the plane came through fine."

One little problem complicated the fifty-mile flight to Kennedy, Tom said. The plane didn't want to decelerate. It behaved itself as long as Tom held it straight and level, but every time he tried to reduce its speed, it tried to nose over to the left and dive again.

"Granted," Tom said, "we wanted to get down to the ground, but we didn't want to do it that way.

"Playing with that kept me occupied all the way back to Kennedy."

Tom was flying a lopsided jetliner that had a long, gracefully tapered wing on one side and a crudely truncated approximation of a wing on the other. It was a bastard configuration, one for which ordinary procedures didn't apply. To kill his speed and descend, he needed to pull the throttles back. But that made the plane slide off to the left and accelerate. So Tom pulled the throttles gingerly, moving them a bare fraction of an inch, then he worked to hold the plane steady while he readjusted the trim. Then, having stabilized the plane at its new throttle setting, he pulled the throttles back a fraction farther, repeating the sequence. In this way, painstakingly, he coaxed the plane to surrender its speed and altitude in small, controlled stages.

"What it flew like," he said, "was a plane with two engines out on one side, only a little worse than that, a little more sensitive. But by kind of feeling my way along, I could keep it trimmed up. So gradually we worked our way down like that, killing our speed a little at a time."

As the plane descended over the north shore of Long Island, the crew members turned their attention to the landing gear. The flight engineer unstowed a crank handle, slipped it into a slot in the cockpit floor, and began cranking, manually lowering the wheels under the plane's right wing. Then he moved to a second slot to lower the wheels under the left wing, and then to a third slot to lower the nose wheels. After that, he opened a hatch in the cockpit floor and cautiously lowered himself into a bay beneath the cockpit.

"There was a window at the back of the bay," Tom said. "[The engineer] could look through it to check the gear, to make sure it was extended all the way and locked.

"Before he went down, he called over, 'Don't land with me down here.' I told him we'd try not to."

Re-emerging as the plane arrived over Kennedy, the engineer reported that the gear looked good. Tom wasn't ready to land yet, though. He hadn't been able to kill enough altitude—the plane was still at two thousand feet.

Tom considered flying past Kennedy, heading out over the ocean until he was low enough to begin a landing approach. He said he didn't like the thought of leaving the vicinity of the airport, though. So he decided on a different strategy. The controllers in Kennedy's tower had told him to land on runway 31L. He flew to the southeast end of that runway and began a three-hundred-sixty-degree turn above it. He intended to spiral down to the runway, bleeding off his altitude as he turned.

"Which way did you bank?" I asked. "Left or right?"

"To the left."

"Wouldn't it have been better to go right, so you wouldn't have to lower the left wing?"

"It didn't make any difference. I had confidence in the plane by that time. I knew it was handling well, so left or right didn't make much difference."

While the copilot operated the electric back-up system to lower the wing flaps, Tom steered the plane along its corkscrew flight path. He monitored airspeed, turn rate, and rate of descent, continuously adjusting the plane's bank and pitch as the compass swung through south, east, and north. When the compass showed 310, Tom leveled the wings and looked out the windshield for the runway.

"The flaps were fully extended by then," he said, "and the altitude was down where it should be, and then here came the runway. So we crossed over the threshold, and you know, it went on smoothly. I've bounced planes that were in perfect condition, and here this messed-up plane decides to land like a dream. Don't ask me to explain it."

The plane's hydraulic brakes weren't working and the nosewheel steering was out, but the back-up air brakes were available. Tom gave them a squirt, and the plane rolled to a stop.

"There were fire trucks and other emergency vehicles all around," Tom said, "and the passengers were evacuating the plane. But when I opened my window, one of the firemen called to me that there was no fire, so I got on the P.A. and told the passengers everything was okay, they didn't have to hurry.

"Some of the passengers got a little carried away after that, when they realized they were safe. They came up to the cockpit to thank us. . . . They made sort of a fuss. I got letters from some of them later. . . ."

Tom's voice trailed off. I asked him what the passengers had said in their letters. "Oh, just what you'd expect," he said. "They were glad we'd gotten them through it, naturally. They wrote to say thanks." He paused. "I appreciated hearing from them. But you know, it doesn't mean anything. If you handle an emergency okay, you're a 'hero.' If you get killed trying, too bad."

Tom said he and his crewmates got out of the plane and walked back to look at the damaged left wing. "When we saw it," Tom said, "I thought 'Jeez.' We hadn't fully known how bad it was before that."

I asked him if the sight shook him. I didn't expect him to answer, but he surprised me. After thinking for a moment, he said, "I don't think any of us had much of a reaction right away. Back in the airplane, there wasn't *time* for anything to sink in. We were too busy. Then when we got out, we still didn't have time to think it over very much.

"You know when it did hit me? I went home, and saw myself on

television, and then the next day it finally had time to sink in. I thought
to myself, 'You know, you're awfully lucky you made it.' "

I envied Tom. The values he and other pilots live by provide a straight-
forward test of personal worth. Do you have what it takes or don't you?
The primary requirement is composure in the face of danger. As Tom
said to me at one point during our conversation, "If you come apart
in an emergency, you've had it. So you just don't. Things happen, and
you react, and then you get ready for whatever else might happen.
Basically, that's all there is to it. You do what you have to do."

Passing the test, as Tom did, must help a pilot answer some basic
questions about himself. He can validate himself, prove himself. I don't
have any comparable proof of my own worth. I've never confronted
a life-or-death crisis, so I don't know how I would do in one. Sometimes I imagine I would measure up well; at other times, I doubt it.
But even when I tell myself that I would certainly pass the test if it
came, I'm left feeling empty. I realize that, in fact, I don't believe in
the test. My standards of behavior are less definite than that, my
conception of manhood less certain. The truth is that if I confronted
a crisis and acquitted myself well, I might emerge feeling that nothing
of significance had been established.

I envied Tom not so much because he had passed his test as because
he subscribed to a set of values that gave the test meaning. Tom struck
me as being wholly sure of himself. He spoke and carried himself much
as other pilots whom I'd met did: with a self-confidence that was
highlighted rather than masked by self-deprecating humor. Despite
their individual differences, most pilots seemed to want to present
themselves this way, as if they thought it was required of them. Before
meeting Tom, I thought I understood that style of behavior pretty well,
and I thought I knew its flaws. But after I visited Tom, my feelings
about these things moderated, and that was important to me.

When I was in high school—during that part of my life when my father and I were most at odds—I came to resent the pilots' style, which my father certainly exhibited. Coolness under pressure seemed like a crock to me. It was John Wayne macho bullshit. I couldn't have explained the anger I felt or said why I was turning my back on values I'd admired so much just a few years earlier. But I had started to perceive, dimly, that those values exact penalties, both from the men who uphold them and from the men's families, and I increasingly resented the penalties that applied to me.

The character traits that a pilot cultivates for his work lose their value at home. Emotional detachment, perfectionism, ice-water calm—these traits may equip a man to operate flying machines, but they are hardly a prescription for success as a husband or father. Home life calls for fundamentally different traits. Perhaps men in some other lines of work, where there may be less disparity between the requirements for professional and personal success, are able to live by one set of values at work and a different set at home. Maybe they can shuck off their business personas when they leave the office and assume different guises when they arrive home. But I can't imagine many pilots doing this. Pilots discipline themselves to fit a rigorous paradigm, the set of values and attributes that constitute the code. They have to prepare themselves to pass the test if it comes—or to pass it again if it recurs. They have to focus their energies on meeting the code's demands. The code is unrelenting, and because pilots have chosen it voluntarily, and because they find potential validation in it, they can't easily set it aside when they happen to be off duty.

I think my father absorbed the code deeply. He was, I think, very much the same man at work and at home. He had admirable integrity, in this sense. He was always himself. But this meant he was never quite comfortable at home. He wasn't harsh or uncaring with my sisters and me. He found it difficult, though, to express much emotion. He remained within himself. I think he behaved with us much as he probably behaved with his crews: He was good-natured but also remote and judgmental. I doubt that he was reluctant to point out his copilots' shortcomings; I thought he was fast enough to point out mine.

I thought he held me to unforgivingly high standards, asking me to be more than I could be. I remember a footrace we ran once when I was very young. As most fathers would do with their small sons, my father let me pull ahead of him. But then as we neared the finish line, he charged past me to win. Throughout my childhood, our other games and contests were similar. He didn't throw them to give me a false sense of accomplishment. If I was ever going to beat him, I would have to do it legitimately, in honest competition. The memory of my many losses stung me for years.

My conversation with Tom made me appreciate some of the benefits of the pilots' code. But my conversations with other pilots confirmed my belief that, in some important respects, the code is deficient. I asked all the pilots I met to tell me what they enjoyed most about piloting and also what, if anything, they disliked most. The answers to the first question varied: authority, travel, accomplishment, freedom. But the answers to the second question clustered around one topic: family life. Repeatedly, pilots told me they regretted the effects their careers had had on their family lives. They didn't go into detail; they made a few quick comments, then they wanted to talk about something else. But a consensus became evident. The pilots referred to divorces; to missed anniversaries, birthdays, holidays; to battles with alienated children; to boredom at being home. "I'd get home from a trip," one retired pilot said to me, "and I'd be bushed. I'd fall into bed and sleep for ten, twelve hours. Then when I was back up to speed, there were things to do around the house. Things to repair or what have you. But I was never too keen on any of that. When I got rested up from one trip, I was ready for another one. I didn't want to hang around the house. That wasn't right. I should have paid more attention to things at home. But you don't think of things like that when you're young."

Besides meeting with pilots during the last three years, I arranged meetings with some of their wives and grown children. I thought I knew what kinds of things the members of pilots' families would have to say—I assumed my own experiences as the son of a pilot had been more or less typical—but I wanted to be sure. I hoped that talking to pilots' wives and kids might give me a better fix on my own situation.

I met Susan D. when visiting her husband, Bob, a DC-10 captain. Bob was helpful to me, discussing at length things he'd seen and done during his twenty-five-year flying career. I visited him twice, once to talk about his airline experiences, the second time to discuss the years he spent in the Air Force. Off and on during these visits, Susan had joined us, listening to our discussions and occasionally reminding Bob of various events she thought I might find interesting: the time Harry Truman was a passenger on one of Bob's flights; the time a snowstorm kept Bob grounded in Newfoundland for a week.

Now I was back for a third visit, but when Susan opened the front door, she told me that Bob wasn't home. He'd gone to the airport that morning to pick up his mail and he hadn't returned yet. She told me to come in, though—she was sure he would be back before long.

We sat at the kitchen table and had some tea. To pass the time, Susan asked me about my family and about the book I'd told her I was working on. She asked how my father was these days, and my mother, and my sisters. She pointed to some photos on the dining room wall, pictures of her children. She told me the children's names and ages, and told me where each child was living now (the youngest, who was seventeen, lived at home; the others had moved away). Then she asked me if I knew the young couple who lived three houses up the block, a USAir copilot and his wife, a former stewardess. She told me that several of her friends were married to pilots. "Or," she corrected herself, "some are married to them and some used to be." She asked if I'd noticed how many pilots got divorced.

"Bob and I have been together fifteen years," she said. "That's pretty good, don't you think? A lot of airline families don't stay together that long.

"Of all the couples we were friends with when we first got married, pilots and their wives, we're almost the only ones who didn't get divorced. I don't know why some pilots get married in the first place, honestly. From the ones I've known, they're bachelors at heart.

"We were friends with six or seven couples on [Bob's airline], and when we would have a get-together, the men would go off on one side by themselves. They really didn't want any of the rest of us with them. They had this very male world and there was no way the wives and the kids could be part of it.

"Bob was like the other pilots and then again he wasn't. He tried, he really did. He brought home toys for the kids after every flight. He brought me things too. But he was so *quiet.* You wouldn't think that now, but that's how much he's changed. For years after we got married, he would hardly ever tell me anything that had happened on a flight. He just kept everything inside. Sometimes I could have brained him.

"But what I did, I would sit him down and *force* him to talk. I said, 'Listen, you're gone more than you're home. If you don't tell me about the places you go, we'll wind up with nothing in common.' Later, when the kids came along, I forced him to tell them, too. I didn't want him to be a *total* stranger to them."

I asked whether Bob's absences had made raising their kids more difficult.

"It was like being a single parent, sometimes," she said. "Which I suppose was good for me, in some regards. I couldn't just wait for him to come home. If something needed to be done when he was away, it was up to me to do it.

"It might have been good for the kids, too, somewhat. They had to be pretty independent too. When they got old enough, I divided some of the house chores among them. That taught them more responsibility."

I asked about Bob's attitude toward house chores. I said I thought most pilots had little patience with them.

"Bob used to be like that," Susan said, smiling, "until we had some heart-to-hearts. He would get very impatient with things around the house.

"Actually, that's one way he hasn't changed very much. But at least he learned to do his part. He has the basement, the garage, and the yard. I told him if he would take care of them, I could manage everything else.

"One thing I insisted, though. I didn't want him to think our house was just the place where he stopped off between flights. Some of my friends said their husbands acted like that, and I wouldn't have that."

I wanted to ask more about Bob's treatment of his children, but I couldn't think of a tactful way to phrase the question. While I hesitated, Susan went on.

"If you ask me," she said, "pilots see so much of the world, they get a big perspective. That's what makes it hard for them to care about minor day-to-day things.

"Besides, even if they want to be involved, it's hard for them. Bob would go on a trip and everybody would be fine when he left. Then all the kids would get sick. Let's say the mumps. But by the time he got home, they would be all right again. So it was like it never happened as far as he was concerned. When I tried to tell him about it, it didn't register, really."

Susan's smile faded momentarily, then returned. "Probably what he really thought," she said, "was that if things had been that bad, he was glad he wasn't around to have to deal with it. But you can't blame somebody for that. I would have liked to miss that kind of thing, too, if I could have."

I said some pilots' kids considered their fathers to be forbidding figures—distant, unapproachable. I said some pilots couldn't quit playing captain when they got home.

"Even if they're *copilots* they're like that," Susan said. "I don't mean our kids were afraid of their father," she added after a moment. "But they were so *shy* around him. I used to encourage them to *talk* to him, but they said they didn't know what to say. When they were around him, they were like clams, the same as he was.

"I got sneaky. I used to think up a topic of conversation, and then at dinner I would go around the table and get everybody to say what they thought. I didn't tell them what I was doing, but that way I got them to bat things back and forth. Sometimes I felt like I was one of those talk show hosts. But it worked."

I met David G. at a used-book store where we were both moving along a shelf of aviation books. We bumped elbows a few times, excused ourselves, and got to talking, recommending various authors to each other and negotiating over a couple of rare paperbacks. Before we left the shop, we discovered that we were both pilots' sons.

We became friends after that. In the following weeks, we visited each others' homes to exchange books and magazines, and we and our wives had dinner together, and David and I attended a small air show in central Pennsylvania.

While driving home from the air show, David told me about his childhood. "When I was real young," he said, "I really looked forward to my father coming home. But later on it got to be different. I got to like it better when he was gone.

"He was a hard guy. When he was home, he would make lists of chores I had to do to earn my allowance. But I couldn't ever do them well enough to suit him. He would inspect what I did and always he would find some little detail to get on me about. He would give me the money, but I felt like such a crud after his lectures, it wasn't worth it to me.

"That's how he was about everything. Nothing suited him. I can kind of admire that now. He thought if you were going to do something, you should do it the very best possible. All right. That might be a good approach. He didn't say it in so many words, though. I thought he was busting my chops for no good reason.

"When he got mad, he didn't yell or anything. He didn't beat up on me. He would just frown and walk away. He had this dark, heavy kind of a frown. I'd almost rather he had hit me, you know? It was like I wasn't worth his time or something.

"Once when I was about eight, I 'ran away from home.' My dad was away on a trip and I had done something wrong. I don't remember what. I broke something or disobeyed my mom, something. But when I knew he would be coming home the next day, I got my sleeping bag and some stuff and 'ran away.' I only got as far as the tree house I had out back. I hid there until my mom came out and took me back inside. But at least that time she didn't tell on me.

"Usually she *did* tell. She used to save up punishments for him to give me when he got back. That was the one time he would spank me, if she said I needed it. The main way she kept me in line was to threaten what he was going to do to me. 'Wait until your father gets home.' I must have heard that a million times.

"I was thinking about that the other day. It was probably pretty rotten for him, as a matter of fact. Come home and have to do that kind of shit.

"The other thing that stays with me, I don't think he liked to be home much. Forget about the punishments or whatever. I just don't think he liked to be around that much. He didn't say anything, but he got restless. He would come home from a trip, and a day or two later he would be pacing around the house, and he would go out for long drives. Stuff like that. You could tell how long he had been home by how restless he got.

"I don't know. I looked up to him and all, but we didn't really get along that well. You wouldn't call us pals, for sure. The best times I had with him, we would go camping sometimes. He was good at that kind of stuff. But usually we would have some kind of fight. I didn't chop up the kindling the right way, or something, and he couldn't leave well enough alone. Whatever I did, it was never good enough."

Midway through my years in high school, the anger that had been building in me crested, and I let loose. I was a dutiful teenager, mainly. A dutiful student, for instance: dutiful grades, dutiful participation in school activities. But sporadically during those years I went slightly ape. I shoplifted from the stores in the neighborhood, and trashed abandoned buildings, and committed small acts of vandalism at school. Late one afternoon, I remember, a friend and I slipped into our math classroom and set off a cherry bomb in the teacher's desk, blasting the papers inside to confetti.

I didn't know why I was doing these things, I just knew I got a kick out of them. But in retrospect my motives seem clear enough. My father was around more when I was a teenager than he had been when I was younger. As planes became faster, flight times were reduced— he was rarely gone longer than a few days in a row, now. But during his days at home, he seemed more withdrawn than he'd once been. He spent most of his free time upstairs in his den or else out on his sailboat taking long, solitary cruises. Either way, I didn't see much of him.

Also, we had gotten awkward with each other as I approached him in size. I had been an average-size kid until I entered adolescence, but then I suddenly shot up. By the age of thirteen, I stood six feet tall, and within a year or two after that, I was shaving, and going out on dates, and drinking beer on the sly. (I could easily pass for legal age. Store managers hardly ever asked to see an ID when I bought a sixpack.) My size probably confused my father. I was at that indeterminate stage between boyhood and manhood—it must have been hard to figure out how to deal with me. Certainly I found my size confusing. I was large, but I didn't feel large. My spurt of growth ended as quickly as it began, leaving me two inches shorter than my father. I was the biggest kid in my class by a considerable margin, but at home I felt undersized, and I didn't know what to make of that. I knew I would be an adult soon—I wanted to be one immediately—but I wasn't sure I felt up to it. Now that I had a man's body, I compared myself to my father more consciously, and more than ever I felt inadequate in the comparison. Was I a hotshot, the way I often felt, or was I a fuck-up, the way I felt the rest of the time? I couldn't sort it out.

Like most adolescents, I teemed with emotions I didn't understand. Gradually, though, one emotion clarified itself and became predominant: anger. I blamed my father for not coming on more of the trips our family took, and for being remote when we were at home together, and for setting standards of size and strength that I couldn't match. I blamed him for things that were his fault and for things that weren't. And from time to time I played out my anger by running amok.

I made sure my father knew what a depraved character I was. I remember that for a while I kept a crime log, a looseleaf notebook in which I recorded particulars of my misbehavior. I thought it was a hilarious document. Each time I raised some new form of hell, I would sneak into my father's den and use his typewriter to write a comic account of the event. Then I would take the log back into my bedroom and hide it in my closet. But one time I slipped up. (I thought it was a slip-up, anyway.) I wrote out a new adventure, and then I returned to my room empty-handed, leaving the log on my father's desk.

His reaction when he found it was low-key. This wasn't his first exposure to my delinquency. Neighbors had complained about me a few times, and once he'd caught me showing my friends a baseball mitt that I had stolen from a sporting goods store. He behaved now as he had then. He let me see that he was furious, but he kept his fury contained. He lectured me, in a tight voice, and asked me what I had to say for myself, and when I remained silent, he imposed various punishments, cutting my allowance and grounding me.

As always, it was effective treatment. I didn't care about losing my allowance or being grounded. But our confrontations always left me shaken. I literally couldn't look into my father's face when he lectured me, and I couldn't find a voice to defend myself. I took whatever punishments he selected, and then I silently retreated. And for weeks afterward I behaved myself. The memory of his fury straightened me out.

The straightening never lasted long, though. When enough time had passed—a couple of months maximum—I would cut up again, and then we would have another confrontation. Thus I arranged for my father to punish me several times a year. Clearly, I engineered our confrontations of my own volition. I maneuvered my father into the role of disciplinarian, but then I held his discipline against him, and I let that feed my anger. So our relationship became increasingly strained and the silences between us deepened.

I realize now that my father tried sometimes to pierce our mutual reserve and reach me. He invited me to go sailing with him once every week or so during the summers, and from time to time he joined me when I was shooting baskets at the hoop he'd erected in the back yard. These were quiet events, generally, but they served as tokens of reconciliation. And periodically he made special efforts, actions that went well beyond tokens. Whenever he did this, however, I unintentionally fended him off. I remember an afternoon when I was seventeen. While watching TV in the living room, I heard the front door close: It was my father, returning from a meeting he'd attended that day at the airport. I heard him hang his coat in the hall closet, then he came into the living room and, switching off the TV, he sat in a chair across from me. He said he had something he wanted to tell me.

During the meeting, he said, a flight instructor had played a cockpit recording that had been recovered from a recent crash. I don't remember the details of the crash. I think it was a collision between an airliner and a small, privately owned plane. In any case, the instructor played a tape recovered from the cockpit of an airliner that had gone down.

"It was awful," my father said. He described the sounds on the first part of the tape: normal cockpit conversation. The crew was going through their normal prelanding drill, checking the instruments, letting down the wing flaps. But then there was a loud, unexpected noise.

"It was a crunching sound," my father said. "You couldn't really make out what it was. A loud pop or a crack." It was the sound of the collision. But evidently the crew didn't realize they'd been hit. They hadn't seen the other plane; they'd received no warning. Everything had seemed to be going normally until they were startled by the noise.

My father continued: "One of the crew said, 'What's that? What's that?'

"And then that was all, that was the end of the tape. The plane must have plunged straight to the ground."

My father stopped speaking. Gripping the arms of his chair, he stared into a corner of the room. I remember his knuckles were white, bloodless. More unsettling—something I'd never seen before—there were tears in my father's eyes.

"I just wanted to tell you," he said.

I knew I should say something. I should make some response to my father. I knew he was trying to share with me something that had affected him strongly. But I didn't know what words to use or what gesture to extend. I had learned too well the lesson that emotions should be guarded; I had become more like my father than either of us recognized.

I turned my eyes away and sat silently until he got up and left the room.

During one of my recent visits with my father, I steered our conversation to the topic of pilots' family lives. I wasn't sure that I should—I'd stewed over it beforehand, but I told myself that I had professional reasons. The topic was going to come up in my book; so many pilots had spoken to me about it, I couldn't very well avoid covering it. Well, then, I was obliged to interview my father about it.

I made my questions impersonal, devoid of references to our own relationship. I said that I'd been conducting an informal survey, asking pilots to tell me what they liked most and what they regretted most about their careers, and I said that a large number of pilots had told me their chief regrets concerned their families. I paraphrased some of the comments pilots had made to me, then I asked my father for his opinion.

Speaking slowly, choosing his words carefully, he took me up on it. Sometimes he began a sentence and left it hanging, unfinished. Sometimes he doubled back on a point to clarify it or change it. But he answered, both the question I'd asked and the question I hadn't, and

I could tell that nothing he said was entirely extemporaneous. He was voicing thoughts that he must turned over, quietly, many times before.

"Pilots make the worst husbands," he said, "and the worst fathers, and the worst citizens in general.

"There are exceptions. There must be pilots who are good family men, and who run scout troops, and get involved in church activities, all that. But there aren't many like that. Most pilots feel that they're above society. They really just don't care anything about it.

"A pilot is never quite free of thinking about his job. If he isn't flying, he's thinking about it. If he's with other people and they're talking about whatever it is they talk about, he's probably still got his job on his mind. Even right now while we're talking, I'm aware that next week I've got a check ride coming up, and I know there are certain things I want to review before then.

"Pilots aren't attached to the same things as other people. They don't live the same kind of life. I always imagine it must be like it was for the old railroad men when that was the main way to travel. You know, that's what boys wanted to be, railroad engineers. Listening to the train whistles at night, wanting to see what was 'down the line.' Or before that, it was becoming a seaman. They had the kind of life pilots have, more or less. Traveling, not putting down roots. If your basic job is roaming, then you become a roamer.

"I know I can't get interested in community events. It might be important for everybody to protest a new landfill or to organize on some other community issue. But basically I just want that stuff to go away, it bores me. That's how I've always felt. I want the 'good guys' to win, I'm all for 'em, but I know I would be terrible at trying to do that kind of stuff myself. I don't want to use my time that way.

"The only place I ever really feel—what? content, I guess—is in an airplane. That's what I want to be doing. Flying. It doesn't make any difference to me where I'm flying to. It could be Cincinnati or Athens or Paris or wherever, I don't care. The name of the game isn't where you're going—it's flying the airplane to get there.

"I think most pilots would agree with me about that. Sometimes there will be a new guy on a crew who gets all enthusiastic and says, 'Hot dog, we're going to Athens. Let's all go out to the Parthenon together.' But the general response among the crew is, 'Screw the Parthenon.' What most of us are interested in is the airplane and the airport, not any of that other stuff out there beyond the airport. I suppose it's sad, but that's how it is.

"The main place a pilot sees when he isn't flying is hotels. Hotels are all right. You check in, and for a few hours you're free of the cares of the world. But that wears off, too—you've probably been to this hotel hundreds of times before, so there's nothing special about being there.

"Sometimes the crews hang out together. They get together for meals and go into town together. I used to do that, but not so much anymore. Generally I'll go for a walk by myself or something like that.

"The thing that makes it worthwhile is the flying.

"But, yes, I agree. There's a price. Pilots cut themselves off from an awful lot. Family, for one. I guess a guy doesn't become a pilot if he's oriented toward family life. It's the wrong kind of life. I've flown with some guys over and over, and I have no idea whether they're married or have children. It's not something most of us talk about much.

"That's why the guys you interviewed said they have regrets. They probably feel guilty about all the time they spent away from their families. They know they cut themselves off from some things and let their families down. I'd bet most pilots feel that way to some extent. *I* do, anyhow."

I knew what my father was saying to me, but I was embarrassed by it. I'd set up the conversation so that we would discuss family life, but then I found I didn't know how to handle the results.

I glanced at my father intermittently while he spoke, but mainly I looked down at my hands or at the floor between us. And I kept quiet. I let him talk until he seemed to be finished, then I changed the subject.

I blamed myself later. Driving home that evening, I berated myself for repeating the old pattern. I knew that I'd chickened out again, shying away again from direct contact.

When I got home, I phoned my father. We talked for nearly an hour, a good talk. And the next time I visited him, we both understood that something basic between us had changed, and we were a little easier.

Now

I LOST MY FREE-FLIGHT PRIVILEGES ON TWA WHEN I TURNED TWENTY-ONE AND COULD NO LONGER SHARE MY FATHER'S EMPLOYEE BENEFITS. Shortly after my birthday, I took the small plastic TWA pass card from my wallet and snipped it in half with a pair of scissors.

After that I didn't board an airplane again for more than a decade, and as far as I was aware that was fine by me. I wasn't aware of retaining any particular interest in aviation. I continued following the space program, watching most of the moon landings on TV, but otherwise I put flight out of my mind. It was a childhood fascination that I'd turned away from before leaving childhood.

I didn't begin flying regularly again until the early 1980s. I had become a writer on the staff of a national magazine, and after I'd advanced far enough to receive some of the choicer assignments, I began traveling around the country to conduct interviews for upcoming stories. I drove to some of these interviews, but whenever the destination was more than a hundred miles distant, our travel department made airline bookings for me.

I was an ordinary business traveler. I boarded each flight with a newspaper in one hand and a briefcase in the other, and I spent most of the time between takeoff and landing with my head down, reading. Initially, I was curious about the planes that had come into service since I'd last flown, especially the jumbo jets. Most of my cross-continent flights were aboard jumbos, either 747s or DC-10s. These were gargantuan machines, with ten-abreast, double-aisle cabins that resembled auditoriums. Other than their size, though, the jumbos didn't seem much different from the smaller jets that I remembered. The sensation of flying in them was familiar. They cruised at about the same altitude, making about the same speed. So before long, I quit paying much attention. I boarded without caring what sort of plane I would be riding that day, and I took whatever seat chance assigned me. A window seat was fine; an aisle seat was okay too. Just give me enough room to open my paper.

A few flights were different, though. If I was scheduled to conduct an interview in a rural community, getting there meant riding part of the distance in a full-scale airliner, then completing the journey in a commuter plane—a cramped miniliner that had seats for only a dozen or so passengers. Commuter planes were uncomfortable and I'd read that their safety record was spotty, but I didn't have much choice about accepting bookings in them. Passenger trains and interstate bus services had all but vanished; the only ways to reach many outlying areas were to drive or take a chance on a commuter airline. Driving took too long, usually—I was working against deadlines. So from time to time I found myself flying over sparsely populated countrysides in odd little planes with names like Twin Otter and Navaho Chieftan. They bounced and rattled, creating the impression that at any moment they might give up and return precipitously to the ground. And yet, after one or two such rides, I admitted to myself that I enjoyed them. The Otters and Chieftans were propeller planes with unpressurized cabins, which meant they flew low. And because they were so small, every seat was near a window. I gazed down at the same toylike scenery that I'd watched from the windows of propeller planes in the '50s. I remembered the pleasure I'd taken from flight then, and I began to experience that pleasure again, compounded now with nostalgia.

Some of the commuter planes had a special virtue. The smallest ones of all were open-plan: There was no partition separating the cockpit from the passenger cabin. If you sat in the first row of passenger seats, you were directly behind the pilots, able to look over their shoulders at the instrument panel and the windshield. I started doing that. It reminded me of the times I'd been invited into cockpits during Connie flights. Leaning forward, I could see the readings on the instruments and observe how they changed as the pilots manipulated the controls. None of it made real sense to me. I'd forgotten what some of the instruments were for, and some of the new gadgets were wholly unfamiliar to me. But I enjoyed trying to puzzle things out. And when I got confused by what the pilots were doing, I could always raise my eyes to peer through the windshield.

I started rearranging my trips to include commuter flights even when it wasn't strictly necessary. I eliminated distance as a criterion: No matter how far or near my destination might be, if I had a choice between renting a car and buying a commuter airline ticket, I bought the ticket. Then I made sure I got to the airport early and I positioned myself at the head of the line of passengers, set to grab one of the front-row seats. To pass the time while waiting to board, I read aviation magazines that I picked up at the airport news counter. I concentrated on the articles written for student pilots: explanations of cockpit procedures, basic piloting know-how. When the agent let us out to the plane and I buckled myself into my seat, I used the articles to help me follow the crew's actions. I made a game of it. Throughout each flight, I watched what the pilots were up to and tried to anticipate what they might do next. I told myself it was good entertainment.

But it was also a mistake. By turning myself into an unofficial, secondhand student pilot, I had set myself up for the fit of melancholy I underwent one evening when, sitting at home, I saw the newspaper headline "Pilot Shortage Hits Airlines." I'd been having fun on the commuter flights, treating aviation as a spectator sport. But now I felt a surge of longing, and self-recrimination, and confusion. I was far too old to switch careers—I was nearly forty, a decade or more older than the pilots I'd been watching. But I wanted to make the switch. At least momentarily, I was convinced that the only thing I'd ever really wanted was to become a pilot.

It was a difficult evening. I told myself I was better off as I was, writing for a magazine. I enjoyed that work and the life I'd made. Anyway, I wasn't cut out to be a pilot. My temperament wasn't right for it. I'd always known that. I still knew it. This attack of the blues didn't change the facts. Okay, so I was feeling sorry for myself. My boyhood dreams would remain unfulfilled. But what else did I expect? Time had passed. It didn't mean anything.

I indulged myself with bourbon and emotion, and went to bed, and during the following days my spirits recovered. But the strength of the remorse I'd felt made me realize that I had unfinished business to deal with. I needed to come to terms with my fixation on piloting. I needed to sort my fantasies about piloting from the reality, whatever that might prove to be, and try to understand what both the fantasies and the reality meant to me. I needed to accept the boy I'd been and the man I'd become.

There was an irony about my timing, I knew. I had renewed my interest in piloting just when many airline pilots were becoming intensely unhappy with their jobs. The aviation magazines I read carried frequent reports about discontent among pilots. Senior captains were taking early retirement, the magazines said, and some of the younger captains and copilots were quitting outright, choosing different lines of work.

Most of the articles ascribed the pilots' unhappiness to the effects of airline deregulation. In 1978, the federal government reduced its supervision of the airlines, intending to let market forces operate more freely. The impact on pilots was severe. Some lost their jobs when their airlines, weakened by fare wars, went bankrupt or were bought out by rival lines. Other pilots kept they jobs but were subjected to harsh austerity measures. Wages were cut, in most cases deeply. Workloads increased. Job security was undermined as airline managements adopted aggressive antiunion tactics. Working conditions deteriorated as the airlines trimmed their operating budgets.

I knew these things, in general terms, when I began meeting with pilots. It was convenient information, offering me easy solace. If piloting had gotten so bad, I was lucky to have avoided it. And, in fact, several pilots said as much to me. They confirmed what I had read; they were angry and dispirited about their profession as it had become; they said I was well out of it. A couple of them even seemed to envy me: They said being a writer sounded swell; they asked how I'd gotten such interesting work. So I was consoled, a little. But only a little. I found myself taking the pilots' losses as, by extension, my own. I didn't feel lucky to be out of it; I felt deprived. The aviation era I'd dreamed about seemed to have ended, and I'd missed it.

Media coverage of tumult on the airlines has spread during the last three years from specialized aviation magazines to general-audience publications. In April 1987, the *Wall Street Journal* ran an article headlined

BUMPY RIDE: PILOTS FEEL THE STRESS
OF TURMOIL IN AIRLINE INDUSTRY

In March of the same year, the Associated Press put out a story that appeared in my local newspaper under the headline

SERVICE COMPLAINTS,
TAKEOVERS, CONTINUE
TO DOG U.S. AIRLINES

Comparable stories have shown up in *Time,* the *New York Times, Newsweek.* One of the most revealing stories was released by the

Knight-Ridder Syndicate in July of 1986. A friend of mine who lives in Connecticut clipped it from the Hartford newspaper and it mailed to me. The headline:

RETIRING, BUT NOT SHY:
PILOT QUITS ON RUNWAY

The story told of the frustrations a DC-9 captain had experienced the previous day while trying to take off from Hartfield International Airport in Atlanta. One crew member was late getting to the airport, causing a short initial delay. Then there was a problem getting the plane fueled—not enough jet fuel was available at the airport. That was delay number two. Delay three came when a door in the galley jammed, requiring some impromptu repair work. And then came delay four: After he had, at last, begun taxiing out to the runway, the captain got word from the control tower that he would have to wait an additional twenty minutes before receiving takeoff clearance. Several other planes were lined up ahead of his at the head of the runway.

The captain had undoubtedly endured many equivalent delays recently—they had become commonplace in the turmoil spawned by deregulation. Until now, hc had taken such things in stride. But somehow on this particular day, this particular sequence of foul-ups was more than he could bear. He was fifty-nine years old, just one year short of retirement, and suddenly the prospect of that year became intolerable to him. He worked for an airline that was racked with labor-management strife, an airline that had incurred millions of dollars in government-imposed fines for safety violations. Every day seemed to bring more bad news, more reasons for dissatisfaction.

Something snapped. The captain picked up his microphone and made a P.A. announcement. "I'm fed up with it," he told the passengers. "I'm sick and tired of the delays, tired of the waiting. I'm hanging it up. You can have it." Then he taxied back to the terminal and got off. He quit.

I carried this story with me when visiting pilots—I would produce the clipping during interviews and ask for opinions. Most pilots told me they sympathized with the DC-9 captain. They didn't endorse his behavior, but they said they knew how he felt—and, often, they proceeded from there to expound their own grievances. Sometimes these seemed as petty as the problems in the news story. Several pilots got exercised about cabin service, for instance: They said the food served onboard now is rubbery; and the utensils are plastic, cheap-looking, not like the real silverware used previously; and the passengers are herded aboard like cattle; and the cabin decor is too chintzy; and the seats are too narrow and stiff.

The pettiness of the grievances was startling, but I thought it reflected the depth of the pilots' discontent. The small irritants that pilots cited were surface indications of larger problems that were the real cause of the discontent. From time to time, some pilots described these larger problems to me. One 747 captain, for instance, picked up a theme that had become prominent in the media: the effects of deregulation on air safety. "If you charted out how safety has gone," he said, "it would look like this." He swung his hand up through a long, gradual climb, and then abruptly pulled it downward. "It's still better than it used to be, twenty, thirty years ago. But it's come down from the high point.

"The airlines are scrimping in too many ways. They've got their eye on the bottom line, which is important, granted. But that's not how to keep safety where it ought to be. I see the signs all around. In our fleet, we used to be scrupulous about things like making sure all our 747s had the same cockpit layout. That's basic common sense. If there's a problem in flight, you don't want the pilot groping around for some switch that's in a different place than he expects. But we've loosened up about that now. We've got some planes with nonstandard layouts, and we haven't changed them because it would cost too much. For every flight, I have to sit down and look over the instruments to see what kind of layout I've got this time. The differences aren't huge, but they could make a big difference in an emergency. One of these days, somebody's going to get confused and throw the wrong switches, and I hate to think what will happen then.

"The company scrimps on fuel, too. It used to be that the dispatcher would suggest a certain amount of fuel to the captain, and then the captain could ask for additional fuel on top of that. We called it 'pocket fuel.' But we don't operate like that now. There's a computer that tells you how much fuel to take for each flight, and that's it. You can request more, but you'd have to justify it up and down, and it's not worth the fight you'd get into. So you take what you're assigned. But the trouble is, the computer cuts it awfully close. If you run into headwinds, you might not have the reserves you need. I know for a fact that some planes have landed with their tanks damn near dry. That's cutting it 'way too close. 'Way too close."

Another 747 captain made similar comments. I had asked him whether he thought flying was actually getting more dangerous or whether today's pilots might simply have grown more sensitive to the issue because the standards for air safety had risen so high. I repeated some of the tales I'd heard about pilots who, in earlier days, had accepted risks as a matter of course. From the old-timers' perspective, I said, flying had become wonderfully safe today, hadn't it?

"Could be," the captain answered. "It isn't the Wild West out there anymore. But there are some trends now moving in the wrong direction. The margin of safety is definitely getting smaller.

"Maintenance is the biggest problem. There are planes going out all the time with open items [i.e., broken equipment]. Nobody says it in so many words, but it's understood that we're supposed to accept planes that a few years ago we would have refused to fly. We're supposed to keep them going until night when theoretically the mechanics will get to them.

"A captain still has the right to turn a plane down, and if it is really unsafe, no one will criticize him. But usually the situation isn't that black-and-white. The plane might have more open items than he'd want, but it might still be technically legal, so where is he supposed to draw the line? He knows that he'll get called on the carpet if he demands repairs when it isn't absolutely, technically necessary. The airline expects him to keep his mouth shut and take the airplane.

"I'll speak for myself. I've taken planes that were questionable, and I'll probably do it again. If one of the autopilots is out but the other one is okay and the weather looks all right, I would take the plane. Or if an oil temperature gauge is broken, I'll think about it, and if I see I've got other instruments [operating] that let me infer whether the oil is getting too hot, I'll say, 'All right, let's go.'

"Pilots always have to calculate the odds. There's always some danger. But what I'm saying is, we calculate them differently now than we used to."

In several instances, the conversations I had with pilots about the 1980s followed a distinct pattern. I asked the pilots to discuss the consequences of deregulation; they responded with a list of complaints, culminating in their concerns about safety; and then they began talking about air piracy. There are no causal links between deregulation and air piracy—terrorists have been bombing and hijacking planes since long before Congress passed the Airline Deregulation Act. But I often found that pilots lumped together these apparently unrelated subjects, seeing them as equally compelling indicators of things gone wrong.

The pilots said the threat of terrorism pervades airline operations today. The elaborate security measures taken at all airports—sealing off departure areas, channeling passengers through metal detectors, probing luggage with X-rays—are a constant reminder of the threat, producing an atmosphere of unremitting tension. They said crews didn't dwell on it—they knew the chance of actually being attacked by terrorists was remote—but still the threat hung continually over the crews, subtly distorting their work routines and souring their dispositions. The pilots spoke angrily. Terrorists are criminally insane, they said. There is no conceivable justification for the violence terrorists commit. "Don't talk to me about the Arabs' problems," one captain said to me. "If the Palestinians want a homeland, fine. But what in hell does that have to do with attacking my passengers?"

Some pilots seemed nearly as angry about the measures intended to stop terrorism as they were about terrorism itself. They complained about the requirement for crew members to remain inside the cockpit with the door locked while a plane is in flight. They complained about the need for pilots to pass through a security screening before entering a plane. ("They used to let us step past the metal detectors," a copilot said, "but now they want us to go through like everybody else. What the hell? Do they think *we're* going to hijack the plane?") They complained about inadequate security training provided by the airlines and the government. I thought they spoke from a combination of practical concern and offended pride. Terrorists rendered them powerless, seizing control of their planes. Aviation bureaucrats compounded the offense, promulgating rules that diminished the pilots' authority and professional stature without providing effective antiterrorist protection in exchange.

I talked to my father about air piracy and the issues surrounding it. His comments were representative of the remarks I heard from other pilots.

"When hijacking got to be a big deal in the '60s," he said, "I bought myself a pair of handcuffs. I carried them in my flight bag. We weren't supposed to arm ourselves (although I knew pilots who did that, too—they carried guns). But I would be damned if I was just going to roll over for some madman who tried to commandeer my airplane. The least I could do was to have some cuffs that I could clap on him if I got a chance.

"We weren't supposed to fight a hijacker. The idea was to try to humor him or wear him down. If that didn't work, you were just supposed to take him where he demanded to go. The main thing was to avoid bloodshed.

"The airline included some stuff about how to deal with hijackers, in the recurrent training classes we had. If you were patient and wore a hijacker down, you might be able to catch him off guard and restrain him. There were also some procedures about secret radio signals you could send, and special knocks. We were supposed to keep the cockpit door locked at all times and only let somebody in if they used the special knock. But most of that kind of thing was worthless. Any half-grown man could kick in the cockpit door. The locks didn't work half the time anyway. As for tiring the hijacker out, maybe that would work if there was one hijacker against a crew of several guys. But when there's a group of hijackers, and they're organized, they're more likely to tire you out than the other way around.

"The government had advice for us too. Not long ago, the FAA issued a proclamation that all flight crews had to get seven hours of antihijack training. So TWA had to pay everybody a day's pay to go down and watch these damned videotapes the FAA had thrown together. Maybe ten percent of the stuff had some value, but the rest was nonsense. They had two long, boring interviews with domestic hijackers who wanted to go to Cuba, but that's not the problem anymore. The weirdo who wants to go to Cuba because he has an economic problem or something isn't the problem. What we face now are organized terrorists who shoot the hell out of people and roll handgrenades down the aisle. They *want* to kill people, as a matter of policy. They want to make a 'statement.'

"The fact is, if the security screening at the airport fails and you wind up with some of these killers on your plane, there's not much you can do about it. That's the most infuriating part of it. You know Russ's wife was involved in a hijacking." Uli Derickson, the wife of one of my father's friends, was a flight attendant on a TWA 727 that was hijacked to Lebanon in 1985. The plane was held on the ground there for several days, during which time the hijackers beat several passengers and executed one of them, a U.S. Navy sailor.

"That crew couldn't do much of anything," my father continued. "They did their best to keep the hijackers from killing everybody, but they really couldn't control anything that happened.

"The thing that stays with me about that episode is the same thing everybody else remembers: that photograph of Testrake." Captain John Testrake was photographed leaning out of a cockpit window, talking to reporters near the plane. He seemed relaxed; his elbow was propped on the windowsill. But one of the hijackers was visible behind Testrake, pressing a pistol against his temple.

"That's what this insanity boils down to. A madman threatening a pilot with a gun."

I knew my father had never had to contend with hijackers, but I asked him whether he had ever been suspicious that any of his passenger might be planning a hijacking. He said he hadn't. He said pilots hardly ever saw their passengers anymore—the locked-door rule prevented it.

"I've had unruly passengers," he said. "Sometimes when the hostesses couldn't handle some particularly obnoxious character, they've asked me to come back to deal with him. But that's nothing extraordinary.

"The one 'terrorist' episode I got caught in was a bomb hoax. I was coming to New York from San Francisco in a 747 when I got a radio message that a guy had left a note at the TWA ticket office in San Francisco. It said he represented an organization that had put a bomb on my airplane. The bomb was very sophisticated, supposedly, and it was set to go off when I descended through ten thousand feet. But the note also said this organization had people on the ground in the New York area who would deactivate the bomb by radio signal if TWA would pay them the ransom. I think they were asking for a million dollars, something like that.

"Anyway, everybody was taking the note seriously. They had called in the FBI and were getting worked up, trying to deal with this threat. So I reduced power and proceeded as slowly as I could, to give them time to either catch the guy or make the payment, so his buddies could disarm the bomb. I told the flight attendants what was going on, but I told them to keep it to themselves. I made some kind of announcement to the passengers, telling them some story about why we were being delayed. (One of the cardinal rules is to never tell the passengers the truth about a bad situation. They'll just go off the handle, which makes everything that much tougher for the crew.)

"I got over New York and held at twenty-five thousand feet, and meanwhile I was getting messages from TWA and the FBI. The guy who had called was dancing around San Francisco, leaving notes, and they were negotiating with him. But they couldn't pin him down. He would leave a message somewhere, telling them to go to some phone booth or other, and when they got there they'd find another note sending them on to some other place. This had been going on for a couple of hours, and we were starting to get a little tight on fuel. I was going to have to come down to land inside an hour, whether or not they got things squared away with the guy.

"But then I got a message that said the latest they had from the guy was that he wanted TWA to leave a thousand dollars in a phone booth as evidence of good faith. As soon as I heard that, I said, 'This is bullshit.' I knew nobody talks about a thousand dollars when he's holding a 747 for ransom. So I called the company and told them I was coming down and I didn't expect to blow up when I reached ten thousand feet. I told them I would be on the ground in twenty minutes. So I got clearance and we came down.

"The crew was calm and collected. I told them I was sure it was a hoax. I imagine they all held their breath as we came through ten thousand, but in fact nothing happened. There was no bomb. So I made some more excuses to the passengers and we landed normally."

I asked how he had felt while he was holding at twenty-five thousand, before he decided the threat was a hoax. "Oh," he said, "it enlivened my day." But then he caught himself and answered me more seriously. "I never really thought there was a bomb," he said. "It was possible, but I just didn't really believe it. Mostly I was irritated at whoever the hell had made the threat. I was mad at having somebody interfere with my flight like that. It didn't make much difference whether or not he had really put a bomb on the plane. I resented the *possibility,* whether or not he had really done it."

One other topic besides deregulation and terrorism came up frequently when pilots discussed the 1980s: automation. The pace of technological change didn't abate in aviation after jets came on line thirty years ago; it accelerated as computer technology was applied to an ever-increasing number of piloting functions. Although few of the pilots I met said so straight out, this struck me as the most basic cause of the dissatisfaction many of them feel now.

Today's airliners are so thoroughly computerized, they can perform most of their functions automatically. Some can take off, cruise to their destinations, and land without human hands touching the flight controls. Indeed, one airliner currently entering service—the Airbus A320—doesn't have that primary flight control, the yoke. It is equipped with computer keypads and joysticks instead. Pilots use these "input devices" to tell the onboard computers how they want the plane to move. The pilots cannot operate the A320's ailerons and elevators directly—they have to route their requests through the computers. Usually the computers will comply; they will evaluate the pilots' requests, approve them, and move the ailerons and elevators to the necessary positions. But the computers have been programmed to overrule any requests that seem, to their silicon brains, unwise. They won't let the pilots push the plane past its maximum design speed for a given altitude and weight, for example. In this sense the computers, not the pilots, have the final say about how the plane is to be flown.

I'm convinced that deregulation and the threat of air piracy would not bother pilots nearly so much if flying remained as fulfilling as it once was. Pilots would shrug off the inconveniences of flight delays and airport security checks if their work still provided the satisfactions they want from it. But now that computers do more real flying than they do, they experience those satisfactions far less often. During the '80s, scientists employed by the U.S. Air Force have been studying pilots' brainwaves. By attaching electrodes to pilots' scalps, they've recorded the electrical discharges that flicker inside the pilots' brains during flight. The goal of the study has been to develop new aircraft control systems that will be more finely attuned to the capabilities of both pilots and aircraft: in newspeak, to improve the man/machine interface. The scientists have learned that when a pilot operates an airplane, his natural inclination is to rely primarily on his right brain, the cortical hemisphere that controls nonlogical functions such as creativity and intuition. But in a computerized jet airliner, pilots must suppress this inclination. They are required to follow rigorously rational, by-the-book procedures, feeding data into computers and abiding by the computers' judgments. This grates on the pilots, not just because it offends their pride but because it violates the mode of consciousness that comes naturally to them when they fly. Rationality and meticulousness are left-brain functions, more appropriate for technicians or scientists than for pilots. Surprising as it may seem (and it would surprise no one more than some of the pilots I've met), pilots are essentially artists.

I should qualify this. Pilots have always needed to heed their left brains. They've needed to be rational, unemotional—that's what the pilots' code is all about. The subordination of air sense to instrument flight in the 1930s was an admission that our right brains aren't wired properly for the environment of flight: Pilots can't trust their intuitions without at least testing them against the objective measurements of speed, height, and attitude provided by instruments. But prior to the jet age, intuition—what pilots called "feel"—still had a place. When flying slow propeller planes, pilots consulted the instruments with their left brains and they consulted "feel" with their right brains. Flight was a whole-brain activity, in other words, thoroughly engrossing. Not so in jetliners. Jetliner pilots must be guided almost wholly by left-brain logic. They must disregard the unreliable promptings of their right brains, in effect nullifying half of their awareness. This nullification inevitably makes the experience of flight much less fulfilling.

Some researchers hope to find techniques that will enable pilots to use intuition in a new, electronically augmented form. They are experimenting with science-fiction-like helmets for fighter pilots. The helmets, which have opaque visors, enclose the pilots in a totally electronic environment, letting them see nothing but data and computer-drawn images that are beamed directly onto their retinas by tiny projectors inside the helmets. The data and images are intended to have intuitively obvious significance, giving the pilots the information they need to make instantaneous, unpremeditated decisions to bank, turn, fire a weapon, do whatever they must in order to survive in supersonic air combat. The helmets sound intensely disagreeable to me—I can't imagine that flying with your head encased in one could be pleasant—but at least they represent an acknowledgment that right-brain thought is important to pilots.

For now, there are no plans to equip airline pilots with sci-fi-like helmets. Probably there never will be. Airline pilots rarely have to jerk their aircraft through harsh split-second maneuvers, therefore little allowance is likely to be made for their intuitions. They're supposed to have time to act with deliberation. Actually, the trend on the airlines is to stress left-brain functions more and more completely. Airline pilots are changing from airmen to airborne computer operators. Their main tasks now are to observe how the computers are functioning and to keep themselves ready for action should the unthinkable happen and the computers break down. A rueful cartoon that has circulated among airline pilots for several years sums up the current state of their occupation: It shows an ordinary airliner cockpit with two seats at the front. But the seats are empty. The pilots are standing inside a glass compartment built into the side wall of the cockpit. A sign above the compartment reads, "In case of emergency, break glass." The cartoon first appeared twenty years or so ago. It gains added poignancy today from the fact that if the computers failed on one of the newest, most automated airliners, breaking the glass would do no good. The plane would be uncontrollable without its computer systems intact.

Charles Lindbergh seems to have foreseen the downturn in pilots' fortunes. He soured on aviation during the late 1950s, at about the time when the first jetliners were being built. "Flying is getting to be too automatic, too push-button," he is reported to have said then. Later, during the 1960s, he opposed the development of supersonic transports (SSTs). He feared that SSTs would pollute the upper atmosphere, and he argued that their sonic booms would prove harmful both to human beings and to wildlife. Most Americans were surprised to learn of his views—they still thought of him as the youthful airman who, after his flight to Paris, had toured the U.S. promoting the benefits of aviation. But that was long ago. In the years since, he had grown disillusioned with technology, believing that it degraded the quality of life. He spent much of his time during his final years studying ecology and the destructive effects technology has had on the earth's ecosystem. In an article he wrote for *Reader's Digest* during the debate over production of an American SST, he asked, "Is civilization progress? The challenge, I think, is clear; and as clearly the final answer will be given not by our amassment of knowledge, or by the discoveries of our science, or by the speed of our aircraft, but by the effect our civilized activities as a whole have upon the quality of our planet's life—the life of plants and animals as well as that of men."

Congress scrapped plans for an SST. Today, however, several U.S. corporations are working toward the development of hypersonic transports (HSTs), planes that will be able to hit speeds as great as eighteen thousand miles an hour—fast enough to enter earth orbit. I wonder whether, if Lindbergh had lived to see such planes built, he would have wanted to ride in one. Maybe curiosity would have gotten the better of him—he might not have been able to resist the chance to see the blue-green globe spinning a hundred miles below. But no doubt he would have opposed construction of the planes, and no doubt he would have considered HST pilots a pitiable bunch. HSTs will be guided by artificial intelligence: Their computers will be designed to emulate human (left-brain) thought processes, but to do so with superhuman speed and accuracy. For the most part, HSTs will be robot craft, making their own decisions and following their own flight plans. The pilots who ride HSTs will be essentially passive. They will scarcely *be* pilots, as Lindbergh understood the term. They will be astronauts, not aviators: Like the crews of the space shuttle, they will have little to do when the engines light up except sit tight and hope.

I knew a guy in college—I'll call him Gary—whose dorm room resembled an Air Force recruiting office. Large posters of jet fighters were taped to the walls, and stacks of *Aviation Week* magazines covered his desk. A model of a KC-135 aerial tanker hung from a string from the ceiling. We weren't close friends. He was gung ho about all matters pertaining to aviation while I pretended to be indifferent. But we got along fairly well. Like me, he was a pilot's son.

I decided to look him up last year. I knew he'd joined the Air Force after college and then taken an airline job. I thought finding him again would let me learn about the kind of life I might have led if I'd become a pilot. It would be like meeting the self I might have been.

I traced him to a Chicago suburb a few miles from O'Hare Airport, the airfield where most of his flights originate. When I phoned him, he said sure, he'd be glad to get together with me. He would check his schedule, and the next time he had a flight to a city near my home, he would give me a call.

Several weeks passed. I phoned him twice during that period to maintain contact, and he sounded happy to hear from me each time. But I couldn't pin him down on a time and place to meet.

I'd about given up on him when, after nearly two months of this wary jousting, he called one afternoon to say he would have a layover in Baltimore on the following Tuesday. He gave me the name of a restaurant near the hotel where he would be staying. He suggested that we get together at the restaurant 7 p.m. Tuesday.

He was waiting in the restaurant's foyer when I arrived. He looked much as he had in college—tall, dark-haired, trim. The only evident changes were the gray patches at his temples and the network of creases around his eyes. He shook my hand, then steered me into the dining area.

For the first hour, our conversation rambled. He ducked most of my questions, replying evasively or declining to make any reply. He acted like he was sorry he'd agreed to the interview. Halfway through dinner, though, he paused, and a look of embarrassment came over his face.

"Listen," he said, "can we make an arrangement?"

He asked me to withhold his name and the identity of the airline he works for. When I agreed, he relaxed visibly. So we began again, and he filled me in on his career.

"I thought getting an airline job was like hitting the jackpot," he said, "I was a hundred percent delighted. It was what I always wanted.

"Some of the guys in the Air Force looked down on the airlines. They said it was like driving a truck compared to the hot flying they could do. But a lot of them looked forward to going with an airline all the same. Their idea was to get their jollies in the Air Force, then settle down.

"I didn't see it like that. I was big on the Air Force, but I was bigger on the airlines. That's where I was headed from the word 'Go.' But sometimes I'm sorry I got out of the Air Force, now. If I had it to do again, I just might stay in.

"The job hasn't turned out like I expected. Sometimes my father and I compare notes, and he can't believe some of the things I tell him about how things are now. He was completely into his job—it was more like he was a partner than an employee. But it's not like that for pilots now. We don't identify with [the airlines] like that.

"Probably I expected too much. I would never have believed there would be *morale* problems. That's probably the biggest letdown. Hell, pilots get paid to fly airplanes! I mean, think of that—somebody is willing to pay us to *fly.* That's fairly damned amazing. But morale has gone through the floor. I don't see guys arriving at the airport all eager to go. They drag in to work."

He ran his hand over his face. "The thing is," he continued, "I'm convinced the airlines *try* to make us dissatisfied. It's intentional. They take the line that there's no special skill involved in our jobs, like we're workers in a factory, doing a job anybody could do.

"It's warfare between management and us. They want to cut us down any way they can." He ticked off points on his fingers. "Salary. Benefits. Hours. Prestige. Work rules. They don't want us thinking we're the airline. *They're* the airline. They make that totally plain. Any way they can drive the point home, they do it.

"Remember how the airlines used to make a big deal out of telling who the crew was on every flight? The hostesses announced the captain's name, the copilot's name, everybody's name. Sometimes the airline had a mimeographed sheet for the passengers with all the crew's names on it, or they would hang a notice in the cabin saying, 'This flight commanded by Captain Blank,' whatever the guy's name was."

I told him notices like that used to be posted at the foot of the boarding stairs for TWA flights. He nodded.

"No airline would dream of doing stuff like that today," he said. "The hostesses might say who the captain is, but don't count on it. The airlines want the passengers to think the front of the cabin is the front of the plane. They don't want them to think there's a cockpit up there with human beings in it."

Gary was interrupted by a waiter who came to remove our plates. When the waiter had gone, I asked Gary what he'd meant about work rules. How did his airline use them to cut pilots down?

"Every time I go in to pick up my mail," he answered, "I have to brace myself. I know there's probably going to be another form letter in there that will make my hair stand up on the back of my neck. You wouldn't believe some of the things the company sends us.

"They just came out with something they call 'Pilot Rules of Conduct.' Section one, section two, section three, with twenty or thirty pages in each section, all of them starting with words like 'Not adhering to this regulation is punishable up to and including discharge from employment.' And they are very serious about it. It includes things like how you have to act in public, and how you can't make less than complimentary statements about the company or the members of management . . . . all kinds of nonsense like that."

I asked whether our present conversation was against the rules.

"Of course," Gary said.

"The company wants to drive us out. If they can get rid of the guys who still make fairly decent salaries, they can hire replacements at a lot lower pay. That's their bottom line."

Gary began playing with his coffee cup, rotating it on its saucer. He squinted at the cup as he spoke, as if he had become absorbed in its circular movements.

"It creates one hell of an atmosphere, I'll tell you," he said.

"They do whatever they can to catch us violating some chicken-shit regulation. If they can get anything at all on one of us, it's grounds for what they call 'progressive discipline,' which is nothing but a paper audit trail that sets you up so they can fire you. It gives them the ammunition they would need. It's goddamned lousy. The result is, we spend half our time covering our asses. You don't try to do a great job, you try to stay out of trouble. Don't let the bastards catch you."

He grew quiet for a minute. He kept rotating the cup, turning it a few revolutions to the right, then a few revolutions back to the left.

"I'm sorry," he said finally, looking at me. "I wanted to make sure I wouldn't be too negative, but I'm not doing very well at it.

"I've got a good job. Some poor bastard who works on an assembly line isn't going to feel sympathy for my problems, and I can understand that. I'd rather be doing what I'm doing than what he's doing. But see, the company knows that. They know that guys like me want to keep flying. It's the only thing I'm trained to do, the only thing I'm good at in a job sense. What other kind of job could I get? I'm boxed in. So the airline knows they can push us pretty hard. Either we'll fall in line or they can force us out and get somebody else who's more manageable."

I said it seemed to me that, despite everything, he still loved flying. He wouldn't be so angry otherwise. I quoted something he'd said: "Hell, pilots get paid to fly airplanes!"

"Absolutely," he said. "When I get into the cockpit, things are okay. I still get charged up when we're at the head of the runway and getting ready to roll. That hasn't changed.

"But see," he added, "almost everything else *has* changed. With all the electronics we have now, flying is a different proposition from what it was.

"I'll tell you how paranoid I get sometimes. Sometimes I think the real reason for the 'glass cockpit' [i.e., computerized flight controls] is exactly because the airlines want to downgrade pilots. If they can get rid of us, they can hire a very different kind of individual as our replacements. I'm not even sure that they'll look for guys with flying skills. They would love it if they could automate the planes to the extent that they wouldn't need pilots, just guys to mind the computers. That would be the ideal solution, from their point of view."

Gary stopped, then laughed at himself. "I get carried away," he said.

Abruptly, he pushed his chair back from the table and stood up. Seeing that he was preparing to leave, I rose too. We put some money on the table and walked together out of the restaurant.

We stood talking for a few minutes more on the sidewalk out front. "When I meet people anymore," Gary said, "I don't tell them I'm a pilot. I don't want to hear their complaints about how rotten the service has gotten, and I don't want to go into my spiel about *my* complaints. I don't want the hassle. It's bad enough dealing with that stuff when I'm at work. I don't want to do it when I'm off. I get sick of talking about it."

I took the hint. We exchanged information about some mutual friends from college, then we shook hands and separated. I unlocked my car and got in while he walked up the street toward his hotel. As I pulled out from the curb, I saw the self I might have been check his wristwatch and then step through the hotel's entrance.

First Flights

MY FATHER STILL LOVES TO FLY. When he reached sixty, the
mandatory retirement age for captains, he refused to quit. He
took a demotion to the rank of flight engineer instead. A loophole
in the retirement rules lets engineers continue flying beyond age sixty.

"I didn't really want to be an engineer," he said to me one morning
last winter. We were driving in his car to an airport on eastern Long
Island. "I'd much rather still be a captain. But if becoming an engineer
was the only way I could keep flying, I would take it. I wasn't ready
to quit yet.

"An engineer doesn't control the plane," he added. "But at least I'm
still in the cockpit. *Any* kind of flying is better than *no* flying."

I told him about the pilots I'd met who were unhappy with their jobs
now. I repeated the things Gary had said to me.

"I know," my father said. "I agree. Things are a mess. One of these
days I'll get fed up and then I'll be ready to retire. But not yet.

"I knew a captain who retired, and he missed the job so much, he
went along on a lot of flights as a passenger, and he would just kind
of hang around the airports where the flights made stops. It was kind

of pathetic. But I'm afraid that's how I would feel—I would miss it too much."

We kept checking the sky as we drove. There was a light overcast that morning, thin layers of pale gray vapor moving lazily inland from the ocean.

I asked my father about private aviation. After his reassignment to flight engineer, he had developed a new hobby: He rented and flew small private planes on his free days between airline flights. I asked if the hobby didn't give him enough flying. At least in a private plane, he was still captain. He could control the machine, fly it as he pleased.

"They're not the same," he said. "On the airline, we cruise along for hours, going somewhere thousands of miles away. In small planes, I usually stay less than a mile from the airport. Mainly, I shoot landings. I enjoy it. But it's not a substitute."

While he spoke, I paged through a manual for the Piper Tomahawk, my father's favorite type of private plane. Then I checked the sky again. I was nervous. If the overcast didn't burn off, we wouldn't be able to fly today. We planned to rent a Tomahawk and take it up. For the first time in our lives, we would make a flight together sitting side by side in the same cockpit. If the weather cleared.

My father had proposed the flight the night before. We'd been sitting in his study, talking about random subjects, when he said that if I liked, he would take me up the next morning in a Tomahawk. "Sure," I said (or words to that effect), trying to be nonchalant. He described the plane to me, then he pulled the manual from a shelf above his desk. We went through the manual page by page—a quick bit of ground school. Then, after we'd agreed to start for the airport at six a.m., I'd gone to bed in the guest room next to his den.

I hadn't been able to sleep. My imagination and memory had been too active. We should have made this flight years ago, when I was a teenager. My father should have offered to teach me to fly, or I should have asked him to. But neither of us had done his part. Now the flight wouldn't have anything like the same significance it might have had then. It wouldn't be my first step toward repeating the choices he had made for his own life, the good ones and the poor ones.

But I was eager for the flight. My father hadn't needed to explain why he proposed it. We both knew that making such a flight was important for us, not because this was the right stage in our lives to do it, but because we had missed the right stage. We hadn't flown together when we should have, as man and boy. But perhaps we could make amends now by flying together as friends.

Lying in bed, I'd visualized the flight. We would be flying just a few hundred feet from the ground. I pictured the views we would see, the suburban landscape swaying below us as air currents jostled the plane. I wondered what the sensations would be and how I would react. I thought the ride would give me my truest experience of flight yet. I'd never flown in a single-engine plane. According to the manual, the Tomahawk's fuselage measured just twenty-two feet from nose to tail. The cabin was smaller than the interior of a subcompact car. The thin cabin walls and curved plexiglass windows would form only a scant barrier between ourselves and the rushing air outside.

I especially imagined our first takeoff. It ran through my head repeatedly, like a film clip. We would taxi onto the runway and park for a moment to run up the engine. Then my father would release the brakes and the surface of the runway would slide quickly under us. The plane would jounce a little as it accelerated. The engine would make a high, thin clattering sound. When my father pulled the yoke inward, the plane's nose would swing up and the horizon would drop away until we saw nothing through the windshield but the transparent disk of the spinning propeller and, beyond it, the sky.

I had spoken to many pilots about their own first flights. I'd wanted to know how the pilots became pilots: what attracted them to flying in the first place, and what their initial experiences of flight were. Generally, they seemed to enjoy remembering. Whether they still flew

or had retired—whether they groused about the current state of aviation or professed to accept it—most of the pilots I questioned lit up
when they recalled their days as student fliers. Their responses made
me think that most of them were like my father and my old friend Gary
in retaining, fundamentally unchanged, their original enthusiasm for
flight.

Joe Tate, a retired Pan Am captain, told me how he took up flying
as a boy in Nebraska in the 1930s. He loved speed, he said. He got
himself a car when he was just a teenager, and he liked to push it to
its limits, whipping up dust on the flat prairie roads. And he yearned
after sleeker, faster cars, and after vehicles that could outpace even
the fastest racers: machines that went so blazingly fast, they actually
shot into the sky.

He said that's why he was willing to give his money to a hard-luck
barnstormer who came to town one day. The barnstormer, who went
by the nickname "Slim," drifted down into Nebraska after losing his
airplane in a poker game in South Dakota. Scouting for opportunities
to pick up some cash, he arrived in Joe's hometown and announced that
he was setting up a flying club. Terms: Any boy could join the club for
twenty-five dollars; if enough boys joined, Slim would use their membership fees to buy back his plane; thereafter the boys would be
entitled to pay an additional three dollars per hour for flying lessons.

Numerous boys—including Joe—went for this dubious proposition.
Slim left town with their membership money in his pocket. But, true
to his word, he returned a few days later at the controls of his plane,
and the club convened.

Joe said the first lesson he took from Slim was a thrill. Slim was a
good guy, really; he didn't try to scare the boys or push them too hard.
He flew with reasonable caution, letting the boys experience the excitement inherent in powered flight—a breathtaking dash across a
grass field, then the surging climb above the town, seeing the plane's
shadow rush along the streets and housetops, watching the earth dip
and twist as the plane banked. Joe was hooked after just one ride. He
wasn't sure how he would scrape together enough three-dollar pay-

ments for a complete course of instruction, but he made up his mind to try. If Slim would keep selling lessons, Joe would keep buying.

That was the catch, though: Slim didn't keep selling. Slim seemed to mean well, but he was unreliable. He had a hardscrabble approach to life, hand to mouth. He was constantly in debt. He tried several expedients to supplement the meager income he made from the club. He challenged the local bloods to evenings of five-card stud—but his poker luck didn't hold much better in Nebraska than it had in South Dakota. He tried coyote hunting, too. Taking a rifle up with him in his plane, he would fly out over the hills, searching for the varmints. When he spotted one, he would swoop low, push the plane's door open with his foot, and fire. If he got a hit, he would land and retrieve the carcass. But the bounty on coyotes was paltry, scarcely enough to offset the wear and tear his hunting techniques put on the plane. So his debts kept mounting.

Eventually, his creditors caught up with him and confiscated the only valuable piece of property he owned, his airplane. That was the end of the club. Slim left town, penniless again, and Joe's education as a pilot was suspended.

The timing could scarcely have been harder on Joe. He had learned the rudiments of piloting, and he was committed. He wanted to go the rest of the way and earn his pilot's license. He wanted to fly for a living. But just when he was ready to start taking more advanced flying lessons, he got left in the lurch. Slim, the only flight instructor in the region, was gone.

Joe brooded about his dilemma for a while, then decided on desperate measures. He traded his car for an inexpensive, homebuilt airplane. It wasn't much of a plane—a fragile construction of wood, canvas, and piano wire, powered by a Model A Ford engine. It was no aeronautical masterpiece, but it had one great potential virtue. If he owned it, Joe could continue flying. Therefore Joe arranged to own it. He kept the plane at the town's small airfield. He hitchhiked to the field whenever he could to take his plane aloft, trying to teach himself a little more about piloting with each tentative flight.

Joe said he kept that plane until one day a troupe of professional stunt fliers came to town and staged an air show. They zipped around above the airfield, snapping off fancy aerobatic maneuvers in fancy factory-built planes. They excited Joe so much that, after they'd landed, he rolled out his own plane, intending to make a flight of his own. But he couldn't get his engine to start. He spun the prop, repeatedly, but the engine wouldn't catch. And as he stood there in the discouraging silence, he heard one member of the troupe say to another member, "I wouldn't ride in that plane for a million dollars."

Hearing that comment bothered Joe. He knew his plane wasn't perfect, but he hadn't thought there was anything downright wrong with it. But when he heard a bold aerobat imply that he'd be afraid to fly in it, he thought again. So Joe sold his plane and applied the proceeds toward the purchase of a newer, sturdier flying machine, one that had been built by professionals. And when he took possession of this plane, he beefed up his private pilot-training program. He got himself a flight instruction manual and set about mastering its lessons. He practiced all the maneuvers shown in the manual—crosswind take-offs, spin recoveries, lazy eights—until he had advanced about as far as he could on his own. His flying still needed polish, he knew. He wished there was an instructor around who could answer a few questions for him and give him a few final pointers. There wasn't, though. He would have to go for a pilot's license on the strength of his self-instruction.

But then he had a stroke of good fortune. Slim drifted back into town. Slim hadn't changed much. He was still living hand to mouth, still searching for the main chance. Joe hired him to administer the final lessons he wanted, then he went out and got his license.

We continued driving east, under a sky that remained low and gray. We switched on the car radio, and while we scanned the dial for a weather forecast, I asked my father what he remembered about his first flights.

He said he took a couple of flying lessons when he was a kid, but they didn't amount to much. "A guy at the Kansas City airport took people up for a couple of bucks a ride," he said, "and I went up with him twice, mainly as an adventure. I didn't really learn much. They were more joyrides than lessons. I didn't get any real training until I got into the Army."

I asked him to tell me about that, then. I asked if he had he enjoyed the Army's version of flight training as soon as he started with it. I asked if he could tell right away that he had an aptitude for flying.

"I suppose I showed some kind of aptitude fairly soon," he said. "I must have, or the Army would have washed me out. People don't stay with flying unless they have a basic talent for it—the rebuffs are too immediate. I know that in primary training, the washout rate was fifty percent or more. Half of the guys found out pretty soon that flying wasn't for them, and the rest of us found out pretty soon that we would probably do okay."

I asked what personal qualities accounted for the difference between the guys who lasted and the guys who washed out.

"I don't know," he said. "I suppose some people just feel comfortable in an airplane and some people don't. Maybe it's as simple as that. If you don't *trust* the plane, you'll never learn to fly it well.

"I know I wasn't entirely comfortable on my first few flights. I didn't really have faith that the air could hold this big, heavy machine up. I distinctly remember having the impression that I was suspended inside this three-dimensional space, you know, and it seemed pretty uncertain—I couldn't see that anything was supporting us.

"But before long, I accepted the fact— the demonstrated fact—that the air really has a great deal of substance and can support you quite well. And once I accepted that, I was perfectly comfortable in an airplane. Actually, today I tend to think of the air as a solid. I don't have any doubts about safety when I'm flying. I always feel that everything is completely under control."

The forecast, when it came, wasn't encouraging: Overcast, possible showers. "But that's for the city," my father said. "It doesn't look that bad out here. It'll clear."

We pulled into the parking lot of a small shopping center. My father got out of the car and went into a delicatessen to buy a couple of containers of coffee. When he returned to the car, he offered a clarification on the matter of control.

"Come to think of it," he said, "the only time I felt out of control in an airplane was during my Army training, and that was because one time we literally *were* out of control. I went up with my instructor one day, and he was going to put me through some of the normal routine, which included recovering from spins. So we went up to a good altitude to get started, and then he said, 'Okay, give me a three-turn spin to the left and then recover lined up with the road below us.'

"Normally that wouldn't have been a big deal. They wanted us to know how to recover from spins, and I had practiced it before this. So I pulled the nose up, pulled the power off, and when I could feel that the plane was about to stall, I kicked the rudder so that we flipped over and started to spin to the left.

"I let it go around two-and-a-half times and then started a standard recovery. What you do—you're pointing nose down toward the ground and going around wing over wing, so you push the rudder the opposite way to stop the spin, and push the stick forward to break out of the stall, and then you level out. So that's what I tried to do. But instead of flopping around loose like it should have, the stick was tight—there was a lot of pressure on it. So when I tried to push the stick forward, it wouldn't budge, and instead of pulling out of the spin, the plane flipped over onto its right side and began spinning in that direction.

"I couldn't understand. I had failed a spin recovery, although I was sure I had done everything right. But we were still up plenty high, so I let the plane make one turn to the right, then I tried another recovery. And I failed this one, too! The damned plane flipped over again and spun to the left again.

"I had never flown this badly. I absolutely couldn't understand it.

"Also, by this time, I started to get a little concerned about our altitude. I wasn't scared yet, but we had spun five times by now, and we were starting to get lower than was absolutely desirable.

"So the instructor said, 'Okay, I've got it,' and I let go of the controls and sat back feeling totally dejected.

"Then the instructor started a recovery, but the plane flipped over like it had for me, and it kept spinning. He tried again, and it did it again!

"Well, by now I *was* worried. I looked around for the red emergency handle to jettison the canopy—I was thinking about getting my butt out of that airplane. We had gotten down low enough so that the instructor would only be able to make one more attempt to recover. After that, we would be on the ground.

"But he made the attempt, and this time it worked. He got the plane straightened out, and got the stick forward, and then very smoothly he leveled us out. I'm not sure how low we were. But *low.* I could see more detail on the ground than I wanted.

"He didn't say a word after he leveled the plane out. He just flew very carefully back to the airport and landed it carefully. And after we landed, he still didn't say anything, either, but I could see that he was whiter than a sheet. I probably was just as white myself.

"I suppose if there was ever a time for me to quit flying, that would have been it. That's as close as an airplane has come to doing me in. But I really didn't give much thought to quitting. I already knew by then that flying was what I wanted to do for a living, so it really wasn't a question for me.

"A couple of days later, the instructor came over to me and said, 'Hey, we found out that that plane was terribly out of rig. Whatever mechanic worked on it last left it in one hell of a mess.

" 'Oh, and by the way,' he said, 'I recovered from it by getting my foot up against the stick and using my leg muscles to push the stick forward. That was the only way I could do it. You might want to keep that in mind in case you're ever in the same situation again.' "

Flight is an act of hope. Few other human activities involve such a complete rebellion against the limitations nature imposes on us. We fling ourselves into the air and expect its tenuous molecules to bear us up. We know that a fall from a second-story window can be fatal, yet we climb miles above firm ground and tell ourselves we are safe there in the void. Flight is an act of hope, and rationalization, and youthful desire.

I thought I detected traces of youthfulness in almost every pilot I met. It glinted beneath the reserved demeanor of even the most imperious captains. Pilots my own age struck me as boyish, while retired fliers two or three decades my senior seemed to be, at heart, my contemporaries. Two of the first dozen retired pilots I interviewed—grandfatherly, gray-haired gents—turned out to own large motorcycles. I don't mean 50-cc motorbikes built for tooling sedately around town; I'm talking about monstrous road-burning powercycles, heavy-metal hogs. Both pilots bought their cycles soon after retiring, and both admitted to me that they had hurt themselves while riding them. One pilot crashed his cycle, breaking a leg; the second was thrown off his cycle, damaging his back. "I always say I never grew up," the second one joked.

Another retired pilot I met owned a hobby shop. He told me he had loved model airplanes as a boy. Building them had been his introduction to aviation. He'd built static models that he displayed in his bedroom, then he graduated to gas-powered models that he flew in a vacant lot near his home. Then he took flying lessons. Then he enlisted in the Air Force. Then he became an airline pilot. And finally, when he reached age sixty and retired from flying, he bought a hobby shop, surrounding himself once more with model planes.

Youthful dreams often lie behind the decision to become a pilot.

Very few of the pilots I met said that flying had been just one of several career options they'd considered. Most said they'd never wanted to be anything except pilots—the desire to fly grew early in their childhoods. Sam Ketchner, a TWA captain who currently flies 747s, told me he'd wanted to be a pilot for as long as he can remember. He wasn't acquainted with any pilots when he was a boy, he said. He didn't receive any encouragement to enter aviation. But his eyes were always set on the sky.

Sam's father was a farmer, a no-nonsense Pennsylvania Dutchman who wanted Sam to become a farmer too. But farm work never appealed to Sam. He told me that as a young boy doing chores on the farm, he would stop and peer upward whenever an airplane flew overhead. The planes set his imagination racing. He said he wanted to get up in one of those things somehow.

Sam plotted how to do it during his final year of high school. He persuaded his father to let him attend college, then he used a pair of carefully balanced criteria to choose the right school. To please his father, he made sure the school had a good agriculture curriculum. To please himself, he made sure it was located near an airport.

When he arrived on campus, he enrolled in his courses, including some in the ag program. Then, without telling his father, he headed for the airport and signed up for the course he really cared about: flying lessons. He told me his father caught on eventually. Flying lessons were expensive. Sam tried to hide the expense, claiming that all the money he spent went for textbooks. But his father saw through the ruse, and he was not happy. "He thought flying was for fools," Sam said. "He thought if I took the money I spent on flying and let the wind blow it away instead, I'd have just as much for it."

Sam went ahead with the lessons anyway and got his pilot's license. But when he graduated from college, he returned home and tried to settle down to farming like his father wanted him to. It didn't work out. "I acted just like when I was a kid," Sam said. "I would be out cultivating the corn, and if a plane flew over, I got fascinated. I would be driving the tractor and looking up at the plane, and when I looked down again, I saw that I'd plowed out thirty feet of corn!"

Sam's father gave in after one year. Those torn-up corn rows and the faraway look in his son's eye convinced him that Sam didn't belong on the seat of a tractor. So one evening when he and Sam resumed their long-running debate, he relented. Sam could go off and try to get himself an airline job.

I asked Sam whether, looking back on it, he thought he'd made the right decision about what to do with his life.

"No doubt about it," he said. "I'll tell you, I have to retire before long, and I'm not looking forward to it. I've got an idea what it'll be like. I'll be watching the planes the same way I used to, and I'll still want to be up there flying them."

I was glad to detect the boyishness in pilots. It formed a bond between us. Often since turning twenty-one, I've felt that I am only a counterfeit adult. Emotions and states of mind dating from my childhood have recurred far more regularly than I would have liked, and I've felt—sometimes despairingly—that I'll never grow up. This is, I know, common. Many adults feel the same thing. They see their friends striding through the world with apparent self-possession and maturity, and when they compare themselves with this image of their friends, they feel a painful sense of insufficiency. They think that only they remain childish at heart. They don't realize that each of their friends also carries a secret child inside.

I hadn't realized it about pilots. I'd looked on them as the very embodiment of mature authority, and I'd dwelt on the differences between us. They'd had the gumption to pursue a goal that had deterred me. They were confident and purposeful, not hamstrung with uncertainty the way I was. But now I told myself that, despite our differences, we shared many attributes. Pilots were nearly as juvenile as I was. They were escapists. They were Huck Finns who used airplanes instead of rafts or balloons to escape the restrictions of society. They didn't want to farm, or hold regular nine-to-five jobs, or submerge themselves in the endless small struggles of family life. They wanted to sail away into the sky.

This insight gratified me, for a while. It gave me a connection with the pilots. I could empathize with them; I knew what made them tick. Later, I intentionally broke the connection. I told myself that I was morally superior to the pilots. They were boyish, like me. But I was trying to do something about my boyishness—to become truly adult at last—whereas they wanted to stay as they were. They had no objective except to repeat the same escape trick incessantly, flying off and then, as soon as they returned, flying off again. I was behaving far more admirably. I was trying to confront reality, trying to face up to the self-doubts that had caused me to repress my childhood dream of becoming a pilot. I was establishing a self-knowledge that would stand me in good stead for the remainder of my life.

I flattered myself in terms like these as I concluded my initial round of interviews with pilots. I enjoyed pinning the pilots with psychological tags. I took my ability to find such tags as a sign of my new maturity. But when I began writing the first draft of this book and went out for a further round of interviews, the pleasure waned. Claims of moral superiority rarely hold up. Once or twice I heard pilots discuss flight in language that reminded me how thin the line is between escapism and a nobler aspiration: the desire for transcendence, and for the clarity it may yield.

Roy Baldwin, a retired Pan Am captain, flew international air routes for more than twenty years. Now he owns a private plane that he keeps at an airport near his home in Allentown, Pennsylvania. "When I fly," he said to me, "I feel like I'm rising above all the crap and corruption. I get in an airplane and close the door, and I can shut all that out. Except for the radio, I'm totally on my own.

"You can't get totally away from the earth today—you've got to have that radio. Years ago, planes didn't have radios. Then the peace and quiet were really something. But today you have to keep that one link with the ground.

"Flying is still a great thing, though. I might be in a bad mood because of some problem that's eating at me, but when I get into a plane, things look better. Problems that look big when you're on the ground look a lot smaller from thousands of feet up.

"I don't know who's going to be able to afford to own his own plane before long. It's gotten incredibly expensive. Maybe private flying will even get outlawed. That's the direction we're going. But it will be a shame if that ever happens.

"It's astonishing how much you can see when you're flying. The views are remarkable. There might be mountains ahead of you, and a city off to one side, and farm fields on your other side. At some angles, the sun hits every little lake and river, and they all glow. If there are scattered clouds, the shadows go across the ground, so some places are bright and some places are darker. If there's a low fog in some of the valleys, then you can tell how the people in some towns are seeing clear blue skies and the people in some other towns are buried in the fog.

"At night, there are the stars, and the sky is deep black. If you're over the ocean, you don't see anything below you—it's black down there, too. If you're over the land, then you see lights on the ground. On a nice, clear night, I've come down over Harrisburg, and I could see New York, and Newark, Philadelphia, Washington, Baltimore, Allentown. I could actually see the glow of the lights from every one of those cities, two hundred miles apart. It's beautiful.

"There's no pollution or ugliness when you're looking at the earth from up there. All of that is gone. The air is clear, and in a way that clears your head. The astronauts talk about that. I read how the astronauts come back down and say you can't see any borders from space. All the political fights and the wars seem ridiculous from up where they've been. It's kind of the same in an airplane. The world looks pretty good and human problems look pretty foolish from up there."

No planes were taking off or landing when we arrived at the airport. A beacon at the top of a metal tower was rotating, signaling that weather conditions were below acceptable minimums.

My father parked his car and we walked into the airport office, a small room in a sheet-metal building. The operations manager greeted us as we came in. He was seated behind a glass case that held flight manuals, maps, aircraft radios, navigation gear: merchandise for sale. The wall next to him was covered with color photographs of student pilots. Inscriptions in the borders of the photos told when each of the students had soloed.

My father said we'd like to rent a Tomahawk if the weather broke. The manager asked our names, then checked his records to see when my father had last flown here. Satisfied, he took our deposit. Then my father and I went back outside and crossed the parking lot to a coffee shop, to wait.

We sat at the counter, near a window facing the flight apron and a runway beyond it. The overcast hung low over the rows of aircraft on the apron. Someone in the shop—another pilot waiting to fly—said the ceiling was just two hundred feet, but it was lifting. "Give it a half hour," my father said. "It's going to clear up."

I studied the planes outside the window, small one- and two-engine Cessnas and Beeches and Pipers. My father pointed out the plane we had come to rent. It was painted dull white, with dark-green stripes running along its sides and a green tomahawk emblem on its fin. It had nonretracting landing gear and fixed-pitch propeller. Its bulbous canopy looked disproportionately large on its slim fuselage.

We ordered coffee—decaf this time—and talked. I asked whether he had done any more aerobatics after he completed his army training, and whether he ever did any now, in any of the planes here. I half wished he would do some today, with me along. Half wished. Someday I'd like to see the earth cartwheel around to hang suspended above me. I'd like to know how it felt to sit in a plane that was rolling and looping through the sky. I'd like to feel a plane shudder as it pulled up into a stall, and watch the nose swing over as the plane entered a spin, and feel the plane grow firm under me again as it recovered from the spin. I'd like to do all those things. But maybe not today.

I told my father about an air show I'd attended a few months previously. It had been a nostalgic spectacle: aerobats flying old-fashioned biplanes and World War II fighters in choreographed routines. I attended in order to see one particular performer, a retired TWA captain named Bob Herendeen. I had read about him in an aviation magazine. He was a celebrity. Twice during the 1960s he had won the national aerobatics championship, competing for the title during vacations from his job with TWA. He quit competing in the early 1980s, and in 1985 he retired from the airline. But he continued to participate in air shows, whipping his tiny red-and-white Pitts biplane through some of the same maneuvers he'd used when winning championships.

Bob flew briefly at the opening and close of the show, and he gave an extended performance at the midway point. His flying stunned me. He seemed not to have heard of the laws of physics—he sent his Pitts into gyrating, fluttering maneuevers that appeared to defy all physical constraints. He did torque rolls, hammerhead turns, tailspins, multiple-turn snap rolls, and a frenzied series of slanted pirouettes called the Lomcevak (in honor of the Czech aerobat who invented it). Each maneuver was more implausible than the one before. The most extraordinary of them, Bob's finale, was an inverted flat spin. Bob ascended several thousand feet above the center of the show area, then turned his plane upside down and set it revolving horizontally, like a record turning on a spindle. And in this posture the plane, canopy downward, fell toward the earth, revolving as it came. The voice of the air show announcer counted the revolutions over a loudspeaker: ten, fifteen, twenty, twenty-five. Finally, after the twenty-seventh revolution, having surrendered most of his altitude, Bob broke the spin, dove vertically, leveled out upside down, and flew low and fast across the airport, rolling rightside up as he went.

I waylaid Bob after he landed, to request an interview. He agreed. But when we seated ourselves on a bench behind a hangar, I found that I wasn't sure what to ask him. I didn't have the right vocabulary to discuss such flying. So, fumblingly, I asked inane, elementary questions. Bob was polite, though—I could see he had sat through many interviews in his time. He took my questions without complaint, answering each one patiently.

I asked which of the maneuvers he performed was the hardest. "The inverted spin," he said. "It's extremely disorienting. It's probably the most disorienting maneuver anybody can do."

I asked how, if that was so, he knew when to break out of the spin. Did he count the number of revolutions as the plane fell? "No," he said. "I don't count. Mostly I watch my altitude and I watch for a reference point that I picked out on the horizon, so I can recover in the right direction. I check the [reference] point each time the plane comes around. When I get down to the altitude I've selected, I wait for the point to come around again, and I stop the spin with it straight ahead.

"The maneuver is always disorienting, but you build up a tolerance for it with practice. Some guys who didn't know what they were doing have gotten into an inverted spin, and they couldn't recover because they couldn't figure out what they were seeing. The ground was spinning around above them, something they'd never seen before. Usually they ended up pushing rudder into the spin, exactly the opposite of what they should have done, so they crashed."

I had to lean forward to hear Bob. He spoke softly, and with apparent modesty. The aggressiveness he'd shown in the air was partially masked here on the ground.

I asked why he liked doing acrobatics. "It's a kind of flying you either love or else hate," he answered. "You know how some people like to go to the carnival and go on all the wild rides? I was the kind who always liked it. Roller coasters and loop-the-loop machines.

Aerobatics is thrilling like that, so I suppose it just came naturally to me.

"But mainly I like the challenge, to be able to handle an airplane in every attitude and know where I am all the time and know exactly what to do."

I asked if there was much physical strain involved. Were the maneuvers as taxing as they looked? "You have to stay in shape for it," Bob said. "If I don't fly for a couple of months, it takes me three or four flights to get back into the swing of it again. You have to keep flying and keep your body tolerances up. But I exercise, and I have some 'gravity boots' that I use—they strap on my ankles and I hang upside down in a doorway at home. They help me stay used to having the blood flow into my head.

"But there's really no way to practice for the G's you pull in the maneuvers. I pull about seven positive G's [pressure pushing the pilot down into his seat, making him feel as if his weight has increased several-fold] and about six negative G's [upward pressure that would pull the pilot out of his seat if he weren't strapped in]. You have to plan your routines so that you alternate positive and negative G's. If you do a bunch of negatives, one after the other—outside loops and maneuvers like that—all the blood rushes to your head and your veins expand. Then when you go positive, all the blood will rush out real fast. That's when you could gray out."

I asked about Bob's crash. The magazine article I'd read told how Bob smashed up a Pitts in 1970 while practicing to defend as national aerobatics champion. He was doing a four-turn snap roll above the desert near his home in Nevada, and he lost too much altitude. The left bottom wing clipped the ground—the plane flipped end over end, skittering across the sand for more than a hundred feet before coming to rest. Bob's right leg was broken and several vertebrae were cracked.

"The crash changed my attitude," he said. "Before then, I thought contest flying was the only thing. You have to devote yourself to it full time if you want to be any good at it, and that's what I did. It was just about my whole life. But after the crash, I decided it wasn't so important anymore. I still wanted to do it, but I didn't put that much importance on it anymore.

"I built myself another plane, but after flying it for a while, I sold it. I decided to give up aerobatics, so I didn't need to own my own airplane. That lasted for two years. But I got itchier and itchier until eventually I couldn't stand it anymore. I had to have another plane and get back into aerobatic flying. So I bought the plane I've got now. I kept the flying more in perspective after that, but I found out I really couldn't give it up."

The ceiling had lifted to six hundred feet, according to a report that circulated through the coffee shop. My father and I finished our coffee, then shortly after ten o'clock we headed back toward the office. The sun was burning holes in the overcast by this time, oval patches of blue that expanded rapidly. Soon the last wisps of cloud would be gone.

As we reached the office door, we saw the airport beacon stop rotating. The airport was open for flying. We entered the office, got the keys to the Tomahawk, then walked out through a side door that led onto the apron. Stepping around rain puddles on the concrete, we approached the plane.

My father climbed onto the left wing, opened the door on that side of the cockpit, and sat in the pilot's seat. I climbed onto the right wing and stood there leaning into the cockpit.

"The first thing to do," my father said, "is a 'preflight.' "

He threw the master switch, turning on the plane's electrical system, then checked the fuel gauges and the fuel pump. Then we both stepped down to the apron again. My father examined the collision warning light and flipped up the stall warning indicator on the leading edge of the left wing. Then he reached into the cockpit and shut off the power.

"Now we go around, looking at everything else on the exterior of the plane," he said. "Just keep your eyes open for anything that is busted, bent, leaking, missing—any obvious problems."

We circled the plane clockwise, looking at the control surfaces, the pitot tube, landing gear, brakes. We drained some fuel from a wing tank to be sure it was free of sediment and condensation. We opened the engine cowling and peered inside. Then we climbed back onto the wings and seated ourselves in the cockpit.

The tension I'd been feeling all morning flared higher, but then it abated. I knew my father intended to let me take the controls sometime during our flight. He would give me a flying lesson: show me how to operate the plane, then observe while I tried. Whenever I'd thought about this during the morning, my stomach had clenched. But as I sat here now, watching my father restart the electrical system and check the instruments, I felt some of the anxiety leave me. I was less anxious now than simply, exuberantly eager.

Talking about Bob Herendeen had been good for me. Compared to his air show performance, our flight would be a cinch. I knew we would fly sedately. We would make gentle climbs, sober turns, cautious descents. I thought it would be almost too sedate. But I was sure I would enjoy it. There had been a point during the show when Bob loitered in the air a few miles from the airport, waiting for another act to end so he could begin his. I was the only one watching him, I'm sure. He was hardly visible, a speck against the high clouds. But while he waited, he celebrated, leisurely looping his plane and easing it through some slow rolls. He performed a short aerial dance, not for any audience but purely for himself—because he was in the air, in a delightfully responsive airplane, on a beautiful summer day. This morning—sticking to the basics, keeping our plane strictly topside up—my father and I would conduct our own version of that celebration.

Finishing his instrument check, my father cranked up the engine and began taxiing toward the runway. "I'll fly it around for a while," he said, "so you can get a feeling for it. Then I'll let you try your hand."

He stopped the plane near the foot of the runway. "I hope you're going to enjoy this," he said.

"For an experienced pilot, a little flight like this is nothing but fun. Everything flows easily. He just has to think of the attitude he wants the plane to be in, and his hands and feet put it there automatically.

"I doubt it will be like that for you. I don't see how it could be. But if you have trouble with any of it, remember that it will come more easily the next time you go up, and even easier the time after that. The more practice you get, the more natural it'll be for you."

I made some kind of reply—I don't remember what. Then he pushed the throttle forward and we got started.